WRITERS OF THE FUTURE

S0-AHH-965

Escape into new worlds. . . .

. . . A tough cop tries to cut it in a tougher century. . . . A terrified young girl wonders what her guardian eats . . . and zoo creatures in a starving world eat what they can. . . .

Escape into new worlds of imagination. . . .

. . . A loving couple in a world of despair pray for a life to nurture . . . the Devil grasps for a pinball-player's soul . . . a Cinderella has no soul to yield . . . and an ancient shaman bitterly witnesses the rape of something irreplaceable. . . .

Award-winning stories from the best of the new breed of science fiction and fantasy writers . . .

. . . An elf woos a princess . . . a man buries his wife, and perhaps his existence . . . a murderous junkie confronts a faithful thing . . . and a theater director plays the highest stake for happiness and fame. . . .

"A story is a ticket to a new universe . . . it is a delight to a tourist such as myself to see the opening of new realms." —ROGER ZELAZNY

"Here the sky is not the limit, nor is time. Here is the gateway to all the space you need. . . ." —THEODORE STURGEON

YOU WILL FIND SOME OF THE BEST SF STORIES OF THE YEAR, BY THE BEST OF THE NEW BREED!

L. RON HUBBARD

PRESENTS

WRITERS

OF THE

FUTURE

L. RON HUBBARD

PRESENTS

WRITERS

OF THE

FUTURE

Commentaries by
ROBERT SILVERBERG
THEODORE STURGEON
JACK WILLIAMSON
ROGER ZELAZNY

Edited by
ALGIS BUDRYS

Bridge Publications, Inc.

Contents

About L. Ron Hubbard

Contest Sponsor

L. Ron Hubbard appeared on the SF scene in 1938 at the age of twenty-seven and immediately became a legend. By then he was already in his eighth year as a professional writer. His ability to consistently produce great numbers of grippingly told stories had swiftly made him a fabulous figure with readers and with his fellow writers.

He appeared at a critical juncture in the development of speculative fiction, and was one of the major factors in synergizing its evolution, which was taking place with blinding speed and mounting excitement on America's newsstands. The 1920s "science wonder" stories of Hugo Gernsback and the 1930s "super-science" machine-adventure sagas of E. E. Smith and his followers were being transformed into what came to be known as "Modern Science Fiction." Simultaneously, the same forces were creating a "newsstand fantasy" literature of a kind never seen before. To the history of these twinned developments, the career of the young L. Ron Hubbard was crucial.

Edited by former superscience star John W. Campbell, Jr., the magazine called Astounding

Stories of Super Science *became its field's leader as* Astounding Science Fiction *magazine, with the "Astounding" de-emphasized and shrinking away and the editorial tone shifting ever farther from mighty machines and toward the philosophical bases of human societal problems and human nature. New ways of writing, new writers, new readers, appeared with every issue, wave after wave. Around* Astounding—*and around Campbell's now-legendary fantasy magazine,* Unknown—*flourished a fabulous Golden Age of creativity that swiftly redefined not only the newsstand media but, by its impact, all of twentieth-century speculative literature.*

In this creative ferment, Hubbard not only found his favorite kind of fiction, he was in the forefront of inventing it. Producing at a pace none of his contemporaries could match, creating now-famous books such as Final Blackout, Death's Deputy, Slaves of Sleep, Typewriter in the Sky *and* Fear, *writing under his own name and under pseudonyms, Hubbard was the sort of intensive phenomenon who appears once in a lifetime, in effect makes his own rules, and transforms everything around him. Among those in SF who knew him, and even among those too young to have met him then, stories about Hubbard— fabulous stories about a man who fountained major ideas and memorable characters at an unbelievable pace—abounded even years later. No one in those days could discuss SF without discussing him.*

Larger than life, Hubbard was impressive not only for his snowballing popularity but for his actual adventures as an aviator, seafarer and technologist.

Pyramiding these various attributes, he became the figure everyone depended on to produce one major exciting work after another, and who delivered. In the Golden Age, he towered over the magazine field as few others had.

His writing career interrupted by service in World War II, he returned to his beloved SF for a few years, successful as ever but increasingly busy with his development of Dianetics. Decades of time passed; succeeding generations of fiction readers knew him only through reprints, losing awareness of his role in SF history. Hubbard meanwhile was prodigiously writing in other fields.

In celebration of his fiftieth anniversary as a professional writer, however, Hubbard returned to SF with the publication of Battlefield Earth, *a massive best-selling adventure novel, that was his first new SF in thirty years. (Two feature movies are being produced of this epic.) Nineteen eighty-five will also see the beginning of the publication of* Mission Earth, *an incredible ten-volume SF adventure. There are many more works to come as he reestablishes himself in a field whose literary evolution cannot be effectively understood unless the nature and roots of his Golden Age popularity are put back into proper perspective and understood.*

Even during the Golden Age, however, few general readers knew of his impressive output of advice and encouragement to new writers. Publishing how-to-do-it articles and features in a wide variety of writer's magazines, L. Ron Hubbard in the 1930s was a respected elder statesman and role model among novices who probably had no idea their mentor was barely a quarter-century old. More advanced in years now, but no less prodigious a producer, Hubbard has returned not only to SF writing but to the encouragement and support of new talent. To this endeavor he has brought both his creative enthusiasm and his characteristic manner of proceeding, as this book demonstrates and as the following introduction sets forth. . . .

—Algis Budrys

Introduction
by
L. Ron Hubbard

A culture is as rich and as capable of surviving as it has imaginative artists. The artist is looked upon to start things. The artist injects the spirit of life into a culture. And through his creative endeavors, the writer works continually to give tomorrow a new form.

In these modern times, there are many communication lines for works of art. Because a few works of art can be shown so easily to so many, there may even be fewer artists. The competition is very keen and even dagger sharp.

It is with this in mind that I initiated a means for new and budding writers to have a chance for their creative efforts to be seen and acknowledged. With the advent of the Writers of the Future competition came an avalanche of new material from all over the country.

And with that came the idea of creating a book that would contain the winners of the quarterly judges' decisions.

Judging the winners for this book could not have

been an easy task, and I am sincerely grateful to those professionals and top-flight veterans of the profession for their hard work and final selections which made this book possible:

Gregory Benford	Robert Silverberg
Algis Budrys	Theodore Sturgeon
Stephen Goldin	Jack Williamson
C. L. Moore	Roger Zelazny

My special thanks also goes to Algis Budrys for the invaluable work he did in editing and putting together this book.

And my heartiest congratulations to those they selected for this first volume. I am very proud to present the winners.

Good luck to all other writers of the future.

And good reading.

—L. Ron Hubbard

Algis Budrys On Shaping Creativity

About the Editor

Algis Budrys, son of Lithuanian diplomat parents, was five in 1936 when he was brought to this country. He discovered science fiction shortly thereafter, and in 1940 wrote his first SF story. During the 1940s, he contributed articles and drawings to various SF amateur magazines including his own, and eventually took college courses in writing. In 1952 he made his first story sale, to John Campbell's Astounding Science Fiction *magazine. His editorial experience began in the same year, at Gnome Press, the pioneering SF book company which brought out the first hard-cover editions of* Fear *and* Typewriter in the Sky *by L. Ron Hubbard.*

An author of adventure, suspense and crime fiction as well as of much SF and of articles on science and engineering, Budrys has also long had a strong interest in working with beginners. He is a frequent lecturer on writing at junior high and high schools, and at colleges. Since 1977, he has been closely associated with the famed Clarion summer workshop in SF writing at Michigan State University.

As editor of this volume, I've written all the introductory material—the opening passages in italics throughout the book—including the one for this essay. That's one of an editor's tasks; putting the text material into an appropriate frame so that it becomes more readily focused and accessible to the reader. That's a species of creativity. But this book would be nothing without the text of the stories created by these various new authors, so another part of editing is in getting out of the way of the major creativities as soon as possible.

We hope—L. Ron Hubbard hopes, I hope, and so do the many people of Bridge Publications who took great pride in their various tasks on this book—that we have done our best for these new writers, as these writers hope they have done for you.

The bottom line here is whether these stories are successful with you—as entertainment, perhaps as something more memorable than mere diversion, but at any rate as the core of a pleasurable and worthwhile reading experience. That's the ultimate aim of a writer's creativity. The details of a writer's personal life, the circumstances under which the story was produced, what will be done with the prize money and the royalties . . . all those are irrelevant beside the need to satisfy the reader with a good story. The Writers of the Future Contest judges were delighted by the high level of the entered work, and by the opportunity to uncover truly effective talent represented by noteworthy works of fiction. We all think this resulting anthology is an extraordinary volume; now we and the writers await the only verdict that truly counts—yours.

That's how it is for creative people; the performance may be judged in many ways, meeting various objective standards, but if there is no applause from the audience—if the audience expresses no pleasure—then the vital thing is lacking. It is with some considerable trepidation, then, that a person attempts to perform before an audience, and when the applause comes . . . or doesn't come . . . the heights and depths of the performer's feelings can make the creative life one in which elation and despair follow constantly on each other's heels. It is not a comfortable life. But for some it's the only life, and from the emotions of that life come the dramas which, translated into stories, create the thrill of good reading.

Those are the thoughts that pass through a veteran writer's mind as one contemplates the debut of these fresh talents. So another purpose of this anthology is to encourage yet additional new writers, to give them a feeling for how others have successfully dealt with obstacles, and to remind them, and the reader, that every writer, no matter how successful now, was once a novice—a writer of the future, in search of readers of the future.

So this book also contains statements on their art and craft by some of the established SF practitioners who devoted much time and thought to deciding the quarterly winners and runners-up. All the competition judges represent top, multiple-award-winning talent from every generation since the pioneering days of SF on the news-stands. They serve virtually without recompense. Why do they do that? They do it because no one ever forgets what it was like to dream of acceptance and recognition, often in the long face of repeated discouragement. And they do it because historically in the SF field, beginning writers have never been regarded as potential competitors; they are new comrades.

The contests continue, as we explain elsewhere in this book, and we look forward to the future. We all owe a special thanks to a talented writer and indefatigable manuscript-reader, Stephen Goldin. Handling the massive workload associated with the competition depended on his patient labor and excellent perceptivity.

We thought that it would be appropriate to select our artwork from among beginning illustrators. All the pictorial work for this anthology is by people who had rarely if ever illustrated fiction before, and who responded to this opportunity with enthusiasm and creative excitement. We have given them their own page of biographical notes, and wish them, too, good fortune in their subsequent careers.

One of our winning stories is not included in this book; Ira Herman's *The Two Tzaddicks* can be found in Del Rey Books' *Stellar Science Fiction Stories*. The 1984 rules did not specify that professionally published stories were not eligible. (The 1985 rules do.) Ira is 36 and has been writing for ten years, but his duties as Executive Director of American Heritage Park in Ashland, Kentucky, have limited his available time; *The Two Tzaddicks* remains his only story sale as of 1984. If this were not an anthology of new stories, we would have been pleased to ask his permission to reprint it for you here, because it's a lively and engaging science fiction tale that richly deserves praise.

We congratulate all the winners and finalists. We wish we could have published more of their work; in years to come, we're sure, someone will.

—Algis Budrys

Tyson's Turn
by
Michael D. Miller

About the Author

Leading off the stories in this anthology is the third-place winner in the third quarterly contest. It's also Michael D. Miller's first fiction sale after fifteen years of trying. This will surprise you when you read this story; it's thoroughly proficient from the beginning to the final thump of its ending. Meanwhile, it's also an intriguing, fast-paced tale in the best traditions of SF storytelling.

For Miller, as for everyone who has long tried to gain the approval and satisfaction of having a story accepted, this story will forever recall a moment only another writer could fully understand. His life has been changed forever . . . by phone calls from a contest director and an anthology editor, but really by what he did himself, over years of perseverance and practice.

Forty-one, Miller has a degree in philosophy, but has always been intrigued by writing. He has worked for AT&T the past eight years. For almost two years, he has been a writer in the public relations department at Bell Laboratories, where SF over the years has been a major interest of many. (Retired director John R. Pierce was known as "J. J. Coupling" to readers of Astounding Science Fiction *magazine during the Golden Age.) Miller learned of the Writers of The Future contest from a flyer on the company bulletin board, under the heading "Risk Takers?"*

Illustrated by A. R. Conway

Tyson was riding the ruins of an old interstate that went nowhere when his high beams lit on something a good half-kilometer ahead. He kicked in the battery of infrared sensors and sonic scanners slung under the front bumper of the police cruiser, and the expert system in the powerful little computer behind the dash came alive.

"Target is a male human with an elevated body temperature," it said crisply, and paused, waiting for more data. "Probably a Drifter," it added, pausing again. "Possibly diseased. Be careful."

Tyson was closing fast, and in a moment saw a vagrant flap of white shirt hanging below the waist of a black jacket. Even at that distance he could tell the clothes were filthy.

A less-experienced Cop would have hit the brakes, popped the emergency drag chute and tried a high-grip skid. That kind of adolescent maneuver might have impressed a hologram audience, but it would not have bagged a real Drifter. A real Drifter would have been over the twisted guardrail and into the jumble of high grass before the tires smoked to a stop.

So Tyson, a Tough Cop with a few smarts and a lot of years, stayed with the high beams, swerved away from the shoulder and accelerated—just like any Anxious Citizen dodging a hitchhiking Vagabond on a derelict highway late at night.

The digital display behind the steering wheel was registering 180 klicks an hour as the sleek black cruiser flashed past the startled Drifter. Tyson glimpsed the figure staggering toward the side of the road, fleet-footed as a slug. And probably about as bright, Tyson thought. He puffed on his big Havana, contemplating an arrest, something he had not enjoyed for more than a year.

Six kilometers beyond the Drifter, Tyson braked hard, wheeled through a gap in the crumbling medial barrier, and sped back the way he had come. Now, however, he was running dark, relying on his sonic scanners to find the pits and bumps, which the computer displayed in eerie shades of red on the windshield. Four kilometers from where he had seen the Drifter he cut the car's speed to 50 klicks and a minute later turned the wheel over to the expert system.

"Go to STALK," Tyson ordered, and stretched. Cramps burrowed in his lower back and nestled in his arms and calves. He knew he'd have to move very quickly. He was in no shape for much of a fight or a lengthy chase. It had been too long.

"Something," the expert system said tentatively. "OK, got it. Range one point five kilometers . . . on the road . . . same profile as previous target . . . repeat, male Drifter, possibly diseased. Caution."

"That's my boy," Tyson said, pleased the Drifter had not remained hidden in the underbrush, or fled across the fields. The Tough Cop's hand caressed the leather-tipped nightstick at his side, brushed the cold metal of the chemical debilitator canister on his belt. Then he felt the hard certainty of his service revolver, a weapon he had never used, and didn't intend to now. A Drifter was too valuable a prize to waste on the Doctors, or the Morticians.

Tyson thought of the Doctors and all the others in the city just over the horizon: the Lawyers, the Bakers, the Orderlies, the Anxious Citizens, the Psychiatrists, all wedded to their callings, which, theoretically, were supposed to mesh like cogs in a great clockwork. While the reality fell a little short of the ideal, Tyson had to admit this setup was a lot better than any of the alternatives. Anyway, he thought, an enterprising individual could always make a few adjustments where the system didn't work.

A century before, when genetic engineers were just beginning to unravel the secrets in the coils of DNA, most people were ill-suited to their work. Productivity hit an all-time low and then nose-dived. Job dissatisfaction was rampant and strikes frequent. White collar crime was bleeding everyone, and everybody was a bleeding white collar criminal. Then the Gengineers, as they were called, discovered how to mold people to professions. The right attitudes, outlooks, temperaments and intellects were there, tied up in the curlicued combinations of DNA. All it took was a little know-how and a bit of labor to turn them loose.

Still, the magic in the giant molecule didn't come up to expectations.

Suddenly, everyone wanted to be international bankers, brilliant scientists, statesmen, great artists. And within a generation or two there were plenty of them. But there also was nobody left to pick up the garbage, wait on tables, clean floors, write orders or mow lawns. Competition between super-geniuses became cutthroat and intensely destructive. Tyson had only to glance out his window at the ruined highway to appreciate the cost of such squabbling.

Civilization, which had foundered in occupational mismatches and killing waste, had been dying of the cure for these ills. In the end, it had barely scraped by. Military takeovers were followed by enforced quotas for essential occupations like Street Cleaner and Store Clerk. Social engineering took over as the heart of a new order, and gengineering was deposed and plunged into disfavor. DNA became a dirty word tolerated out of necessity.

Shortly after Tyson's conception, his mother visited the Family Doctor, who took his orders from a government computer. The computer wanted a Cop, subclass Tough, and the Doctor made the appropriate adjustments in the zygote that was Tyson. Nine months later he reported for duty, the Little Constable, as his parents fondly called him. From the beginning that is all Tyson had wanted to be. And he was very good at it. If Mr. and Mrs. Tyson were a bit startled by the vigor with which their son pursued his vocation—he could get rough with any child who got in his way—they consoled themselves with the knowledge that their brutal little boy was a product of predetermined nature, not nurture. After all, they were Perfect Parents.

As a youngster, Tyson instinctively despised Drifters, who at best were shiftless, prone to petty thievery, vandalism and worse. Drifters had been known to kill, to molest children, and some had been Rapists. Still, they kept Cops, Psychiatrists and Social Workers gainfully and happily employed. And in the end, that was all that really mattered.

Tyson tried to think like a Drifter. What would he be doing now if the computer had put him in the other man's shoes? Probably sticking to the shoulder, close to the guardrail, ready to head for the safety of the high grass.

"Seventy-five meters," the expert system said, interrupting his thoughts. Tyson squinted, but could see nothing in the darkness ahead. He ground out his cigar and wondered briefly whether he was cruising into a trap set by Criminals with the Drifter as bait. Tyson's hand brushed the handle of his service revolver. Unlikely. The kind of Criminals who would go after a Cop would not sully their reputations with a Drifter.

"Twenty meters," the expert system whispered. "I've got his profile. Estimated weight: 100 kilos, height about 190 centimeters."

Big, Tyson thought. He considered calling for a back-up, and instantly dismissed the idea. First, he was a Tough Cop and could handle any Drifter ever conceived. Second, the Firemen, the Doctors, the Psychiatrists and anyone else monitoring the police band would be all over him before he got close to the city.

And he had to get the Drifter to the City and down a certain narrow side street. At the end of the street he would swing right into an alley that led to a courtyard ringed with modern apartments and offices, guarded by ever-vigilant security robots backed up by snarling Dobermans. There is where Tyson would find the Fixer, the one occupation not specified—in fact, outlawed—by the Social Engineers. The Fixer bootlegged genes.

The reason for the genetic black market was simple: the Social Engineers made mistakes. A small slip in planning here or a tiny miscalculation there could send shortages rippling through the whole complex social fabric.

Tyson first visited his Fixer five years before, during the great Criminal shortage, when thousands of

Lawmen were thrown out of work by a shortfall of Hoods. Soon, Cops were snatching up Bums, Drifters and Vagrants and running them over to the Fixers, who transformed these social dregs into Hardened Criminals. Tyson had even grabbed a couple of Average Citizens.

That shortage eventually disappeared, but others cropped up. Sickness declined and the Doctors started a plague. Fires were few and Firemen began prowling the streets looking for candidates for the position of Arsonist, First Class. "Twenty meters," the expert system whispered. Tyson shook his head and blinked. Daydreaming again; losing his edge. He eased his gullwing door open on well-oiled hinges, stepped gingerly onto the highway and patted the car on the rear fender, a signal he was out and ready.

Suddenly the car's headlights blazed, the sirens screamed and the overhead strobes lashed the darkness with a sterile brilliance. Startled by the cascade of light and sound, the Drifter spun and, as Tyson hoped, faced his attacker. In an instant he was blinded and deafened, bent over with both hands pressed to his ears.

Tyson charged past the cruiser, which braked abruptly. The Drifter tried to turn toward the guardrail, but Tyson was quick. He snapped the leather-tipped nightstick smartly against the Drifter's head, and the man collapsed in a heap.

"Stay!" Tyson shouted at the cruiser, which was creeping forward. The car stopped, the strobes dimmed, the siren fell silent. The engine purred menacingly.

Tyson examined his catch. The Drifter's scalp was gushing blood, but his pulse was steady and strong. His face bore the regulation two-day stubble, ground-in grime and old scars of his trade, and his hair was stringy and long. The man's breath reeked of strong whiskey, a government dollop Drifters loved.

Still . . . Under the grime, beyond the stubble, in spite of the stringy hair and general dishevelment, there was a healthy glow to the face Tyson shone his light on. He touched the Drifter's forehead, and it was hot. Of course, Tyson thought, the rosy glow of a fever. The Big Cop dragged the man to the car, ordered the expert system to open the back door, and pushed the unconscious heap inside.

"I want a checkup," Tyson said as he pressed a bandage on the bleeding head wound. A small panel slid open on the rear of the front seat, and Tyson removed a pair of wire leads and a small needle trailing a clear plastic tube. He pressed the leads against the Drifter's limp left wrist and slid the needle into a vein. A moment later the expert system offered a diagnosis.

"He's got a fever of 103.5, pulse is 90 and his blood pressure is 110 over 75. No contagions or other pathogens, and the cause of fever is unknown. He's a little anemic, too. He needs a Doctor."

Tyson cursed. He did not want a Doctor cutting in on him. If one, or, which was more likely, several Physicians intercepted them, however, Tyson would have no legal defense. Drifter or not, by law the man was a Patient.

Tyson could be in the city in fifteen minutes if he pushed it. Trouble was, Doctors hungry for Patients, or Social Workers looking for Clients, might be waiting for him. And they would have plenty of legal help. Tyson knew a dozen Lawyers who would turn a simple arrest into a federal case.

When all was said and done, though, speed seemed his only defense. If he could get to the city before too many of the others got organized, he might push through to the Fixer.

Tyson swung into the cruiser, sealed it, and brought his big steel-toed boot down hard on the accelerator. The car shot forward, spewing chunks of rotting roadway in its wake. He ran fast with lights out and the sonic scanners probing ahead for the big pits and boulder-sized chunks of rubble. The steering wheel, now in the hands of the computer, twisted wildly as it weaved the car over the invisible obstacle course.

Tyson heard a sound behind him, and turned to see the Drifter clawing on the wire-mesh screen between the front and back seats.

"Hey! Hey! What's going on? You, why am I . . ."

"Shut it, Bum," Tyson growled. He tapped a button on the dashboard, and a voice droned mechanically from the radio speaker. "You have the right to remain silent. You have the . . ."

"Please," the Drifter whined, his voice surprisingly high for such a big man. "Gimme a smoke." Tyson casually tapped another button on the dashboard, and the Drifter screamed as 20,000 volts of low-amperage current burst from a thousand tiny electrodes sprinkled over the back seat. The Drifter spasmed and flailed futilely at the tiny pinpricks of excruciating pain. Tyson held the switch down a moment, then released it. The lights on the dash, dimmed to near-darkness by the drain of the punishing shock, brightened. The tape recorder, which had automatically paused, resumed. "If you waive the right . . ."

Tyson didn't care about the Drifter's rights. He was squinting at something far enough away to be an illusion concocted of darkness and fear—or real trouble. At first, a dark shape seemed to span the interstate where the crumbling highway met a road ringing the city. Then, as the cruiser drew closer, the shape became a metal wall, and then a fleet of ambulances.

"So," the Drifter said, "the Doctors have arrived." His voice was lilting, laced with a gentleness that seemed out of place in his massive frame.

Tyson ignored him, rammed the brake pedal down hard and barked at the computer to begin a violent fishtail skid. The Drifter tumbled backward and bounced off a window with a heavy thud. Ten meters from the sparkling wall of rescue wagons, the cruiser slid to a stop, and Tyson gunned the car backward, braked abruptly, spun the steering wheel hard and bounced over a curb and into the high grass. The ambulances rushed after the police car, their headlights blazing furiously, sirens crashing through the peal of Tyson's engine. The strobes burst on their rooftops like tiny bombs of light.

"They've come for their Patient," the Drifter said almost lightly. "Mustn't hog me to yourself."

"You're no Patient while you're still my Prisoner," Tyson growled.

"You can run, but you cannot hide, not in this town," the Drifter said. Tyson set his big, muscular jaw and veered sharply toward the ring road. The police cruiser scrambled effortlessly up the steep bank, burst across the highway just ahead of a pack of ambulances, and dashed down the other bank and into a maze of streets. The pack was right behind them, and, Tyson realized, probably radioing for reinforcements.

"If the Doctors don't get you, then the Firemen will. Or the Social Workers. Or the Dentists. All those Do-Gooders out there, dying for someone to blame, to pity, to make well. To make work."

Tyson ignored the Drifter's patter and bounced the car onto the sidewalk to avoid an ambulance that darted from an alley. The cruiser clipped a bicycle set against a wall, tore the front wheel off and sent the sparkling pretzel of metal wobbling violently off in a long, flat arc.

"This is the toughest city I've ever been in," the Drifter said, "excepting Central or South America."

"Yeah," Tyson grunted, swerving to avoid a turbo-powered emergency wagon that had fought its way to the head of the pack and now sprinted ahead, nearly running the cruiser down. A hydraulic ram protruding from the wagon's blunt snout barely missed the police car's rear window. The Drifter gasped.

Tyson spun the steering wheel viciously and led the car through a 100-meter skid that ended with the vehicle staring into a galaxy of starry headlamps and burning red flashers.

"Lights," Tyson shouted, and two silvery glass eyes popped out of sockets embedded in the grill of the cruiser. Each eye was a xenon lamp delivering 100,000 foot-candles sustained, with 400 million candles of strobe power. With the blinding lights blazing, Tyson whooped, snapped the gearshift into full accelerated drive and plowed into the midst of the startled Ambulance Drivers. They scattered almost in unison as the lights of the cruiser cut through their ranks. The Drifter turned to see first one then several of the cumbersome vehicles careen out of control and crash through storefront windows, hammer into unmoving walls or slam into utility poles. Glass was flying and metal shrieking when the Drifter caught a glimpse of one of the ambulances ripping through the thin metal skin of an illegally parked tanker truck. A moment later a dazzling light swelled through the street, followed by a thud powerful enough to have been a heavy blow from a powerful man's fist.

Tyson rounded the corner just ahead of the first blast

of superheated air, which burst into the intersection with a wall of iridescent dust rolling ahead of it.

"What was that?" Tyson asked.

"Tanker," the Drifter replied breathlessly. "Gasoline."

"That'll keep 'em busy," Tyson replied, suddenly buoyant with relief. The street behind them was full of flame and bereft of ambulances. "Doctors'll be swarming over that mess like sharks after a shipwreck." He glanced at the Drifter's reflection in the mirror, and grinned at the other man's expression. "Like action?" he asked.

"Not much," the Drifter replied. "This is out of my league."

"Happens all the time. Especially in the city. Especially in *this* city. Unemployment hit 15 percent last month. Keeps everyone on their toes."

"Well, at least it's over," the Drifter said. His eyes were downcast, his look distant.

"Not quite," Tyson corrected him. The Drifter looked up. "Trouble is, there are still 5,000 Firemen, 10,000 Psychiatrists, the government only knows how many Dentists. . . ."

"Oh."

"'Oh' is right. Before we get to the Fix . . ." Tyson bit off the rest of the word. "Before we get anywhere . . ."

"The Fixer?"

Tyson shrugged. "Sure." The Drifter stared back. "I thought you knew. There's a million people out of work. We gotta look out for ourselves."

"An arrest isn't enough?"

"What have you got to lose? You're only a Drifter. Suppose the Docs get hold of you. You'll be sick the rest of your life. Or the Social Workers. They'll pamper you until you can't even feed yourself without an interview. If you become a Criminal, though, you could score big. Syndicate, maybe. International drugs. Hit Man. Money. Women. Hell, travel."

The other man stared back. "I want to be a Drifter."

Tyson shrugged. "OK, but you have to admit, it's still better than the Docs getting you, or the Airline Pilots. Spend the rest of your life in tourist section eating poisonous food."

"Oh, good God," the Drifter moaned, looking past Tyson.

The fire engine must have sneaked up on them. Now its head-high balloon tires rested firmly on the sidewalk, its nose pressed smartly against the wall of the building beside the cruiser. The rear of the truck was angled against a closed garage door across the street. A big, gold number "101" was emblazoned on the side of the vehicle. Tyson spun around and saw a long, black shape skidding across the road behind him. They were caged.

"No," the Drifter said. "No, no. I won't go . . . can't go with the Firemen . . . they'll . . ."

"OK, OK," Tyson said. "Don't panic."

But the Drifter cried out and shrank back in the seat. Tyson turned to see a figure fully two meters tall swing down from the cab of the fire engine before him. Despite a torso the size of a clothes chest, the man descended gracefully, bounced lightly and strolled toward the police cruiser. He was fully bearded and wearing a pair of Holocaust goggles dark enough to reduce the brightest xenon to a comfortable glow. Tyson flicked the lights on anyway, and a figure atop the fire truck immediately played a stream of foam on them. The foam sizzled evilly on the hot lenses, sending up acrid white fumes. Tyson countered the stream by playing a jet of hot water against the lights. But he turned off the water and the

lights when he saw the broadhead ax swinging from the Fireman's hand.

The giant grinned and brushed off his goggles. Then he stepped forward and with one practiced sweep of the ax knocked out the lights, shaking the cruiser with the force of the blow. A xenon bulb swung limply at the end of a thin strand of electrical wire.

"Ohhhhhhh," the Drifter moaned.

Tyson didn't wait for an encore; he slammed the gearshift into reverse. The giant, now illuminated by flood lamps on the fire truck, paused as the cruiser raced backward, then slid to a stop, its path blocked by the second fire engine. Someone on the second truck jabbed at the rear window of the cruiser with a metal-tipped pole.

The Fireman moved forward, alone. With a growl of rage, Tyson slapped the gearshift into drive, stomped the accelerator pedal, and aimed the cruiser at the hulk. An ugly look formed on the giant's face as he watched the wheels of the cruiser spin frantically, spewing clouds of blue smoke. It took Tyson only a moment to realize the quick-witted Firemen in the second engine had chained the rear of the cruiser to their vehicle. The car didn't budge.

"Think," Tyson hissed to himself. "Don't panic. Think."

"I'm thinking. I'm thinking," the Drifter replied. "Ohhhh, I don't . . ."

The huge Fireman paused by Tyson's door, stooped and tapped on the side window. Tyson stared at him.

"We can't fight our way out of here," the Drifter hissed. "We can't muscle out. Let me weasel out, squirm, sneak, anything."

"Great! Great!" Tyson snarled. "But he wants me to

open the window."

"No, no. Not the window. Wait! I've got it, maybe. Let me out."

"Are you crazy?" Tyson asked, twisting in his seat to face the Drifter.

"What choice have we got? They'll kill us in here. Let me try something. Just follow the fire trucks. Yeah, drive around the block and follow the fire trucks. I have an idea."

Tyson shook his head. "You're my Prisoner."

The big Fireman tapped on the glass of Tyson's window with the lean, hard edge of the ax.

"Not for long," the Drifter countered, and Tyson had no answer. The giant outside was warming up for the first killing blow when Tyson popped the back doors and the Drifter scurried out. The giant grabbed his prey by the throat and hurled him toward the nearest fire engine. A moment later both men were aboard, Tyson heard a clanking sound, and when he pumped the gas his cruiser shot forward and quickly accelerated away.

But he did not surrender. There was a quality of certainty about the Drifter, a hint of something solid that sparked a glow of hope in the great stretches of Tyson's pessimism. The man did not, when the chips were down, fit snugly into the Drifter stereotype, Tyson thought. There must be something more, a twist inserted by a clever Gengineer bored with stamping out standardized strings of DNA in some federal penitentiary.

From six stories above him, the dark faces of tenement buildings stared blankly at each other. Tyson felt very alone. Nothing moved. He turned a corner and started up the long side of the block, his turbine engine hissing softly in the darkness of the barely lit street. When he reached an intersection, he turned left again and nudged the cruiser forward at a crawl. At the next intersection he braked gently and peeked around the corner. The two fire trucks were trundling away.

Tyson took a chance, played his infrared spotlight on the back of the trailing truck and saw a big gold "102."

Tyson took the corner slowly, patiently allowing the cruiser to melt into the darkness. At first his pursuit was cautious, almost timid. He allowed the fire engines to open the gap. Then, when he was sure the Firemen had not seen him and were not looking for him, he carefully crept up on the trucks, whittling down the distance between them meter by meter. He did not know what to expect or when to expect it, but he was willing to gamble a little bit on the Drifter.

His faith was rewarded. Suddenly the rear truck swerved and drove straight into the wall of an apartment building. The cab rammed partway through, and the truck stopped with a shudder. Glaring white plaster swept over it and ragged chunks of structural concrete rained down. A living-room-full of furniture cascaded down through the gaping hole in the wall and a sink rattled along behind the furniture. A television set exploded in the rubble, and a human form rode a bed to the sidewalk, bounced hard and hobbled into the darkness.

The Drifter hopped down from the cab and trotted toward a disbelieving Tyson. The Drifter seemed almost calm as he scrambled into the front seat beside the Tough Cop.

"What happened?" Tyson asked as he swung the cruiser around the rear of the fire engine and shot off down the street.

The Drifter stared straight ahead. "Easiest thing in the world," he replied. "They weren't expecting me to do anything, so I got a shot at the steering wheel. One good yank and we went into that building. I saw it coming. They were knocked silly." He turned to Tyson. "Thanks for hanging around."

Tyson glanced at the Drifter. "We were damned lucky. How'd you stop from going through the windshield?"

"Like I said, I saw the building coming and let loose of the wheel and ducked. They didn't." The Drifter sighed. "I've been thinking over what you said about being a Criminal. I've been knocking around and been getting knocked around a long time. Maybe I'm ready for something better. I think maybe you showed me that."

Tyson glanced at him, then down the empty thoroughfare. "You should be in the back."

"Sure," the Drifter said with a shrug. "But don't you think I'd have run by now if I were going to? Besides, I can help out up here."

Tyson eyed him coolly. "Maybe."

"Well, then, stop," the Drifter said. "I'll get in back."

Tyson glanced around. They were less than a mile from the wreck of the fire engine, and heading away from the Fixer's laboratory. That meant Tyson would have to double back, something he did not want to do. The Ambulance Drivers were after him, and by now so were the Firemen. He probably had a price on his head, and he wanted to get this over with.

"No time," he snapped. "We're going to make a run for it. Straight line back to the Fixer's."

"Fine," the Drifter said.

But the straight line was broken five blocks later. A gang of Social Workers operating out of a nearby settlement house had thrown up a barricade. The cruiser was pushing 160 klicks when Tyson saw it, and he had no time to think.

"Left," the Drifter shouted, and Tyson swerved the cruiser into an alley, which opened into a courtyard. For a moment Tyson thought they had stumbled into a dead end, but the far side of the courtyard emptied into another alley, and Tyson squeezed the car through it and swung onto a street. He was lost, unsure of which way to turn.

"Right," the Drifter offered helpfully.

Tyson hesitated only an instant before turning. "Where are we?" he asked.

"No sweat," the Drifter said. "I've been in and out of this city a lot in the last 20 years. I know it as well as you. I know some parts better, because Cops don't go there."

Tyson concentrated on his driving. He was very sure they were heading away from the Fixer's. He turned sharply once, picking a side street at random, and almost ran into a cluster of ambulances. Their Drivers poured out of an all-night bar and gave chase.

As Tyson had feared, word had spread. The Ambulance Drivers were no longer content with a Patient. Several of their colleagues were dead, incinerated or crushed between steering wheels and unyielding concrete walls, and the Tough Cop was the culprit.

"That way," the Drifter said, alarm in his voice. The ambulances were drawing close. Tyson swerved sharply, almost rolling the cruiser. An Ambulance Driver who tried the same turn was not so lucky. His vehicle flipped, tumbling hard and smashing into several parked cars before skipping to a stop in the middle of the street.

"Nice work," the Drifter said. "I think I know a safe route. If I can remember. . . ."

"That'd be nice, because I don't know where the hell we are," Tyson growled.

"Left now," the Drifter said. Tyson swung the cruiser hard left and sent it bumping down a badly rutted street, bouncing past a line of decaying warehouses, and abruptly sailing up the smooth concrete surface—an entrance ramp to a high-speed highway that skirted the harbor.

"Open 'er up and go," the Drifter said. Tyson took the cruiser to 200 klicks, then went to full infrared and full sweep radar. They sailed into a wall of fog, and the highway beneath them blurred.

As the cruiser slid through the darkness, Tyson remembered to douse the headlights. Night closed like a vise, and the Drifter seemed to relax completely. But Tyson remained alert. He wished he knew where they were.

Gradually, he became aware of a lightening around them. Dawn. It would be coming out of the sea on their left.

"How far have we come?" the Drifter asked.

"Nearly 50 kilometers," Tyson said. "It's a long way back to the Fixer's."

"We'll run down the coast road," the Drifter said. "There'll be other traffic in a little while, and we can blend in. We'll be at the Fixer's in less than an hour." He paused. "Just take the next exit."

Tyson slowed the cruiser and the sleek car rolled off the highway onto a rural two-lane road that drove straight through banks of rolling fog. Tyson kept the speed up, just in case they needed it. But after five minutes he had encountered no other cars, and the radar and infrared sensors showed no one behind them.

"Turn here," the Drifter said.

"Here? But that's toward the ocean."

"There's a town about five klicks down the road, and

the police chief there will be glad to take me off your hands. Think you have a Criminal shortage in the city? Imagine what it's like out here. Take the road that runs along the beach. We'll be OK there."

Tyson thought about that, then turned onto a gravel road that became packed sand, which gave way to loose dunes. Then the road disappeared.

The cruiser was clawing its way over the crest of a dune when the curtains of fog parted and a brilliant sun blazed at them across a cobalt blue sea. The ocean opened like a vast stage, and Tyson paused momentarily to look at it. Rollers foamed onto the beach below, and far, far away a ship crawled over the horizon.

The Drifter slipped a tiny ampule out of his sleeve and snapped it open. Instantly, a pale yellow cloud spilled out of the broken neck of the skinny glass tube and filled the inside of the cruiser. Tyson saw it a moment before he recognized it. The cloud would be harmless, but the invisible, odorless gas it propelled was a fast-acting neural toxin. First it would shut down the voluntary nervous system, paralyzing Tyson's arms and legs, his toes and fingers, neck, head and tongue. Then the gas would begin ravaging the involuntary nervous system, and his digestive tract would die, followed quickly by his heart and lungs. In the last moment of life, the higher centers of his brain would collapse.

The Drifter turned and studied a paralyzed Tyson. An ingested antidote, Tyson thought; probably brought on the fever. Probably how he got the Firemen. Tyson's thoughts felt strangely alien, like shoes that no longer fit. He was abruptly cold and very tired. Not long now.

The Drifter gently touched the rough bristle on the Tough Cop's face and rotated Tyson's head so his eyes were looking out the side window.

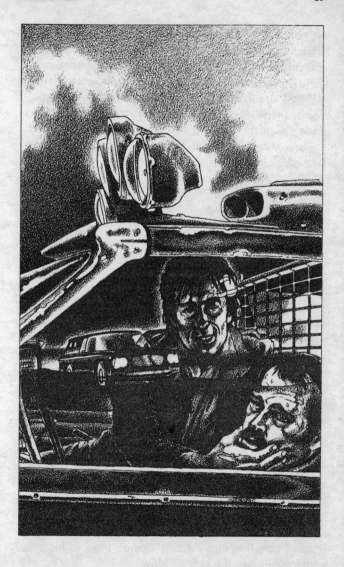

"You have been very helpful," the Drifter said. "You are an exceptionally violent man, but you have a place in this pitiful society. You've given us enough work in one night to feed many of us for some weeks." He paused. "Thank you, friend. My wife, my children thank you."

As Tyson's hearing faded, he saw a sleek, black vehicle with just a touch of chrome top a dune and trundle toward them. It was a hearse. The Morticians were coming.

A Step Into Darkness
by
Nina Hoffman

About the Author

Nina Kiriki Hoffman at first glance appears to be a quiet if bright-eyed person with a recent B.A. in English. She is in fact a guitar-playing, song-singing photographer who has worked as a cook and a proofreader, and been an extra in a Burt Reynolds film. She can often be found behind the wheel of her CB-equipped station wagon, roaming the scenic areas of the West and Northwest. Winning third place in the first quarter has enabled her to move to the Pacific shore in Oregon, a state that houses a number of her fellow graduates from the famous Clarion Writers' Workshop, which she attended in 1982.

While at college in Moscow, Idaho, she had become a prominent member of the "Moscow Moffia," a prolific and populous amateur writers' group. Despite Moscow's relatively small size, the group thus far has had three members accepted as Clarion students, a testament to what hard work, acute criticism, and dedication can do.

Nina's writing career may very well become a long and important one; editor after editor is beginning to respond to her highly individual touch on a story. Something of her Balkan family heritage also shows in A Step Into Darkness, *which may be called science fiction by some, and fantasy by others. Whichever it is, it is unmistakably a tale by Hoffman. . . .*

She's starting something," said Goblin, plunking her bony elbows down on Sylvia's wooden kitchen table and propping her chin in her hands.

"What do you mean?" Sylvia put down the dishrag and sat in the chair across from Goblin. She stared at the twelve-year-old.

Goblin was used to the concentrated gaze of those golden eyes. She liked the attention. She stopped in at Sylvia's apartment after school every day.

"Mom," said Goblin. "She's going all starry-eyed over this guy, and she's started bringing him home, and I can't stand him. I don't know why. I just hate him."

"Tell me about him."

"He's really nice. He has a deep voice and a big stomach and thick brown hair and his mouth gets crooked when he smiles. He's really nice, and I hate him. Mom cooks him big dinners and he says thank you and brings wine." Goblin looked down at the table, began scratching at some dough thinly crusted on the wooden surface.

"Are you jealous?"

Goblin stared out the kitchen window at the driveway. The lilac hedge had lost most of its leaves. "No," she said. Sylvia studied her profile, the large green-brown eye under the fierce brow, the smooth tilt of nose, the thin pale lips. Goblin's gold-brown hair was twisted into short tight pigtails. The part in her hair looked serrated, and her bangs were spiky.

"What is it, Goblin?"

"He looks at me this way, and it makes me feel creepy. Like I wish I could roll up in a cocoon to get away from his eyes."

Sylvia stood up, went around the table, and took Goblin in her arms. The little girl's shoulders began jerking in dry sobs.

"I'm sorry. I hate being so stupid. I'm sorry," Goblin muttered.

"Shhhhhhh," murmured Sylvia. She began humming.

Goblin relaxed as the song seeped into her. Sylvia kept doing things like this to her, singing to her, feeding her odd things, studying her with those big golden eyes: Goblin had seen her lift a dresser once to catch a mouse beneath it. She had all sorts of suspicions about Sylvia, but none of them marred the overriding feeling she got that Sylvia loved her and cared about her.

Sylvia nested the sleeping Goblin in the furry orange beanbag chair in the living room. She covered the child with a quilt. Then she went into the kitchen to make pastry dough and shape odd little meat-and-parsley dumplings until her husband Alex came home.

Goblin felt she was in some giant furry lap when she awoke. She opened her eyes to half-light, recognizing the cluttered living room, the climbing devil's ivy that blocked most of the twilight out of the window. "Carol?" Sylvia's voice called into the hall.

"Yes?" said Goblin's mother.

"Can I have Goblin for supper?"

Carol laughed; a masculine chuckle joined her. Goblin

Illustrated by A. R. Conway

frowned, wishing Sylvia would learn better English so people would stop laughing at her, and resenting Silas for laughing at someone he didn't even know.

"As long as she comes home safe afterwards," Carol said.

"But Carol, I bought her something special," said Silas.

"Is this important, Sylvia? You been working extra hard?"

"I made brepri," said Sylvia. Goblin heard a mournful note in her voice. What was brepri?

"Is Gretchen down there now?"

"Yes."

"Why don't you send her up to us for a few minutes? We'll send her right back down. Is Alex home yet?"

"He comes in ten minutes," said Sylvia.

"Right. She'll be back by then."

"That is fine." Sylvia closed the door. Goblin heard her take deep breaths.

In the hall, Silas was saying, "Who the hell was that?"

"Oh, they're foreign, but extraspecial nice; it's great for me that Gretchen has somebody to come home to," said Carol. Then the door closed upstairs, muffling their conversation.

"Did you see him?" Goblin asked.

"I saw him." Sylvia moved across the room. Goblin heard glass grate on metal. She smelled kerosene. Then a flame touched a wick, and Sylvia set the lamp's chimney back on the lamp. She turned to Goblin and the fire danced in her golden eyes. "Goblin, I guess you must go upstairs for a few minutes. But you do not have to stay."

"All right." Goblin rubbed her eyes, then climbed out of her nest. Goosebumps rose on her arms. "Guess I'll get my sweatshirt. Brrrr."

"I will turn the heat up."

"Thanks." Goblin had noticed that Sylvia never got goosebumps. She just moved slower when cold weather set in.

Goblin opened the door and stepped out into the lime-sherbet-green hall. Her mother had turned on the stair light. For a moment Goblin looked out the front door toward the tree-dark park across the street. She would rather run away into the trees than climb the stairs to face Silas. But Silas made Mama happy—early morning songs in the shower, perfume in the air, periods when her mother stared at nothing and smiled, making the whole apartment feel like the week before Christmas. Goblin turned and scuffed up the stairs, feeling threads of pain in her knees at each step, her feet dragging like they did when she wanted to slow a merry-go-round or stop a swing.

"There she is, the little sunbeam," said Silas when she walked into the living room. He was sitting on Mom's red sofa. He patted the cushion beside him. "What did the neighbor lady call you? Goblin? You like that, honey?"

"Only from her."

"She don't espeaka de English real good, do she?"

"She learns fast," said Goblin. She went and sat on the edge of the sofa, pressing against the sofa's arm.

"Look what I got for you, sweetie."

It wasn't fair. It really wasn't fair. He held out a penny whistle. Mom knew that was on her Christmas wish list.

"Take it, baby. A little bird told me you'd want one. Can you play anything on it?"

"Not yet." Goblin squinted at him. Silas grinned and waved the whistle in front of her in that peculiar limp way that makes long straight things seem to wobble like rubber. Then, tiring of that, he put the whistle in her lap without really letting go of it.

"Thank you," said Goblin, grasping it. Suddenly the silvery flute seemed filthy. She wanted to throw it across the room.

"Please. A note or two," said Silas, watching her.

Goblin looked up. Mom stood in the doorway to the kitchen, grinning like a pumpkin. Goblin raised the blue plastic mouthpiece to her lips, feeling an intense desire to retch, and tootled a little. Then she stood up, feeling breathless. "I have to go downstairs," she said. "Sylvia needs me to set the table."

"Don't you love that whistle?" Mom asked, her voice just a touch too bright.

"I love penny whistles," said Goblin. "Thank you, Uncle Silas." She ran out of the room and pounded down the stairs, pushing away from the wall as she rounded the turn in the staircase. Sylvia was waiting in the doorway of her apartment. Goblin rocketed past her, fetched up in the beanbag chair, and collapsed. The little brass bell on the door tinkled as Sylvia clicked the door shut.

"He gave me this," Goblin said, holding the whistle out with just the extreme ends of her fingers touching it.

Sylvia breathed on her fingers, then took the whistle from Goblin. She held it up and sniffed it. Goblin watched her face. Suddenly it looked alien, the golden eyes half-lidded in concentration, the nostrils wide, the tip of the tongue out just a little. Goblin felt all the agitation in her settle and still. She was almost afraid.

"The contamination does not go very deep," Sylvia said, becoming human again. "Come into the kitchen."

Goblin watched Sylvia one-handedly put the kettle on

the stove. A firmly lidded Dutch oven on a back burner resonated with simmer. Something smelled brothy and good. Sylvia took the saltshaker off the shelf over the stove and sprinkled salt on the penny whistle and in her palm. Then she rubbed her salt-gritty hands over the whistle. The kettle began to shrill. She opened the spout and passed the flute through the escaping steam. "Did you play it?" she asked.

Goblin nodded.

"Hold out your hand."

Mute, Goblin held out her hand, and Sylvia sprinkled salt on her palm. "Kiss the salt. It cleanses," she said.

As Goblin brought her palm to her lips, she heard a key in the apartment door. The salt bit her tongue. The bell on the door tinkled, and Alex came into the kitchen. "Hi." He touched Goblin's head and moved toward Sylvia.

"Wait," she said, holding up a hand. He paused. She held out the penny whistle, grasping it at either end, and sang something to it in a hissy, slithery language.

Goblin watched Sylvia's shoulders untense, then glanced at Alex to see how he was taking this. She was still a little frightened by what she had stirred up in Sylvia. The new strangeness did not scare her quite as much as Silas did, though.

"Where did that come from?" Alex asked, pointing at the flute.

"A man gave it to Goblin." Sylvia handed the whistle to Alex, who narrowed his brown eyes to study it. "Is it clean?"

"Cleaner than new," he said, holding the whistle out to Goblin. "Who is this man?"

"He is achini," said Sylvia. She spat in the sink.

Bewildered, Goblin rubbed the flute on her jeans and

looked up at Alex. He frowned and knelt so that his eyes were level with hers. "Where did you meet him?" he asked.

"He's my mother's boyfriend. What was that word she said, Alex?"

"Something very bad."

Goblin stood up straight and glared at him. "I am not a baby."

"No. You can't be. It means child-molester, Goblin."

Goblin stared at him, then sucked in breath. She began to tremble. She had felt it all along, but the words put a face on her suspicion. She felt angry and scared. She had heard stories. But why her? Everything seemed ugly. She looked at Alex. He was too close to her, and Sylvia was too far away. She took two steps backward, bumping into the kitchen table, and hugged herself, pressing the flute against her arm.

Alex stood up and faded back.

"Oh, Goblin, you are safe here, little one," said Sylvia, her voice edging up toward crooning mode.

Goblin knew that tone of voice, knew it could knock her into a nap. Everyone could do things to her she felt powerless to prevent. She gulped, glanced toward the living room. The kerosene lamp hissed a little. The apartment smelled like dinner, and she was so hungry. Outside the windows, the early autumn night had fallen. Yet here, in this kitchen, were two people she didn't really understand, and upstairs, in her home, was a monster. She took two steps, then looked at Alex and Sylvia. Alex looked very worried. Sylvia suddenly held out her arms; her face was twisted with pain.

"No, no," said Goblin, and ran away, past the bell, out the front door of the building, across the street.

The cold wrapped around her as she crunched across

frosty grass blades. The park had bright lights in it, but the trees had shadow sides. She ran to her favorite maple and huddled against the dark side of its trunk, then let herself think.

What did they want? Everybody wanted something.

Alex had given her a word for Silas: child-molester. But she had felt that.

She gave herself a word for Sylvia.

Witch.

She wasn't sure what Alex was, but she knew he knew about Sylvia. He had understood what Sylvia was doing when he came into the kitchen.

She tried to think of some place to run away to. The tears froze on her face.

A little later a man stepped into her strip of shadow. Fear gripped her. She held the flute tight in her fist, tried to raise her arm so she could hit him.

"Goblin," he said. It was Alex. "I brought you a coat."

"I'm so cold," she said, and began to cry. Her fist dropped to her side.

He wrapped the coat around her and lifted her in his arms. She leaned into his shoulder.

When the storm of weeping had passed, Alex said, "Is there any place I can take you?"

"I'm hungry," she said. She felt too tired to protect herself.

"Can I take you home?"

"All right." His shoulder was warm against her face. She could smell soap and aftershave. She felt his muscles moving as he crossed the park. The chill had gone deep into her: even his coat did not warm her; she could feel her whole body shivering against his arms.

Sylvia was waiting to open the front door for them,

and then the apartment door. When Alex settled Goblin in a kitchen chair, Sylvia pulled the coat off her, lifted a blanket off the radiator, and wrapped it around Goblin. She put a mug of beef broth in the child's hands, then sat down across the table from her.

Goblin sipped, feeling warmth trickle down her throat, and melt into her numbed skin. She was still shivering. The broth was just right: not hot enough to burn her tongue, but a radical difference from the cold outside. She gulped it, savoring the tingling spread of warmth that slowed her trembling. At last she looked up.

Sylvia's hands were twisted tight together on the table. "I didn't mean to frighten you," she said.

"You're a witch, and you do things to me without asking me."

"I am an adult. Sometimes I think I know what is good for you."

"What language are you a grown-up in?" Goblin put down her mug and Alex took it away to refill it.

Sylvia laughed. "Oh, Goblin, you are right. In English I am still a child."

"Don't laugh at me. I'm scared."

Sylvia closed her eyes. "I am sorry. I am scared, too."

"Where you come from, they have these—these achini people?"

"Very rare."

"What do you do to them?"

Sylvia opened her eyes, gold discs with hairline pupils. "They become dead, and their seed is watched."

"But they're people." Goblin gripped the mug, pressing her palms against its warmth. "What if your mother loves them?"

"It is very different there," said Sylvia. Her pupils

widened, and Goblin realized that they were slit, like a cat's. For months she had been watching Sylvia's eyes without letting herself see them. "In some ways, it is terrible. I would not go back there. But it is pressed into me, under the skin. I would still say a child is more important than a—a briznoi? Alex?"

"A boyfriend," said Alex. "I'd say that too." Goblin looked at him carefully. His eyes were normal—no gold, no slit pupils. "And I come from around here," he said, nodding to her. "I think we have to talk to your mother."

"No. You don't understand. She felt so awful after the divorce; she's just been dragging around. Now she's happy."

"But she would feel terrible if something happened to you."

"If I make Uncle Silas leave, she'll hate me."

"If you let Uncle Silas stay, he'll hurt you."

"What can I do? What can I do?"

"You don't have to do anything, Goblin," said Alex. "We'll tell her."

She looked at Alex, then at Sylvia. They were doing it again, taking the choice away from her, making her feel helpless and small. In a way, she wanted to leave it in their hands, have grown-ups take care of it. In a way, she wanted the decision to be hers.

"I'll tell them about Sylvia," she said. "I'll tell them she's a witch and comes from another planet." She looked down at her mug. Her stomach churned. She remembered that she had drunk Sylvia's broth, and was wrapped in Sylvia's blanket.

They sat silent for a little while. Goblin began to feel sick.

"We cannot let that stop us," Sylvia said. "If this Silas hurts you, it will—it will slash you in your soul, and that is very hard to heal. Then if you had an Alex walk through your life, you would probably run away from him, and never know that it can be wonderful. I am an adult, and I know this."

"Mama will hate me," whispered Goblin.

"Better she hates you a little while than she hates herself the rest of her life," Alex said.

"Maybe he won't do anything."

Sylvia stood up and went to the stove. She ladled dumplings out of the Dutch oven and into a bowl. On her way back to the table, she fished a fork out of the dish rack by the sink. She set fork and bowl in front of Goblin. "These are brepri," she said.

Goblin picked up the fork. She jabbed a dumpling. "I said, maybe he won't do anything."

"You're not a baby, Gretchen," said Alex. "Please don't lie to yourself."

"Good night," Carol's voice called, out in the hall. Alex folded his hand of cards and laid it on top of the go-fish pile. For a minute Goblin was mad; she needed another eight, and she was sure he had just picked one up.

"Good night," called Silas. The building's door slammed.

Goblin heard the bell on the apartment door ring as Sylvia opened it. "Carol?" she called up the stairwell. "Could you come please down?"

She does it on purpose, Goblin decided, and wondered why.

"Has Gretchen been bothering you?" asked Carol, a lilt in her voice. Goblin heard the step-click of her mother's high heels on the stairs.

"It is not that."

The sound came from the living room now. Goblin looked at Alex, then at her lap, feeling she would rather shrivel up and blow away than face what was coming.

Sylvia, wearing the gray-tinted glasses she always wore when she went outside, went to stand behind Alex, laying her hands on his shoulders.

"Gretchen, honey, did you help with the dishes?" asked her mother, rubbing Goblin's head. Goblin dropped her cards and covered her face with her hands.

"What is it, baby?" Carol said.

"Please sit down," said Alex.

The kitchen table stood against the wall, under the window. Carol took the seat between Goblin and Alex, then leaned over and touched her daughter's shoulder. "What's the matter, Gretchen? Can you tell Mother?"

Goblin shook her head. She lowered her hands and looked up, feeling a tightness behind her face.

"We need to tell you something," Sylvia said. "This is not Goblin's choice."

Carol looked at them, then at Goblin. "I don't understand."

"Goblin thinks you love that man, the Silas."

"I'm beginning to think so, yes," Carol said, and smiled. In the silence that followed, she lost her smile.

"Goblin likes to see you happy, but this man, this man is dangerous to her. He is a child-molester."

Carol's grip tightened on Goblin's shoulder. "Has he done anything to you, baby?" she asked in a low, tense voice.

Goblin shook her head. "He just—he just makes me feel creepy. I'm sorry, Mom. I'm sorry."

Carol took a deep breath. "Let me get this straight. Silas makes you feel creepy. You tell the neighbors. Now—who decided he was a menace to children?"

"I did," said Sylvia.

Goblin watched her mother's face. She recognized the terrible smile there. It was the smile Carol got when she was behind her cash register at the supermarket and some customer was being completely unreasonable, but Carol couldn't talk back. "Well, now," she said. "You know, I was glad Gretchen made friends with you folks. It's nice to have a community sense about a building. But I can't have you making my child's life ugly with these filthy suspicions. A child ought to have her childhood. God knows kids have to grow up fast enough these days. Gretchen, I don't want you visiting these people any more, dear."

"But, Mom——"

"I'm sorry you don't like Silas. Maybe he and I can go out to dinner instead of eating at home. I'll find you a reliable sitter if you don't want to be home alone. You just try to forget anything these people have told you tonight, all right?"

"Mama." Goblin pushed her chair back and stood up. She rubbed her eyes.

"Carol," said Alex.

She smiled brightly at him.

"Don't let it happen with your consent," he said.

She grabbed Goblin's arm and dragged her out of the apartment. "Kerosene lamp in the living room," Carol muttered as she marched Goblin upstairs. "They'll burn the building down some day."

Goblin hugged her books and scuffed her moonboots on the sidewalk. School was out, but she didn't want to go home. Carol had been very firm over the Special K that morning, telling her to be polite, say hi, but not to get into an involved conversation with Alex or Sylvia again. Goblin said nothing. She had not slept. The conversations played over and over in her mind. She kept wondering who was right. Were Sylvia and Alex out of their minds? Was Goblin? Was Silas really just a nice man? Her mind kept giving her questions but no answers. Whenever she started to relax, she saw Sylvia sniffing the penny whistle, or salting it, or steaming it. She worried about what sort of weird space alien Sylvia was. Sylvia might have told her, but she wasn't supposed to ask Sylvia any more questions.

School had been a total washout. Her best friend Dave had had to poke her awake all day.

The sun had not melted the frost. Goblin cut through the park, looking up at the trees, which were starting to turn. She picked up a maple leaf with a green star in the center and spiky yellow edges. Sylvia would like it. But——

Sylvia, wrapped in a puffy maroon quilt and hiding behind her large gray glasses, sat on the front stoop. Her lips looked pale.

"Come inside. You're cold," said Goblin.

Sylvia rose in slow motion. Goblin held the door for her, watched her stiff movements as she started down the hall, then followed her into her apartment and put the kettle on. "It doesn't get cold like this where you come from, does it?" she asked.

"No," Sylvia whispered, shedding the quilt and lowering herself into a chair at the kitchen table.

"You shouldn't sit outside."

"I wanted to give you something."

Goblin found some tea and made a mugful. She gave it to Sylvia. "I'm not supposed to talk to you," she said.

"I know." Sylvia took the mug in one hand and held out the other. Goblin opened her hand. Sylvia dropped something into it.

It was a ring, a thin band of gold. Goblin studied it, saw faint, worn lines that made it a snake biting its tail. She tried it on the middle finger of her left hand. It fit so snugly she couldn't get it off.

"If you are in trouble," Sylvia said, her voice thawed by tea, "rub this ring and wish. It summons a serpent. I do not know how else to help you, Goblin. I am so worried."

"Mom doesn't hate me, but she doesn't like me, either. It's like we broke this picture she was making in her head, and she can't fix it. She's not happy. So she's treating me like a baby, telling me not to talk to you."

"She thinks we are bad people."

"I don't think she really does," Goblin said. She twisted the ring on her finger, watching her hands. Then she looked up. "I don't like snakes."

"I am sorry." Sylvia took off her glasses and smiled at Goblin.

"Do you have a ring that summons a tiger?"

"No."

"I'm not a baby," Goblin said, looking up at Sylvia. "I can make my own choices. But I don't think I better stay today. I have to talk to Mom some more."

"I think you are right."

"Thanks for the ring," Goblin said. She took a breath, gave Sylvia a little hug, picked up her books and dashed upstairs.

"Your mom asked me to pick you up today," Silas said. He was leaning against his car, which was parked a block up the street from school. Maple branches laced above the road here, shielding it from the sky.

"No, she didn't," Goblin said. She clasped her left

hand in her right hand across her books. She glanced back over her shoulder toward the school, but she had been one of the last to leave. The buses had gone. No one milled around down there. No witnesses.

"Sunbeam, I'm not kidding. She wants us to have a serious talk. She told me what those weird people at the apartment said the other night." He looked so earnest, so harmless.

"What do you think, that you can do it to me and I won't tell anyone? You're crazy."

"I'm not going to do anything to you, Gretchen. I just want a chance to prove myself. I'm really in love with your mother. I want us to get along."

She couldn't believe he was standing here saying these things. She searched his face for signs of deception. She couldn't find any.

He held the car door open for her.

"No," she said, backing away. "If you want to prove something, leave me alone."

"All right." He smiled, shut the door, got in the car, and drove away.

When she got home, Goblin knocked on Sylvia's door. "How do you know if someone is—achini?" she asked Sylvia's spectacled face.

"It is a taste, a smell in the air around them. What is the matter?"

"Nothing." Goblin flashed her a half-second smile, then turned and ran upstairs. How could she trust Sylvia's sense of smell? She turned on the lamp in the living room, got a glass of milk, and settled herself on the sofa, opening her history book. A little later she emerged from the Federal Constitutional Convention to look at her hands. She had been twisting Sylvia's ring around and around.

By the time Carol came home, Goblin had finished all her reading and put a sectioned chicken in the oven. A bell pepper was turning into raggedy slivers under Goblin's knife. Carol dropped a kiss on Goblin's head and took the knife away from her.

"How was your day, Mom?"

"Long."

"Did you see Silas?"

"Not today. I talked to him on the phone. Why?" Carol stopped chopping and lifted the seedy core free of the green shards. Her voice had a wary note in it.

"Did you ask him to pick me up after school?"

"Of course not. I know you don't like him." Carol froze, then set the knife on the breadboard and turned to face Goblin. "Did he—? You're not just making this up?"

"No," said Goblin, shaking her head. She twisted the ring. "No."

"Oh, baby." Carol opened her arms and hugged Goblin. They stood motionless a long time as the night leached light out of the day. At last Carol relaxed a little. "I shall have to revise my social calendar," she said. Goblin looked up at the tear tracks on her face, then away. "Perhaps we should invite Alex and Sylvia up for dinner."

"Not tonight." Goblin didn't want to see her mother apologize so soon after losing her dream.

"Will you . . . talk to them? After dinner?"

"All right."

"Go wash your hands. The chicken smells done."

A week later, on a day when the white mists had smoked free of the ground, he caught her. She was just crunching across the gravel, past the park restrooms, and the park lights were already on to fight the early dark and the fog, when he stepped out and pulled her against him. Something pricked her throat. "Scream and I'll cut you," he murmured. Her books slid out of her arms. She closed her eyes, feeling her knees and elbows and shoulders lock up. Ice crept up her spine. If his arm hadn't been snug around her, she was sure she would have collapsed.

He half-carried her into the men's room, then wedged the door shut with a broom handle. He pushed her away. "You make any noise and I'll cut your throat," he whispered. She could see the knife now. It looked a foot long and freshly sharp. "Take off your clothes."

"Why?" she whispered. "Why?" She was already numb with cold.

"None of your business," he said. He looked tense, but not really evil. Then he licked his upper lip and stepped closer, the knife ready. "I was really trying. I wasn't going to hurt you. You told your mother. You screwed it up. It's your own fault. Take off your clothes."

She looked at his pants, then away, and pulled off her gloves. Then she held her left hand in her right and rubbed the ring. Serpents. Serpents.

"Come on," he said, and drew the point of the knife down the back of her right hand, leaving a shallow bloody scratch.

I wish for a serpent to save me, she thought, and squinched her eyes shut. And suddenly all the open space at her back and over her head was gone, the echoing emptiness behind her muffled by something alive and breathing and huge. She heard the movement of something smooth and dry against the smooth damp concrete of the floor.

Silas screamed. Goblin heard the knife clatter on the floor. She heard him run back to the door and scrabble with the broomstick, all the while moaning. A rush of cold air hit her as he opened the door. His footsteps crunched over gravel, then faded, muffled by mist and grass.

Goblin opened her eyes.

Dark shadows blocked the light from the bare bulb above. She raised her head, looked up at three pale, scaled throats. The heads were as thick as her waist. She stepped away, out from under them, and turned to look.

Its massive coils were thick as tree trunks, the color of golden brown sugar, with darker diamond-patterned traceries along its back. Despite the three heads, it was all one beast. Three forked black tongues flickered out and in. She could have slid down any of its throats with room to spare.

"Oh, God," she said, wishing she could stop shivering, and unlock her knees, and run after Silas.

One head lowered. She stared at a round gold eye with a slit pupil, saw the pupil flick wider. She gasped. She reached out and laid a trembling hand on the head. "Oh, God," she whispered. She stood there a moment, struggling for breath, then stooped and retrieved her gloves. She took five steps and reached the open door, then turned to look at the serpent. Three pairs of golden eyes stared back. Its tail shifted, hissing across the concrete.

"Thank you," she said, edging outside. She bent and scooped up her books. "Oh, God. What do you eat? Oh, God."

She ran all the way home, stumbled in through the building's front door, and leaned against the post at the foot of the stairs, her breath aching in and out of her. A

faint tinkle of bell. Sylvia, bare-eyed, stepped out of her apartment and glided toward Goblin. Goblin stared.

"Brepri," said Sylvia.

"Oh, God," Goblin whispered. She looked back through the glass-paneled front door towards the park, where the trees stood faint shadows in the fog, some silhouetted by the lights. "Sylvia." She turned back, to stare at those golden eyes. Sylvia's face bore no expression. Goblin wrestled with herself, trying to figure out which scared her more. Silas probably wouldn't come back, but Sylvia still lived downstairs. Goblin looked at the ring, a thread of gold under the stair light. "Was that you?" she asked.

"An aspect of me."

"Well . . ." Goblin dropped her books and gloves on the bottom stair. She paused a moment to pull herself together. Then she hugged Sylvia, burying her face in the folds of Sylvia's silky beige dress, breathing in her strange burlap scent. After a moment, Sylvia's arms came around her.

"Can't do a tiger, huh," Goblin said.

"No," said Sylvia, releasing her and looking down at her face.

"Can I keep the ring?"

Sylvia gently pulled one of her pigtails. "Until you learn your own aspects."

Tiger Hunt
by
Jor Jennings

About the Author

First-place winner in the second-quarter contest, Jor Jennings says: "Characterize me (if you like) as a respectable, middle-aged San Fernando Valley matron who enjoys the outdoors and the alien minds of animals." While all that seems true, it also seems insufficient to describe Ms. Jennings, a pleasant and bright person who graduated from Stanford in 1957 with a B.A. in "humanities with a concentration in art."

Tiger Hunt arises from her experiences as a volunteer at the Los Angeles Zoo. It was extensively workshopped by two writers' groups to which she belongs, one academically sponsored and the other supported by the Los Angeles Science Fantasy Society, one of the oldest and most active clubs in SF fandom. An earlier story placed high—but did not win—in our first-quarter contest.

Other Jennings stories have appeared over the years in Galaxy *magazine (twice) and in* Twilight Zone *magazine; the latter piece was later reprinted in* Year's Best Fantasy Stories #9. *So with* Tiger Hunt *Jor Jennings bids farewell forever to the ranks of "New and Amateur Writers" . . . quite deservedly so.*

We rode out from the zoo as night fell, and the lights of Los Angeles winked on in the valleys below our mountain park. Although my elephants must have been terribly hungry—they've been on short rations since the famines began three years ago—most of them plodded docilely up the fire road, each trunk holding the tail of the elephant ahead. The one exception was Susie, my big Asian matriarch, who led the way. Her trunk was free, and she used it to uproot clumps of grass, slap them against her knee to knock the dirt off the roots, and then stuff them into the V of her mouth. Soon she was leading the column of elephants from one side of the road to the other as she searched out the tastiest tidbits.

Why had I let Keith, my least experienced mahout, ride the lead elephant? Well, because Susie, an old circus performer, is the easiest to control. And because Keith, with his tall, lean good looks and frightfully upper-class British accent, quite naturally strikes you as officer material, even after you learn he comes from Oregon, and the British accent is an affectation.

"Keith! Control your elephant!" I shouted.

Keith turned his head and called a reply. With four elephants between us, all I caught was, "Robin, old girl," and "What's the point . . . ?"

"The point is," I told Big Joe, who was riding the

elephant ahead of me, "you *must* keep control of your elephant at all times, so she won't ever learn how easily she can defeat you. Besides, Susie is setting a bad example for the other elephants. Pass it on."

If only I could change places with Keith! But I didn't trust anyone else to ride Ajax, my huge old African bull. He's too unpredictable. Too unpredictable for me to ride, too. I should have left him behind and cut forage for him, as the keepers of the ungulates do. Lately, however, he has seemed poorly and dispirited, moping about, lying down a lot, his spine beginning to show. Granted, he's old, and his last set of teeth is wearing out. He was about four when the zoo acquired him fifty-three years ago, the last survivor of a culled herd—that is, a herd that was massacred by park rangers when the elephant population grew too large for the carrying capacity of its range. Sometimes, when Ajax and I are exchanging long glances, I wonder what goes on in that enormous skull of his. Do forgotten childhood memories come back in old age to elephants, as they do to us? And does Ajax remember once again that terrible day long ago when his mama and sisters and playmates and all were slaughtered in that elephant Auschwitz, and he himself was trucked away, bleating and terrified, to an unknown fate? Is that why he seems so dispirited, so depressed?

News of his condition has gotten out, and the keepers of the carnivores have been asking after him. However sympathetic they try to look, I know what they want. They want elephant steaks for their snow leopards, jaguars and wolves. That's all my beautiful old Ajax is to them, five tons of cat food. So I'm going to keep him alive just as long as I can.

Maybe all he really needed was fresh air, exercise, a

change of scene, and a chance to select from nature's bounty those tender shoots and succulent herbs that would be gentlest to his failing teeth. At first I was nervous, riding out from the zoo on the neck of that huge bull. But then, when Ajax was so quiet and well-behaved, plodding peacefully at the end of the column with Jill's tail in his trunk, I soon stopped worrying about him. And started worrying about Keith.

"Robin?" Big Joe had relayed my message to the next in line, and turned back to me. "Robin, Keith says to tell you you're a bossy broad."

"Is that what he says! Well, you just tell Keith Baxter —hey, wait a minute! There wasn't time . . ."

Big Joe roared with laughter, and I realized that this was one of his jokes.

"Hey, look, Joe," I retaliated. "When you're dealing with dangerous wild animals that are bigger than you are, you *must* keep control at all times. You just have to. You know that from dealing with rhinos."

"Yeah?" said Big Joe, suspiciously.

"And Joe, I'm only five foot two. Nearly all men are bigger than I am," I reminded him.

It took awhile for that to percolate through Big Joe's brain (or what passed for it). One of our jokes, when we're kidding each other, is how much the keepers resemble the animals in their charge, and Big Joe the rhinoceros keeper is everybody's favorite example. (That skinny little blonde in charge of the elephants is the exception that proves the rule.) Finally, Big Joe got around to replying. "Robin? You trying to tell me you think *men* are dangerous wild animals?"

"The bull human," I told him, "is the most dangerous wild animal of them all."

Put that way, it was a compliment (I guess). Anyway,

he shouted "Aw *right!*" and kicked his heels on Jill's neck exuberantly.

To a trained elephant, "All right" is a command which means, roughly, "As you were." Jill, who is so perfectly obedient that we used to let children ride her when the zoo was still open to the public, stopped dead in her tracks, let go of Kikki's tail, and reached around with her trunk as though she might smell what her rider wanted. Then she bleated and swerved sideways when Ajax, coming up behind her, jabbed her butt with his tusks.

"Hike, Jill, hike! You stupid bitch!" Big Joe shouted angrily, whacking Jill's shoulder with his bull-hook. (Why did I have the feeling that his "stupid bitch" was meant for me?) Jill, who had never been ordered to "hike" before, did her best to please her rider: she sat down, and raised the foreleg on the side Big Joe had whacked.

At this, Susie, Ganny and Kikki, totally ignoring the commands of their frustrated riders, stopped and turned around to see what was happening.

"Joe," I said, "please don't do anything more. Just sit there quietly, okay? Ajax! Come here (Go left). Good boy. Move up. Easy, Ajax, easy . . . Steady (Stop). Good Ajax." Ajax seemed to understand exactly what I wanted him to do. Obediently, he stopped beside the confused cow, and put the tip of his trunk in her mouth, reassuringly.

"Jill! All right! All right, Jill! All right!" I ordered her. Finally Jill heaved herself to her feet, then sent her trunk to explore my face as though to ask, "Is that really what you wanted?" "Good girl," I said. "Move up. Move up. Good girl. Easy . . . Tail up, Jill." Once again Jill took Kikki's tail in her trunk, and I could spare some attention for the head of the column.

Without waiting for my orders, Keith had dismounted and lined up the first three elephants. He was now walking beside Susie, leading her (and keeping her out of mischief) with his bull-hook looped around her ear. Part of the time he walked backwards, to keep an eye on the following elephants. I was so impressed I nearly called out, "Good boy, Keith!" (The last time I said that, he replied, rather testily, "For your information, Robin, I am *not* one of your elephants!") Maybe my new caretaker would turn out to be a good elephant handler after all.

Finally we reached the hillside below the observatory where the fire department had asked us to clear brush. We all shouted "Steady!" and "Foot!" and "Lift!" The elephants all sat and raised a foreleg so their riders could dismount. Then I gave the command "Go play!" The elephants ambled off and began to feed on the grass and weeds that had grown so deep in the spring rains. The keepers spread out around them, cutting forage for their deer and rhinos and stuffing it into sacks. I stayed on Ajax, unsure that I could trust him, and Keith remounted Susie. Controlling the matriarch would control the herd. Susie seemed nervous with her unfamiliar rider, circling among the herd and sniffing each elephant over carefully as though vacuum-cleaning it with her trunk. I called to her several times to reassure her, concerned that she might not get enough to eat. That wasn't Ajax's problem, though. He had decided that a spring tonic of dandelion greens and wild mustard was just what the veterinarian ordered, and trunked up clump after clump of the delicacy, dribbling green saliva as he stuffed the weeds in his mouth.

His patch was soon gone and he moved in on Ganny,

prodding her butt with a six-foot tusk and grunting dangerously. Ganny, a quiet little Asian cow who manages to remain the fattest elephant in the herd in spite of being number zilch in the pecking order, yielded ground to him but moved as slowly as she could by way of protest. The two elephants were nearly side by side when a man jumped up out of a bush they were about to step on, raised his pistol, and fired.

The shot sounded like thunder in the quiet night. Ganny gave a sort of stifled squeal and dropped to one knee. Then Ajax, his great ears flaring out like airplane wings, let out a bellow and charged. Although I was in a better position to see than anyone else, I confess I am not quite sure what happened next.

Very distinctly I remember that the man was screaming "Help! Help!" when Ajax wrapped his trunk around his waist and raised him high aloft, but Keith, from nearly as good a vantage point, swears just as sincerely that Ajax had slammed his victim against three or four trees before brandishing the limp and silent body. Ajax must also have tusked him through the belly, then put him down and stepped on his head. We figured that out later, when Ajax had quieted down and we got a chance to look at the body.

For the next hour no one could go close to it. Squealing and trumpeting, with his ears flaring madly and his five-foot penis snaking about like a fire hose, Ajax circled the meadow, smashing down trees on its periphery (On the off chance that there might be poachers behind them?) and doing his best to rape the cows. None of them was in heat, so whenever he reared to mount one, she ambled out from under him and resumed munching the greenery, while I clung to the folds of thick, wrinkled skin on Ajax's vast neck and wondered just how I was going to administer the syringe full of M99 I had brought along in case Ajax became uncontrollable. The tranquilizer, and a second syringe containing the antidote, were in a pouch on my belt. They might as well have been on that full, beautiful, unconcerned moon. I needed both hands to hold on.

Ajax likes me, in his way. At least I'm the only keeper he's ever had that he hasn't tried to kill! Several times during that wild ride, when I felt myself slipping, his muscles bunched up under me and returned me to my seat, so I think he wanted me to stay there, safe on his neck. Once I had learned to anticipate his movements, I looked around for the others. Ganny seemed to be all right. Susie and Kikki had gone to her, one on each side, to push her back up on all four feet. Susie briefly ran her trunk over the leg that had given way, and then the three cows ambled off together, Ganny no longer supported. Later, when Ajax reared to mount her, Ganny moved out from under with her customary quickness.

Keith was no longer on Susie. I had a brief, horrible fear that he had been crushed when Ajax tried to rape her, and then I heard his voice from somewhere high on the hill, shouting, "Jump, Robin! Jump!" I let go with one hand long enough to wave, then grabbed hold again as Ajax reared, this time to crash down on the poacher's bush, smash it to bits, and kick the fragments this way and that.

Finally Ajax did calm down, and I was able to dismount and go to Ganny. Inspecting her leg with my pocket flashlight, I could see nothing wrong, and the only gun we were able to find was a .25 caliber "Saturday night special." Maybe the bullet had bounced off her hide.

Meanwhile, the other keepers had come down from

the wall around the observatory and gathered about the body. The poacher was beyond all help. His skull had been crushed like an egg and ground into the ground. As Big Joe remarked, "Jesus Christ couldn't bring this one back from the dead." We debated what to do. It was a long ride back to the zoo where we could telephone the authorities. Meanwhile, the elephants had to eat, and the other keepers had to gather forage for their charges. Finally, we did the only thing we could do. We stuffed the body into one of the forage sacks, packed it well with dead leaves to absorb the blood, and tied it on to Jill's homemade pack saddle. (We had made pack saddles for all the elephants as soon as we realized that the city council was really going to pass the law forbidding the purchase of food to feed zoo animals, as long as there was one hungry person in Los Angeles—as though humans were the endangered species, not them! Believe me, if people were an endangered species, the world would be much better off!)

Keith took the flashlight from my hand and turned its pale beam on Ajax's forehead, where a streak of dark goop streamed from a gland above and behind his eye. "I say, Robin old girl. I hate to be the one to tell you, but it looks like Ajax is in musth."

"Nonsense!" Only the Asian bulls have musth, that unpredictable, belligerent and dangerous condition signalled by secretions from the temporal gland. African elephants, both bulls and cows, secrete scent continuously, but most copiously when they are excited or alarmed. Didn't that inept Oregonian know *anything?* "Keith," I snapped, "do you think you could manage to talk like a human being, for once in your life, instead of—instead of——" I couldn't think of anything with a British accent that wasn't a human being.

"Righto! Sorry about that! Oh, I say! I really *am* sorry!" Maybe he couldn't help it. I began to feel guilty about losing my temper. It wasn't Keith's fault I was worried about the man Ajax had killed. What would happen when word got out? Would we lose our foraging privileges? "If you think my accent's bad now, you should hear me when I get upset," Keith told me. "Sis says she can always tell when I'm worried about something; I sound like Winston Churchill." ("Sis" was carnivore keeper Karen Baxter, Keith's twin.)

"And when I'm worried I lose my temper—that's why I snapped at you. Keith, I'm sorry. I hope you didn't take it personally."

"Wouldn't dream of it," said Keith. Then, curiously, "You worry a lot, don't you?"

Well, yes, I do worry a lot. Every day I must scrounge a ton of food for those five big lugs, who aren't just animals; they're all my friends, or, more than that, my children, for they all depend on me. I've been so tired lately, so close to total exhaustion! Yet, if I collapse, what will happen to my elephants? This is the thought that keeps me going. I wanted to cry, but not in front of Keith! So I hugged the foreleg of the nearest elephant instead. Elephants feel so substantial, like living mountains that will be there forever. Although I know from sad experience that they're surprisingly delicate, and can drop dead without warning, their great strength seems to flow into me when I hug them, and gives me the strength to go on.

Restored, I turned to Keith. "I say, Keith old thing, that does *rahthah* give us something in common, righto?"

I meant we were both worriers, but Keith misunderstood. "Right—um." With an effort, he left off the "o." "I like elephants, too," Keith said softly.

The full moon, sinking in the west, faded to match the brightening sky around it, and we knew it was time to go back to the zoo if we wanted to avoid confrontations with the public. The keepers loaded the last sacks of forage onto the elephants' backs, ordered up a foreleg, and climbed onto the wide, wrinkled necks. Then we queued up the elephants, trunk to tail, and lumbered off.

Back at the zoo, we hung the body, still in its sack, in the meat locker to keep cool until we had done our chores and could afford to spend the next umpteen hours answering cops' questions. Then we went off, I to hose off and bed down my elephants. The other keepers opened their daytime paddocks to their bongos, Arabian oryxes, dall sheep, gerenuks, giraffes and Indian rhinos—to name just a few of the rare and endangered animals we're trying so hard to keep alive for an uncooperative and unappreciative world.

Karen Baxter, Keith's keeper twin, was waiting for me in the elephant barn. "How's Ajax?" she asked, as usual.

"Much better," I told her. "Killing that poacher did him a world of good."

"Ajax killed a poacher?" Karen screeched.

"Some goofball who attacked the elephants with a twenty-five pistol, last night when we were out foraging. We've hung the body in the meat locker until we get a chance to notify the authorities. Didn't Keith tell you?"

"Haven't seen him." Karen shook her head. "Isn't that going to be kind of a shock, I mean if somebody who doesn't know about the body walks in the meat locker?"

"We put it in a forage sack." I wanted to change the

subject, so I asked, "How's Katy?"

Karen shrugged. "She's alive, that's about all you can say. I caught her some rats last night, eight of them. She gulped them down, swallowed them whole, too hungry to chew them, and, well, they came right back up. So she ate them again. That time she chewed them, and they stayed down—so far. Rats aren't enough for her. She needs some real meat, Robin!"

Katy (short for Catherine the Great) is our clandestine Siberian tiger, maybe the last of her race in the whole world. Siberians are thought to be extinct in the wild, now that the greenhouse effect has wiped out their last remaining habitat. When the worldwide food shortage began to affect the provisioning of zoos, the International Zoo Association agreed on triage. The animals that could still be saved in the wild—leopards, jaguars, ocelots and the Bengal tiger—would be fed whenever possible, but zoos were ordered to destroy their Siberian tigers, on the grounds they had no natural habitat remaining. On the other hand, African lions are doing better in Africa than the people, so we don't have them in zoos anymore, either, in order to have more meat for the cats we need to save for the future.

Karen had bottle-fed Katy when she was a furry, feisty handful abandoned by her mother, and she refused to see her tiger destroyed. There were still Siberian tigers in the wild, Karen maintained; she had seen them in her dreams, while floating over Asia in her astral body. And, surely, other zoos had Siberian tigers hidden away, perhaps even a handsome young male, who would be delighted to meet Karen's pretty female as soon as mankind had learned to cope with the great inland seas that had drowned the world's best farmland, and food was plentiful again. If not, why then, Katy could be bred to Bengals and the offspring backcrossed until a true-breeding Siberian strain reemerged. Why not? As soon as food was plentiful again . . .

Would food ever be plentiful again?

Like most of the other keepers, I felt sorry for the great, starved beast, and thought Katy ought to be put out of her misery. But that was Karen's business, and as long as she could keep her tiger alive without taking food away from the approved carnivores . . .

"Karen," I said, "I would give Katy my left arm—not my right, just my left—if I thought it would keep her alive until things get better."

"Yeah. Well, I'm glad Ajax's feeling better . . . hey, I really am!" Karen waved goodbye, flashing her diamond ring.

How long after the death of her fiancé should a young lady continue to wear his engagement ring? "Concerned Mother" wrote columnist Etta Kitt. I forget the answer. It wouldn't apply in Karen's case anyway. Whether or not Karen's fiancé was dead, or had ever existed, Karen needed to go on wearing the ring, to prove she had once been loved, and by a man.

The trouble was, she looked so much like Keith that people who didn't know any better assumed they were identical twins. "The only difference between Keith and Karen," Big Joe so wittily remarked, "is Keith has a beard and Karen shaves." Karen really did have a scraggly, immature wisp of beard, which she didn't always remember to pluck out. However, the main difference between the twins is that on Keith a beard looks good. And Karen? Well, when Big Joe saw me having lunch with her, he took me aside to whisper, "You don't want to hang around Karen Baxter, a pretty little thing like you. Folks will get the wrong idea!"

But, no. I take it back. The *main* difference between the twins is that Karen has always known what she wanted to do with her life, and Keith hasn't. (Karen once told me that Keith had never shown any interest in animals at all, until he met me. If so, that was a remarkably quick conversion. Two days later, he was working at the zoo.) While Karen was getting a B.A. in zoology as her credential in wildlife management, Keith was bumming around the world, or working at odd jobs, one of the great mass of young people who were "trying to find themselves" in those innocent years before famine set in and made the quest seem superficial and irrelevant.

Freemartin though she was, Karen was no homosexual, which was a pity: a woman might have loved her as no man could. That is, we assumed no man could love her. One day she showed up with a magnificent diamond ring on her left hand, and said she was engaged to an officer in the National Guard. Yes, she would bring him by to meet us. When? Soon. Very soon. Only, somehow, he never could come, and finally Karen told us that he had been killed in the food riots of '98. Karen went on wearing his ring on her big, square hand. Then Big Joe told us she had bought it herself, from his uncle the jeweler; she was behind on the payments. We all have trouble telling whether Big Joe is joking, lying, or telling what he thinks is the truth, but this time everyone believed him. Even me.

I finished cleaning out the elephant barn, and checked Ganny's wound one last time. This time I was able to see the tiny bullet half-buried in her hide. When I touched the area she shuffled about in pain, so I gave her a shot of lidocaine before I dug the bullet out, and one of antibiotics afterwards. The skin of an elephant may be thick, but it is as sensitive as ours, and more susceptible to infection.

Once my chores were done, I went off to a meadow behind the Administration Building where I knew I could catch a few hours' sleep without interruption. If I try to nap in my office at the elephant barn, someone invariably wakes me with some problem that can't be put off. The only problem I can't put off is getting a few hours of uninterrupted sleep every day or two.

At noon I was startled awake. Something was wrong. The noise of the crowd at the front gates, the crowd that gathered every day to protest the continuing existence of zoo animals in a time of human hunger, had taken on a new note. Then I heard the squeal—of an elephant! As soon as I identified the sound, I was on my feet and running toward the gates.

All those people pressed against the inner gates made them impossible to open. Instead, I climbed over. As soon as I was on top, I could see what was the matter. Among the crowds of people, their shirts blinding white in the blazing sun, loomed the towering gray bulk of Susie. Keith, on her neck, had obviously lost control; all Susie would do in response to his commands was shuffle backward in a circle, trumpeting all the time. Elephants can't see behind themselves—they can't turn their heads far enough—and it makes them very nervous when they think something dangerous is just behind them and out of sight.

Susie was more than nervous; she was on the verge of panic. A panic-stricken elephant may bolt, or charge. Either way, people would be trampled.

Shouting "Excuse me," and "Let me through," and using my elbows so much they were bruised the next

Illustrated by Frank Ferrel

day, I finally reached Susie's side. "Keith Baxter!" I screamed, "You get down from my elephant this instant!"

"I say, old girl," Keith said in his phoney British accent, "you can't get down from an elephant, you get down from a——" the noise of the crowd increased just then, so Keith had to shout, "Duck!"

I dropped to my knees as I whirled around, but nobody menaced me.

"Sorry about that," said Keith. "I really must stop making stupid jokes in emergencies, what?"

Meanwhile, Susie was sniffing me over with her trunk, as though she could hardly believe it was really me, at last. I patted her reassuringly while I glared up at Keith. "Goose!" I snapped.

"Who, me?" said Keith.

"You get down from a goose. So. Are you going to give me the bull-hook or would you prefer to stay here all day?"

"Bossy broad," I heard him mutter as he leaned down to hand me the bull-hook.

Stationing myself at Susie's left eye, where she could easily see my reassuring presence, I called to her over and over, "Susie! Move up! Easy, Susie, easy. Move up, Susie. Good girl. Good Susie," and touched her gently and repeatedly with the bull-hook, when I wasn't using its handle to push back someone who stood in our way. Most of the people fell back when I glared at them, and the rest when Susie seemed about to trample them underfoot.

Slowly, the great elephant shuffled her way through the crowd. It must have taken a good half-hour, but we finally passed the outer gates. I scared the people out from between the two sets of gates by putting Susie through her circus tricks of rearing and handstands.

(Keith kept his seat surprisingly well, I must say.) Once everyone had fled, Keith climbed down and closed the outer gates. Then and only then could we open the inner gates and take Susie home to a well-earned rest. Only then could I let my attention stray from the task of controlling my elephant.

"All right, Keith Baxter," I said. "You may now explain what you were doing outside the gates on my elephant."

"*Your* elephant?"

"The elephants are mine because I'm in charge of them. The fact that you work for me does not mean that you may ride them without my permission. Is that understood?"

"Righto, quite so, knew it all along," Keith said, not at all apologetically. "Fact is, we did try to find you, but you had disappeared, and we didn't have much time. Eric, you see, got zapped by the boomslang. We had to get him to the hospital fast."

Eric was our curator of reptiles. The boomslang is a pretty damn poisonous snake. "Don't they have boomslang antivenin in the reptile house?"

"Righto, and it went along with Eric to County General. You see, old girl, shooting it in his arm with a needle won't do the trick. Antivenin must be perfused in slowly with an i.v. if it's to work, We'd called for an ambulance, but the crowd wouldn't let it through. They wouldn't let us drive Eric out to it, either. We even called the cops and the fire department, trying to get a helicopter—those blighters don't give a bloody damn about us, do they? They thought they might have one available in two or three hours. . . ."

"So you volunteered to take Eric to the ambulance on Susie?"

"We did try to find you, Robin, but you weren't around, and Eric couldn't wait. We got him out to the ambulance all right; saw him off and all that. The problem was getting back in. What ho?"

A man in a policeman's uniform blocked our way. He held up his hand. "Are you Roberta Day, the head elephant keeper?"

I said I was.

"Then what have you done with the body, Ms. Day?"

"What body?"

"The body of the man your elephants killed this morning. The one in the meat locker. What have you done with it?"

Oh, *that* body. "Susie, foot!" I said, to gain time. Susie lifted her foot and I bent over its thick callus pad. Actually, it was a good thing I looked. She had picked up some fragments of broken glass, which might have lamed her if they had worked up into the quick. I dug them out with my jackknife while I decided what to say. Maybe the innocent approach? I looked up suddenly, as though startled, and a veil of blond hair fell over my wide blue eyes. "You mean," I said, "there's a *human* body in the meat locker?"

"In fact, there isn't, but we got this report. . . ."

"Well, I didn't put it there!" I blurted, truthfully enough. It was Big Joe who had hung up the body. Still, if the body had disappeared from the meat locker, that was a stupid thing to say. My next remark wasn't any smarter. "If there's a body in the meat locker, it sure isn't mine!"

"The body in the meat locker seems to have disappeared, Ms. Day. And so, if you would kindly help us find it. . . . We think it may be a robber we've been looking for," he explained lamely. Looking at them through my hair does it. "That's why—you'll be doing us a favor. . . ."

"Will somebody please tell me what's going on?" I said, when I couldn't think of anything else to say.

Keith came to my rescue. "Robin, there's a rumor going around that the elephants killed somebody and you put the body in the meat locker. I would have told you, but I thought you'd heard it. Still, I don't suppose anyone would bother to tell you, would they? Not if they thought you did it. Sorry about that, officer. You know how it is with rumors," said Keith, with his disarming smile. Good boy, Keith!

"If you don't want my elephants killing people, you've got to do something about that crowd at the gate," I told the cop. "This morning we had to take a snakebite victim out to the ambulance by elephant; the crowd wouldn't let the paramedics through. These are zoo elephants, officer. They're not circus elephants, they're not used to dealing with crowds. Can you imagine what would have happened if Susie here had panicked and bolted? You wouldn't have just one dead person, you would have hundreds, trampled, dead and injured. It really is a very dangerous situation."

"Yeah, sure, but you gotta understand how they feel! I mean, all these animals up here living in the lap of luxury while people go hungry." It was not very professional of him to express his own sentiments; for that moment he was not an officer of the law, he was one of the mob at the gate.

"Most of the animals here eat grass, weeds and shrubs we cut from the hillsides," I retorted. "Anybody who's hungry is welcome to eat that too. We've cut our carnivore stock down to a bare minimum; we're feeding them on mice, rats, coyotes—pest animals we trap or shoot." I didn't tell him that a lot of our "pest animals" are abandoned pets; dogs and housecats turned out by their owners. They walk into our snares all the time, half-starved. "If people are hungry, why don't they catch rats? Or pigeons?" It's a good thing they don't, or there wouldn't be any food left for the zoo animals. Not to mention their keepers. "Instead of looking around for someone to blame—Susie! Stop that!"

While I was distracted by my speech, Susie had been feasting off the blooming acacia tree overhead, grabbing trunkful after trunkful of the fragrant yellow blossoms and stuffing them into her mouth. The other keepers and I have agreed that we won't let our animals feed off the foliage inside the zoo itself, as that should be saved for when no other food is available at all. I felt the most need to abide by this understanding, as I have the largest animals to feed. Let's hope nobody else had seen Susie stuffing herself with the zoo acacias while her keeper stood at her left ear!

"Yeah? Well, I don't know about that, I just do my job," said the policeman, looking around for a way out of a conversation he was beginning to realize he should never have begun.

"Of course you do!" I tried to sound enthusiastic. "I know you can't set department policy. Still, when you go back and make your report, you might mention that there's a potentially life-threatening situation up here. Our elephants aren't trained in crowd control. If we have to use them for that, somebody's going to get killed. Now, if you'll excuse me, I really must get poor old Susie back to the barn before she falls asleep on her feet and I have to carry her," I joked. Catching the corner of her ear with the bull-hook, I led her at a fast shamble toward the elephant barn.

Keith came jogging after me. "Robin," he whispered when we had left the policeman far behind, "what do you think happened to that body?"

"Keith, I don't know. I don't want to know. I don't even want to think about it."

"Righto. That's what I think, too."

I unlocked the gate to the elephants' paddock. "Keith, Susie's rather warm. You're going to have to give her a bath before you bed her down."

"Who, me?" said Keith.

"You took her out." You risked your own life to save Eric's, I wanted to say. What actually came out was, "And while you're bathing her, think long and hard about how that crowd would have behaved if Susie had trampled——"

"But this is my last clean uniform!" Keith protested.

I shrugged. "Take it off."

Keith's face split into a grin. "I will if you will."

The day was so hot, its tensions so immense, that suddenly the idea of going swimming with my favorite elephant was irresistibly appealing. "Last one in is a rotten egg!" I shouted, shedding shirt, slacks and shoes as I ran toward the elephants' pool.

Keith dashed past me as I struggled with the last shoe, already stripped down to his underwear; and, I must say, that was a revelation. Who would have guessed that the big, bearded oaf wore, under his invariably rumpled zoo-keeper's uniform, a leopard-print bikini! Nor had I guessed—well, I knew he was strong. I hadn't known he was *built!* With his gorgeous tan, he looked like a bearded Tarzan.

So the rotten egg was Susie. Keith and I were so busy splashing each other and playing "shark," stalking each other in the murky water, that we didn't realize Susie had joined us until the half-full pool suddenly over-flowed. In retrospect, I wonder what she thought, she who had always been the center of attention from humans. (Never take your eyes off your elephant, that's the first rule. Not that elephants aren't the sweet, lovable, friendly, sociable, only slightly temperamental beasts they're reputed to be. But that slightly temperamental bit can get you killed very dead, very fast, by an awfully large animal who isn't always aware of what its 10,000 pounds can do to your 100.)

Susie ambled into the water, lay down, rolled over onto her side with a great sigh, and rolled all the way over onto her other side while the two humans who should have been scratching her back with big, stiff brushes shouted and laughed at each other, and dived over her trunk. Then, when she defecated in the water, the same two humans picked up the strawy turds and pelted each other, ignoring poor Susie. Poor Susie!

Afterward, Keith and I made love on an old patch of straw in the elephant barn, while the elephants slumbered around us, their bellies rumbling in the gloom.

A few nights later, Ajax went down. We were just starting out, and barely half a mile from the zoo, when it happened. I told the other keepers to go on without me, then I waited with Ajax until he had rested, talked him onto his feet again, led him back to the elephant yard, and left him there with a handful of dandelions and wild mustard that I had snatched along the way.

The zoo seemed quiet and peaceful by moonlight, its humans long gone to dreamland or out with the elephants, its animals napping in their paddocks or acting out their immemorial rituals, according to species. I should have gone back up the fire road and joined the other keepers, harvesting forage for their beasts. Instead, I loitered, seizing the chance of a brief vacation, and slipping guiltily from shadow to shadow lest my conscience spy me and upbraid me for goofing off.

Someone else was doing that too. A bull human I didn't recognize, a chunky white man with his Levis and T-shirt parting company at the belly button. Was he one of the new assistant keepers? We'd brought some in to replace those traitors to Conservation's cause who had deserted us, preferring nights at home with their spouses and families to cutting forage for endangered animals by moonlight, or to patrolling the zoo grounds to discourage poachers.

I stalked him from the shadows, wondering who he was.

Presently I realized that I was not his only stalker. There was someone or something else; a faint gleam of white here and there in the shadows, a scent on the air that didn't quite belong—not in this part of the zoo, at any rate. Something mysterious.

I strolled on, slipping unobtrusively from shadow to shadow, enjoying my secret game of cat and mouse. The man I was following stopped by a fenced-in grove of eucalyptus and stared intently at a branch overhanging the road. Or rather, he stared intently at something moving along the branch. That eucalyptus grove was the new home of the zoo's koalas, who had been turned loose to fend for themselves, something they do quite nicely. The pale, furry lump moving so slowly along the branch, flashing an occasional white patch in the moonlight, must be a koala.

Suddenly the man raised a rifle I hadn't seen he had, and fired a muffled shot. A plump, round body plummeted from the branch. The man broke into a run, scooped the koala up in passing, and ran on down the road.

A tiger burst out of the shadows and leaped at his back. The man went down on his face with a startled yelp. His rifle skittered across the pavement and into a drainage ditch. Somehow the poacher managed to roll over and sit up. I heard him say, "Nice kitty. Velvet paws . . ." Then he let out a horrible screech. The startled tiger raised a muzzle dripping gore from his fat, exposed belly. He rolled out from under her and scrambled to his feet. Hunched over his torn belly, he started to walk away. The tiger seemed puzzled as she watched him go; no one had ever taught her that your dinner gives you a lot less trouble if you kill it first. She backed up to a tree and sprayed; the reek of cat spray stained the perfect moonlit night. Then she trotted after her prey.

For a minute or so she padded at his side like a dog at heel. This made him nervous. He lost whatever common sense he had about the folly of running from an animal, and broke into a jog. She slapped at him with one of those dinner-plate-sized paws rimmed in sharp knives. The claws caught in his jeans, which tore with a loud rip. So that's what you do with clothes! This time, when she knocked him down, she began to feed on the thick, fleshy thighs, inadvertently hamstringing him, so that the next time he got away from her, all he could do was haul himself along by his arms. And, finally, even that was beyond him, and he could only push feebly at the great striped head that tore at his rib cage, ever nearer his lungs and heart. . . .

Unarmed, and therefore helpless, I watched all this from the roof of a long-closed snack stand. How I got up there, and when, I have no idea, but presumably I climbed up on the roof when I realized that my fellow stalker was the zoo's half-starved Siberian tiger, and my fear lent me wings.

Hours—or minutes—passed. The tiger, becoming sated, slowed her feeding. Her victim sank to merciful death. Then Karen drove up in her little pickup truck. "Katy, back!" she cried. The tiger backed off her kill. Karen picked up what was left of the man, hauled it into the back of the truck, and tapped the metal sides with her stick. Obediently, the tiger leaped into the truck and resumed her meal. Karen slammed the tailgate shut with a metallic clang. Then she unrolled a hose and washed the blood and gobbets of flesh off the pavement into the drainage ditch. The diamond on her finger glowed, full of moonlight. Some icy cold portion of my mind told me that nothing good would be accomplished if I interfered, so I stayed where I was until they drove away.

Sooner or later I would have to confront Karen with what I had witnessed, but first I had to see if Ajax was all right. On my way back to the elephant barn I picked him a bouquet of acacia blossoms, climbing up into the tree to break off boughs whose absence nobody would detect from the ground. Ajax was still standing, but with his head down, his trunk and those enormous tusks resting on the ground. He blew on my bouquet as though in appreciation, then, with a great, tired sigh, he lay down, rolled over on his side, and fell asleep.

Now, elephants can sleep standing up, and much of the time they do. Even a tired old elephant won't usually lie down unless another elephant is nearby to stand guard. That night all the other elephants were out foraging. Yet Ajax lay down. That was his way of saying he trusted me to keep him from harm while he slept.

Well, there was nothing for it. I would have to stay

there and deserve his trust. I could talk to Karen the next day—or the next. In the meantime, if I tried real hard, I might even be able to forget all about what I had seen. As I had forgotten about the body in the meat locker.

I jerked awake as a soft, damp trunk tip gently caressed my face. Now it was Ajax who was standing over me! Dawn had come. I could hear the shouts of the keepers bringing the elephants home, and Ajax had thoughtfully awakened me so that I would not become a bad example for the less-experienced mahouts. (If I told them once, I told them a thousand times, to stay alive around elephants you must watch out for them every second of every minute! Had they found me asleep at Ajax's feet I would never have heard the end of it.)

It wasn't till afternoon that I finished my chores, rested, showered, ate lunch, and ran out of excuses for putting off my confrontation with Karen. Well, if you have something unpleasant that has to be done, the best thing to do is to stop thinking about it and just go ahead and start doing it. So, in the stifling afternoon heat, I set off for the grassy, moated, tree-shaded pit where Katy was supposed to be only at night, when our illegal tiger could not be seen from the air.

During the day she had to be kept inside, in one of the massive steel cages that had once housed half a dozen tigers, so I went there first. Katy was not in her cage, nor was her keeper sleeping on a mat in an adjoining cage, which was where Karen was usually to be found during the heat of the day. The door to the pit was unlocked, which meant the tiger could not be out in her yard. Karen must be out there, cleaning up. I opened the door and climbed up the steps into the tiger's pocket forest, calling "Karen? Karen?"

A low growl answered me.

Then I saw them, in the deep grass under a tree, the tiger's back blending almost too perfectly with the dappled shade. The blanched hand she held in her bloody muzzle caught the sun and flashed with a diamond's rainbowed light.

A chair and a whip! I need a chair and a whip! I thought irrationally. Back in the cage area, I helped myself to a stool and a leather strap. Holding the stool out in front of me, I advanced on the feeding tiger.

Keith's arms closed on me from behind. "I say, old girl! Just what do you think you're doing?"

"That's your *sister!*"

"Quite so. But we can't help her now," and Keith led me out of the pit, remarking gently as he closed and locked the door: "Sis would have wanted it this way."

"Then you know . . . she's dead?"

"Rather! I was here when it happened." Keith seemed almost cheerful, and his fake British accent was thicker than ever. "Just like me, actually, rushing in where angels fear and all that. I was passing by, you see, and happened to notice Mademoiselle la Tigre chomping away on some poor chap who must have fallen in during the night. Not much left of him. Still, undeniably human. Next thing I know, I'm over the fence, swimming the moat, walking up to Katy and saying, 'Katy, give me that!' or some fool thing, all the while with a curious feeling of being, actually, up in the palm tree, looking down on myself and thinking, *That bloke must be out of his mind!* Katy backed off her kill and crouched in the grass. All the chap on the ground could see of her was the tip of one ear, and perhaps a bit of eye. But—and this is the curious part—the 'I' in the tree could see the whole tiger, her legs gathered under her, the tip of her tail lashing. I knew she was about to spring, and I couldn't seem to warn the chap on the ground! Then Sis rushed out, shouting, 'No, Katy, don't!' just as Katy leaped for my throat—and got Sis instead. Damn near bit her head off. Don't think she intended to do that, not at all. She backed off hissing, glaring at me as though to say it was all my fault, while blood spurted out of Sis's neck like a geyser. . . .

"Next thing I knew, I was running down the road muttering, 'Must find help, I've got to find help!' while the bloke from the tree hovered over me, sneering, 'You lost your nerve! You lost your nerve!' You don't think I really did, do you?"

I started to say something about "a prudent withdrawal," but Keith wasn't listening, or not to me, at any rate.

"I'm sure she was dead before I left, she had to be, nobody could survive . . . her whole throat was torn out, it really was," he assured himself, looking around as though that detached fragment of his personality was still floating overhead, criticizing him in a voice only Keith could hear. Abruptly he was talking to me again. "On the way—to find help—I had second thoughts about it. What could help do? Retrieve the body, give it a proper burial, all that—but is that what Sis would really want? Wouldn't she rather become one with the tiger she fought so hard to save? So instead of fetching Big Joe, I popped off to Administration and asked Dr. Keeler for her job. The most likely result, if someone else got it, is that Sis would be put down, and we mustn't have that!"

I was momentarily confused, and then I realized that Keith had mistakenly called Katy "Sis." Unaware of his error, he went on, "Dr. K. says it's all right if you can spare me in the elephant barn—you can, can't you?"

"Well, yes, but—Keith?"

"Jolly good," said Keith in his customary cheerful, careless manner, "because I'd much rather fall in love with you than work for you, and I really don't think I shall be able to do both."

That fast curve of his left my head spinning. "Keith," I said, "I really don't think I can deal with that right now."

"Quite all right, old girl," said Keith. "I couldn't deal with you dealing with it."

"Right. Now, look. If you take on Katy—Keith! She can't go on eating people! Even if they're only poachers, and, I agree, poachers are the lowest form of life. I would much rather feed the big cats poachers than *nice* animals, like deer or coyotes. . . . But, Keith! If the word ever got out that we're killing *people* to feed the zoo animals, that would be the end, Keith, it would really be the end. However morally justifiable it may be, feeding poachers to our big cats is *not* good public relations."

"Righto! No people. Couldn't agree more. I might even go farther than you and say that feeding poachers to the cats isn't even morally justifiable. But then, I haven't been here as long as you have," Keith hastened to add. "Not to worry, Robin old thing. If I can hold out a few months longer, a game farm on the Mohave Sea is about ready to begin marketing. It'll be a while before people get used to eating crocodile and capybara, and they've promised me all the meat they can't sell. So, if I can hold it together at this end two or three months longer, six at the outside . . ."

"I have to get back." I held my hand out for him to shake. "Good luck in your new job."

"Quite—uh, may I walk you home? Fact is," Keith said, taking my arm, "while I know I'm doing the right thing, and all that, I really don't think I can take much more of it, hearing old Katy munching away." His voice was calm, steady, even cheerful, yet when he turned to lock the door, his hand was shaking so badly he could hardly fit the key in the lock.

We walked side by side under the flowering trees, me with my eyes on the ground, looking for pebbles to kick. Finally I said, "I take it there's a male Siberian hidden away somewhere?"

"Next best thing. San Diego has sperm on ice."

"Sperm from how many males?"

"Three or four, I think. You're worried about inbreeding?"

"You bet I am! Just what do you illicit tiger hoarders intend to do about the next generation, anyway? Backcross to Bengals?"

"Well . . . rumor has it," said Keith, "that Bronx and Cincinnati have Siberian embryos in the fridge, all ready to thaw out and pop into lions as soon as the meat shortage eases up and we can feed them again. Not that Katy isn't necessary," Keith added quickly, anticipating my doubts. "She's the only intact, full-grown Siberian tiger we know about. She's doubly necessary."

"Of course she is." As the only intact Siberian tiger, and as all that's left of Karen Baxter. I kicked a few more pebbles. Finally I said, "Look, I hoped I could keep Ajax alive until the cows come into heat again, but it looks like he's not going to make it, and I guess I might as well put him down while the meat's still good for something. I'd like to electroejaculate him a couple of times before I do him in, though. Will you be able to help me?"

"Rather!" said Keith. The ecstatic hug and kiss he gave me made me feel that I had been conned. Well, maybe. Still, he was right. Some must die that others may live. It's that sort of world.

Poor Ajax. Well, that's what you deserve, for trusting a human to stand over you and guard you while you sleep.

Robert Silverberg Speaks of a Writer's Beginnings

About the Author

Once a prominent science fiction "fan" and amateur magazine publisher, Robert Silverberg then began appearing in all the science fiction magazines as a short-story writer when barely out of his teens in the early 1950s. Soon thereafter, he became an anthologist and novelist as well, and soon after that began winning the awards that continue to come to him. For many years one of the most productive writers in any field, he "retired" for a period of contemplation, then returned triumphantly with a major novel, Lord Valentine's Castle, *and has since maintained a steady output of equally high-caliber work. Success in his career, however, has not dimmed his sense of the process whereby the new writer learns from the old, and of how the tradition is handed on.*

What a wonderful idea—one of science fiction's all-time giants opening the way for a new generation of exciting talent! For these brilliant stories, and the careers that will grow from them, we all stand indebted to L. Ron Hubbard.

We were all new writers once—even Sophocles, even Homer, even Jack Williamson. And I think we all must begin in the same way, those of us who are going to be writers. We start by being consumers of the product: in childhood we sit around the campfire listening to the storyteller, caught in his spell, lost in the fables he spins, envying and admiring him for the magical skill by which he holds us. "I wonder how he does that," we think—concerned, even then, as much with technique, the tricks of the trade, as we are with the matter of the tales being told. So we go off and wander in the woods by ourselves for a little while, thinking about the storyteller's story and how he told it, considering his opening few words and how they drew the audience in, and how he developed his narrative, and brought it to its climax, and how he managed to finish it in such a way that when he looked up, eyes glowing, and grinned at his listeners, everyone in the campfire circle knew beyond doubt that the story was over. We ponder such things, perhaps even tell ourselves a little story just to see what the process feels like, and then, perhaps the next day, we turn to a couple of our classmates and say, "I heard an interesting story last night," and so we begin.

We begin young, most of us. That's most notably true, I suspect, in the field of science fiction, where prodigies are the rule rather than the exception. It's not hard to understand why: science fiction, like other forms of fantasy, is uniquely favored by the young reader, and so by the young storyteller. Thus we see Isaac Asimov selling stories at eighteen, and writing the classic *Nightfall* at twenty-one; we have Algis Budrys on every magazine's contents page before he was twenty-two, Harlan Ellison doing the same, Bradbury famous for his weird tales at twenty-three, Theodore Sturgeon turning out *Microcosmic God* at about that age, Frederik Pohl not only a professional writer but a magazine editor at twenty-one, and so on and so on.

Of course, there are those professional writers whose first published stories appeared when they were thirty or forty or even seventy years of age. I think here of Robert A. Heinlein, starting his career at the age of thirty-two after leaving the Navy, or Gene Wolfe, who was thirty-four when he sold his first story, or Ursula K. Le Guin, first published at thirty-three, or "James Tiptree," who must have been about fifty. But even late bloomers like these, I'm quite sure, were writing stories long before they ever bothered to get them published. Perhaps Heinlein was different—it's my guess that Heinlein had never written a story in his life until he sat down to turn out a completely satisfactory one on his first try one day in 1939, because that's the way I imagine Heinlein has always done things—but surely Le Guin and Wolfe and "Tiptree" were storytellers from childhood on, furtively scribbling curious little things and hiding them in desk drawers, or at best sharing them with a trusted playmate. Every professional writer I know—again, with the possible exception of Heinlein—began telling stories as soon as he knew what a story was.

And how does one know what a story is? By listening to them, before one can read; by reading them, insatiably, a little while later; by taking them apart, soon after that, to find their essential components; and, finally, by writing them. I remember that process in myself: the appetite for vicarious experience that could never be sated, the stacks of books carried home from the public library at age six or seven, the sheets of lined paper clumsily covered with "stories" that were really just reworkings of things I had read or heard, and, finally—by age eleven or twelve—the first stories that were something more than imitations, however crude they might be and however much they might owe to my previous reading. Out of all this came the awareness, by the time I was thirteen, that I might actually be able to create stories that other people would want to read, if only I could discover the secrets of the trade. And then, all during my adolescence, the single-minded quest to identify those secrets and penetrate to the heart of the storytelling mysteries.

I remember reading books with titles like *The Narrative Art* and *The Structure of the Novel* and even *Writing to Sell*. They taught me useful things, sure. So did a book called *Greek Tragedy*, by H.D.F. Kitto, which taught me nothing at all about science fiction but everything in the world about the relationship of plot and character. (I often recommend it to young writers, who look at me in bewilderment when I do. Generally they shrug my recommendation off, I suppose. So be it.) But I really learned about fiction by reading it. If a story held me and moved me and awed me and startled me, I read it fifty times to see how the writer had done those things to me. I looked at the opening paragraph and the closing paragraph and hunted for relationships between them; I measured the mix of dialog and expository narrative; I checked the length of paragraphs, the quantity of adjectives and adverbs, the use of punctuation, and a lot of other things. I counted the number of characters, and how many of them appeared on stage per thousand words. I studied the way complications piled up as a story unfolded.

Oh, I worked at it! I read Heinlein and Asimov and Clarke, Henry Kuttner and James Blish and Cyril Kornbluth, Fritz Leiber and Jack Vance, Bradbury and Sturgeon. I read Conrad and Faulkner, too, and Kafka, and Thomas Mann, and Joyce and Ibsen and especially Sophocles. In particular the writers I studied closely were the ones just a few years ahead of me—Robert Sheckley, Poul Anderson, Algis Budrys, Philip K. Dick, and a few others: I figured their secrets might be easier to isolate than those of the more experienced writers. (It wasn't so.) By the time I was eighteen I had absorbed this great mass of words, I had derived from it a handful of basic principles so simple I could list them on a single page (but I've never let myself be talked into doing it), and I set out to write some stories.

Since then I haven't given much thought to theoretical matters; but I don't need to, because the theory is as much a part of me as the marrow of my bones, and can be taken for granted just as readily as one's bone marrow is. I know no other way to go about the business of becoming a writer. Sit by the campfire, listen to the storyteller, arrive at some sense of what is being done, and start doing it yourself. And very shortly, if you really are a writer, you will have so deeply internalized the principles you sought so hard to find that you stop thinking about them at all; you merely tell your stories, in what you know to be your own way. And it *is* your own way: but also it's the way in which all tales have been told from Homer and Sophocles down through Kipling, Hemingway, Bradbury, Sturgeon, McCaffrey, Zelazny, whoever. Once upon a time, you say, there lived so-and-so in such and such a place, and while he was minding his own business the following absolutely astonishing thing happened to him. And so you begin; and they gather close about you, for they cannot choose but to hear.

—Robert Silverberg

In the Garden
by
Anna Jean Mayhew

About the Author

Anna Jean Mayhew manages an opera company in North Carolina—a project of which she is justly proud, and to which she devotes a great deal of her time. Nevertheless, she has also been writing since 1975, and repeated a writing course four times "on the theory that even if I didn't learn to write, my credentials would be authentic." The story she sent to the contest did not win. But it was one of the finalists in its quarter, and we bring it to you here.

She has been published in a volume of North Carolina poets, and in Space Grits, *an amateur magazine where she serves as associate editor. In that respect, she is following a classic pattern in the field; many a professional SF writer has emerged from amateur publishing, and many have backgrounds including unusual occupations. What this tells us is that SF people have far-ranging interests, and a bent for the unconventional; it also tells us that some of them want so much to express themselves as writers that they will work hard and long to achieve their goals. In hindsight, when we look at the long series of successful breakthroughs by a long line of would-be writers, it all seems logical and inevitable. It seems rather different from inside the aspiring person, however; it seems unlikely, perilous, promising, hopeless, agonizing and wonderful, all at the same time, and until the day of professional publication arrives, it seems, sometimes, as if it will never arrive.*

Here is A.J. Mayhew's first professionally published story. It seems particularly appropriate that it should be a story of doubt, and dreams, and despair, and hope. . . .

I **met a young one."**

"Healthy?"

"Abundantly."

"Age?"

"Fifteen. And pregnant."

"Where was she the week of——"

"In her mama's belly. She was born healthy to affected parents one month after."

"What did she say?"

"She's willing to discuss it."

"When?"

"She'll be here in the morning." He passed his hand over his eyes. "I like her."

She sat down in slow motion, every movement precise. "This one is different."

"Yes." He touched her shoulder, then began to pace. "This one is different. She is gentle. She is polite. She is tough and rangy and broad shouldered, and I suspect she's not through growing. She's sensible and independent. She's bright and witty. Not like the others."

"How far along is she?"

"Not quite two months. She's wearing a pillow. It's a custom now in other places, she tells me. The pregnant ones begin to pillow almost immediately, so they can be protected by the rest of us. They are deferred to everywhere, so she says."

"You talked to her at length, then."

"Yes."

"Did you lower your veil?"

"I dropped it at once. She never missed a beat."

"David, she may really be the one."

"Yes." And in that word was fifteen years of hoping. "If she'll have us, she is the one. I have no doubt. Marie, she liked me, really liked me. We laughed and chatted and hit it off just fine. Oh, and Marie, she's lovely, beautiful in the way of the perfect young ones."

Marie reached for his hand, then stroked his gnarled and pitted arm, a caress he could not feel through knotted scar tissue. He pulled her up. "Let's go sit in the garden."

They walked through French doors onto a wide lawn which bordered a large garden. They were ordinary people walking in their garden, and except for the horror of their sores they could have been any couple in any garden in any year.

They seldom spoke of what they called the week of death. Whenever they did discuss it, everything before that epoch became real again, clearer in memory than it had ever been in reality, and desirable to the point of painful longing. They learned to walk away from such discussions, to embrace the reality of today, to dwell on what might come tomorrow.

They sat on the lawn in weathered wooden chairs, chairs like large mushrooms growing in the grass. Marie picked a dandelion and twirled it. "I miss teaching children things, like dandelions are flowers and they are yellow and they smell like spring rain, but their seedpods dissolve into snow flurries. I wonder if it will be a boy or a girl. Did she say where she found the father?"

"Hm?"

"What are you thinking about?"

"Oh, you know, here we sit, making plans to get a baby. Get a baby. We'd never have put it that way before. But babies are so scarce, and healthy babies such a rare miracle. It never would have happened if we had known how precious and wonderful a healthy baby is, but there was such a glut of babies that our values got skewed. It seemed natural to get rid of the excess masses but to preserve their things for the hardy few who survived. What a twisted rationale! Yet it seemed to make sense to so many of us. It let us design weapons built 'just in case.' How twisted we were!"

He rose and walked away from her, away from the drift of his words to be among the flowers. He grew daisies, which reminded him of a green field ringed with daisies around a perfect baseball diamond. The baselines were as equal and the bases set as precisely into matching angles as nine boys with compasses, protractors, geometry books, papers and pencils and ropes and rulers could make them. One need not complain that it was further from third base to home plate than it was from first to second, or that the southpaws had an unfair advantage because of the lay of the bases; the others knew it simply wasn't so. But those games were in the days when it was easy to round up nine boys to spend hours marking off a large green field running wild with daisies, when it was even easier to find another nine boys with bats and balls and maybe even a few regulation caps to challenge the first nine to a regular game, turning a pasture into a ball field running wild with boys. Many times he pulled a daisy from the ground and carried it with him till it fell apart, gathering memories from the sharp green smell, hearing once again shrill boy voices raised in protest over a close call at home plate.

While David coaxed the daisies to develop from a blossoming weed into a lovely flower, Marie grew a small but special patch of vegetables within the larger crops of the garden. Her choice tomatoes she cooked and puréed and cooked again with spices and a mysterious broth she had learned to make at her grandmother's side. It was a smooth red soup the color of fresh tomatoes, a soothing soup with none of the acid taste of the thick orange liquid that flowed from cans, a peaceful soup that began a happy meal, teasing the stomach to look forward to the next course. She remembered sitting around her grandmother's groaning table for long Sunday dinners beginning with the soup served hot or cold. Her sister liked to slurp the steaming soup from a large spoon, while her brother drank it cold from a cup. Sounds of children playing in a neighbor's yard blended with the clinking of spoons and rattling of cups and the happy chatter of her family. She remembered these things as keenly as she recalled the orange juice toothpaste taste of girlhood mornings.

The summer David tamed the daisies, Marie captured and trained some blackberry vines to grow on a fence along an old and wild grape arbor. After several failures the arbor again produced grapes which yielded a sweet lavender wine, reminding her of a blouse she wore as a girl, a blouse with sleeves tied in lavender ribbons above elbows on tanned arms that never knew a scar or scab or running sore. She could almost see her sister's quick fingers tying the ribbons for her and saying, "Someday I'll wear a wedding gown that moves in a white cloud around me and has somewhere on it a lavender ribbon just for fun. Wedding dresses shouldn't be taken too seriously, after all."

She grew melons which reminded her of the laughing,

squealing midnight playing of a dozen summer cousins who knew of a cold stream where cantaloupes and watermelons were stored to be cracked open on nights too warm and mysterious for sleeping.

Food from the garden was necessary for life, but the process of growing it was equally vital. They rejoiced together each spring when the first green shoots showed on the rise of long brown rows.

They had met in a care center in Pennsylvania shortly after the week of death, and from their first meeting they were a pair as they wandered among the miserable survivors. They filled the long painful days with plans to leave as soon as their bodies would let them. They left the center in early spring and headed south through Virginia to North Carolina and looked for a house. They finally chose one with large windows and high ceilings, a house sitting gracefully atop a long, low ridge beside a river, a stone house surrounded by grandfather oaks which guaranteed tolerable Southern summers in a world without air conditioning. Three chimneys rose proudly from the slate roof, and they agreed it was a good home, a sturdy home that would serve them well.

When they had lived there about three years they met a pregnant young one, a pale and sickly twelve-year-old girl who was nonetheless determined to bear her child. They worked tirelessly to improve her health, but she died giving premature birth to a puny, wet little rat of a baby whom they loved intensely and relentlessly from the moment it made its first feeble move, a flutter of a tiny finger which to their hungry and sensitive eyes was a flag waving for the battle hymn of life.

The baby was, like its mother, flawed. Though they fed it with eyedroppers and let it suckle at Marie's dry but sugared breasts, and slept in shifts for eleven weeks watching and listening and nurturing and healing, their little Hope died one afternoon with the sun. They laid her to rest down by the river next to the child who was her mother.

Marie cried, as she always did at the memory of Hope, silver tears sliding and hiding in the valleys of her face. She wiped the tears with the hem of her gown, one of dozens she and David made and wore interchangeably. They were flowing cotton gowns which sometimes got in their way, but which moved gently on their tender sores. She called to David, who had wandered deep into the garden, "If she'll be here tomorrow, we must talk."

He walked back to her and his eyes were as red as hers. "Yes, we must talk. We must list all the things we need to tell her, to convince her to stay."

So they talked. Through the beginning of evening and into the fullness of night they talked. They ate tomatoes off the vine and blackberries wet with dew and they talked. They talked through the dark and into the dawn until they had convinced themselves that the coming day would make reality of a favorite daydream. They talked and they cried and they laughed and they touched, and the touching grew into caressing, and they lay in the grass in the soft light of morning and for a sweet space of time became one.

They woke to a soft voice. "Good morning."

A shadowy figure stood just within the French doors. They scrambled to their feet in confusion and, mixing up their gowns, began to dress. Marie grabbed her face. "Oh, my God, where's my veil?"

"Why?" David pulled her hands down. "You'd only drop it immediately anyway. And she has to see you sooner or later." He opened the doors.

She was so beautiful Marie was temporarily speechless, ashamed to stare and afraid not to, afraid she would never again see such a lovely sight as a healthy fifteen-year-old girl. David took her hand and placed it in the hand of the girl. "Marie, this is Irish."

Irish looked at Marie, not at her ravaged face but directly into her eyes. "My father was afraid we would forget there ever were Irish, a thought he could not bear. He was going to name me Dublin, a thought my mother could not bear, so my name is a compromise."

David laughed and stepped back. "Well, Irish, would you like to see our garden before we talk?"

Irish gasped, then ran into the garden, stopping at first one spot, then another. "It's a wonderland! How did you do it?"

They followed the beautiful child in among the flowers. Marie stopped to pick a rose, which she gave to Irish. "We had professions which were rather useless after the week of death. David was a physicist and I was a dancer. He was 25, I was 20. The garden was not always like this. We tried and failed at many things, but lived on what scrawny vegetables we could grow until we got good at growing what we wanted."

Irish smelled the rose. "I know this is a rose, but I've seen so few of them. Not every place is like this, though there are other good people trying to make a decent life. I've been to many places since long before I knew I was going to have a baby, looking for just the right place to stay. My parents were affected as you are, but their sores finally defeated them and they died, one after the other, just before my thirteenth birthday. So I set out on my own. The father of my baby is a boy I met in southern Kentucky, a healthy boy who stayed with me until we were sure I was pregnant, then headed west."

She patted the satin pillow she wore at her waist. "I

don't really feel pregnant yet, except I'm hungry all the time."

Her words stirred David to action. "What hosts we are! We've been away from others for so long we've forgotten our manners. Have you had breakfast?"

"No, and no supper last night. I eat well on what I can find, but seldom more than two meals a day."

He headed for the house. "Sit in the garden and talk with Marie. I'll return with a feast."

"May I help you?" She turned to follow him.

Marie stopped Irish with a gentle hand. "David is king of the kitchen. He quickly learned that as a cook I was a good dancer. I have a way with soups, but even fine soup gets boring three times a day. It'll be David's pleasure to prepare a wonderful breakfast."

Marie and Irish settled in the wooden chairs and were comfortably silent, enjoying the sights and scents of the lush garden in the ripe warmth of a Southern morning. Irish broke the silence with a question.

"What do you know of the rest of the world?"

"Not much. When we found our home we were too busy surviving to explore. We know there must be others who were able to leave the care centers as we did, but we've met very few. We became accustomed to our life here, our solitude, and except for our longing for children we've been . . ." she paused, searching for the right word, ". . . contented. David has been in contact with others more than I have. I simply cannot bear to see how pitiful others look to me, because it reminds me of my own affliction. And the very few healthy ones we've seen have shied away from us, as if we were contagious. We are the unclean of today as lepers were in years past."

Irish spoke slowly, choosing her words with care.

"I'm going to tell you of some of the things I've seen. If I tell you more than you want to know, stop me. But when I'm through I believe you'll understand why I'm being so cautious in choosing where I'll raise my baby. When I told David we pregnant ones were protected by the others that much was true, but it's not always for good reason."

"What bad reason could there be?"

"Greed. Babies have become the new commodity, impossible to mass market and therefore very scarce. Every baby is a limited edition of one, to be bartered to the highest bidder."

Marie gave a low moan, then spoke in a strangled voice, "Go on."

"I've been to places where girls are captured when their bellies are big and locked up until they give birth. Their babies are stolen and whisked away. Some girls bleed to death. Some nurse themselves back to life with help from no one."

Marie's eyes filled with tears, and she shook her head as if to deny the possibility of such horror.

Irish continued, "I can't understand why people who are so kind and protective of children are so wasteful of mothers."

"What happens to the girls who survive?"

"If they're smart they leave in the dark of night. Those who don't leave understand they will be locked up again as soon as they're capable of growing another baby."

"Have you seen many places like that?"

"Enough to know that others exist. There is one such colony north of here in the place called Virginia. I saw many children, which made me suspicious at once. I dressed like a boy and hid my pillow and looked around.

Several people said I'd be treated to a comfortable life if I located and brought to them a pregnant one. And for my second such 'contribution to the growth of the family' I was promised the virginity of their oldest girl-child, who was eleven. I left there with visions of that sweet little girl haunting me."

Marie rose from the chair, stumbling on the hem of her gown and taking a deep breath to calm herself. "Irish, surely you have no doubt that David and I would love and protect you as well as your baby."

Irish jumped up and put her arms around Marie, patting and soothing her, the girl comforting the woman. "No doubt, none at all. My baby and I would be lucky to share your home."

Marie stepped back and drew a breath to fill her soul with hope, then asked the question: "Will you stay with us?"

Irish looked down at the limp rose she still carried. "I can't answer that. The three of us, you and David and I, could offer my baby everything but community. Wherever I settle there'll be a mixture of young and old, healthy and scarred, men and women and children—the way I think it must have been before. And among us there'll be hearty boys and girls to make an abundance of healthy babies. If I can find another pregnant young one, happy and whole as I am, and persuade her to settle with me, that will be a good start. Then later we'll find healthy boys to make more babies and perhaps stay with us. Until I choose a home I'm going to wear my pillow and meet as many people as I can. Then for a while I'll put my pillow aside and live as if there is no child."

Before Marie could reply there was a loud interruption as David kicked open the French doors and appeared carrying a large tray. "Come and get it, a fine breakfast from the king of the kitchen!"

While they ate, nothing was mentioned of the conversation between Irish and Marie. The girl ate with the gusto of health, youth and pregnancy. When she finished, she picked up the rose she had carefully placed by her plate. She looked at David and spoke.

"I've explained to Marie why I must leave you today. I'm willing to answer your questions, but I'll leave before dusk. I can't say whether or not I'll be back."

The three of them, the man and woman with their chunked and ragged faces and the girl with her satin pillow, talked into the afternoon until finally silence settled among them with only one question not answered.

David watched the lovely girl playing with the limp rose, then took Marie's hand in his own scarred paw and asked, "How will we know what you've decided?"

"If I'm going to return to you I'll send you a sign by the middle of September, something to let you know I'll be back in January."

"And if we hear nothing?"

"Then I won't be back."

David and Marie nodded, accepting the decision of the girl they loved already.

After Irish left them they sat in the garden until long after dark. In the weeks that followed they seldom spoke of her. They worked in the garden and preserved the produce. Their life was no different in the presence of hope than it had been before, with two exceptions. Marie began to make small clothes which she hid from David; David began to build a cradle which he hid from Marie.

In the late summer, when they were preparing for the cold months ahead, they woke one morning to find at their door a small pillow. Resting on the pillow as if placed there with great care was a withered rose.

They laughed and they cried, and spent the rest of the day in the garden.

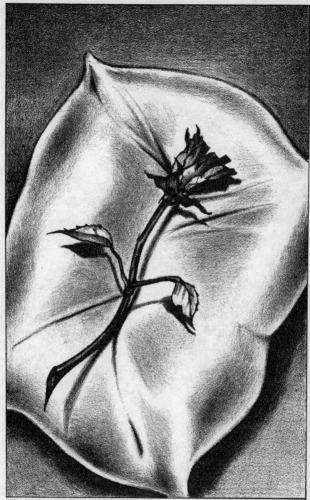

Illustrated by Frank Ferrel

Arcadus Arcane
by
Dennis J. Pimple

About the Author

Here is the First Prize winner of the first quarter's contest. Fittingly, it's the first published short story by its author, a married 29-year-old engineer. But Dennis Pimple's literary career began with editing his college newspaper, and continued through a self-imposed "creative correspondence" program in which he sent more than 1500 pages to his friends over a two-year period. Writing and editing constantly, he has now for several years been editor of Acme Comics, the ambitious Denver-based amateur magazine devoted to the world of comic books.

His storytelling technique here is the relentlessly propulsive kind that makes fast, tense reading. It isn't easy writing. To perform it, an author needs to fall into an almost compulsive mode that typically leaves him on the brink of exhaustion, wondering whether what he's created could possibly affect the reader as much as it gripped the writer. Dennis says that after learning of his win, "I didn't stop bouncing off the walls for two weeks." In the light of what you are about to read, that seems disquietingly appropriate. . . .

Illustrated by A. R. Conway

The arcade has a sentience of its own. A life of electricity, neon, glass, metal. A life of zaps, bongs, deep thuds. The machines wait for you. They beckon with slicing laser lights and harsh, garish colors. They call with bright bells and cheerful whistles.

Pinball. Breath of life, sanity in an insane world. Stability amid vertigo.

Sharp shadows slice through the deep confines of the arcade. Lightning flashes and is gone from the machines. Thunder rolls through the air, momentarily muffling the music from the ceiling speakers. One can sense danger there.

Especially in this one, John thought. I thought all of this type was gone. It's dark inside, dark. No electronics, all the old five-for-a-quarter machines. He smiled, remembering hours spent in arcades like this one, before the video games changed them. This one is like the old arcades, he thought. Nothing here to pervert the nature of the game. Nothing here to dilute the essence of pinball.

The music was blaring, savage. Rock-and-roll; acidic, pounding, vicious, almost drowning out the pings and bongs and thumps of the games. The smells were dust, smoke, alcohol, metal, glass, electricity, neon.

The arcade inhaled and drew John in. He had found

himself inside again, after such a long time. The machines blinked, winked, grinned, flashed amber and white and scarlet greetings. The machines welcomed him home.

John stepped slowly forward to claim a machine as his domain. He felt his coat slide from his shoulders, fold once, and drop beneath the machine. His watch untwisted itself from his wrist and pounced upon the coat. His sleeves rolled themselves up to his elbows. He looked down into his right hand. He held a quarter.

The coin separated him from the game. He found the slot, deflowered the machine. "Bing-bongde—bing ———bong." It greeted him, challenged him to a game. John slowly reached down and pushed the start button. "Bingde—bong—bong," it announced. Score: 00,000,000.

The music thudded, pounded, bounced, whipped around and through and into him. The silver ball was a dull gleam in the plunger chute, waiting for action. John's trembling hands caressed the flipper buttons, testing resistance, responsiveness, coordination. His palms cradled the machine's corners, feeling cool, smooth metal. The machine blinked and flashed a laser challenge into his eyes. He could feel the electricity, the power of the waiting machine. John sighed, remembering.

After all the years, he could again feel the power. He reached down and encircled the plunger handle with strong fingers. He pulled it back slowly, fully. He released the handle, and the dull gleaming ball shot and spun into the playing arena. It bounced off the far bumper, recoiled against the chute gate, dropped into a lighted hole. "Bingbingbingbingbingbing," the machine said. Score: 00,006,000. The ball was ejected, skipped and rolled against a lighted pin. "Ding!" the machine told him. Score: 00,006,100.

John remembered. He played the machine like a familiar lover; caressing, pushing, grasping, shuddering, until it yielded to him a free game.

And John smiled.

He was back. Back in the womb he had created for himself many years ago. His breath was again the breath of cigarettes and alcohol. His head again pounded with the music, the rock-and-roll, thudding in counterpoint to the staccato zaps and dings and bongs of the pinball game. His eyes flashed lasers, scarlet and white and blindingly bright blue. The arcade dust settled into the lines of his face and into the crooks at his elbows. His life became the life of electricity, neon, metal and glass. His movements were as those of the machine he played, the machine he would caress, cajole, pound and shake into the nirvana of a free game, time and time again.

Seven games, seven free games, dropped seven years from his life, and he was the man he was before.

Pinball. Breath of life, sanity in an insane world.

John paused and sighed with relief after the sensual intensity of the games. He smiled again, surprised how easily the reactions, the stance, the instincts for the game returned to him after seven years. He looked about him, hands still gently in contact with the sides of his warm, bright, metal and glass machine. It was the same. The shadows sliced the arcade into sections, each with a machine in center. There were only a few other players in the room, bending over their own machines. To John they didn't matter, they were more shadow than substance. Far, far in the back of the room, huge and round and dangerous, a creature of smoke and dust sat on a tall stool, eyes glowing, watching. The proprietor. John shuddered when he saw him.

John turned back to his machine, ready to again flick his hand across the start button and then allow it to drift easily up to the plunger handle, ready to pull, release, and begin the game again. But then he paused, because there was something in the air that had not been there before. His machine trembled in a different sort of way, and went ever-so-slightly colder beneath his gentle, strong, skilled hands.

John looked up and met the gaze of the proprietor, who was leaning forward on the stool, watching through the flash shadows and cigarette haze. His eyes were aglow, reflecting the bright scarlets of the machines. John flinched, startled. He dropped his hands from the sides of the machine, a machine that suddenly was strange to him. The power was gone; the memory of a dream.

His sleeves unrolled themselves back over his forearms. His watch sprang back upon his wrist, his coat shrugged itself back onto his shoulders. John turned, and walked toward the exit.

The arcade exhaled and John found himself outside. He reeked with a sweat of fear, embarrassment, failure. He shrugged his shoulders with wonder and relief. It wasn't the same, after all. In a way, he was grateful for that. He turned, and walked away.

Twenty-one steps down the street, he stopped. He turned back, looking toward the arcade. "Shit," he muttered.

He had left a game on the machine. He knew the rule. You never leave a game on the machine. Never before had he left a game on the machine. "Oh, shit."

Tradition, ritual, the mysticism of pinball drew him back. He stopped outside the building, again peering

inside, allowing the lasers to flash across his eyes, smelling the smoke and alcohol and dust, hearing the throb and pulse of the music. He looked at the window, and for the first time read the fading, chipped letters that named the place:

ARCADUS ARCANE
S. Beezle, prop.

Mr. Beezle, you cannot cast me out, he swore to himself. The arcade inhaled, he found himself inside again. He strode to the machine, saw that it remained untouched, waiting, challenging. He jabbed at the start button. "Bingde—bong—bong" came the reply. His coat shrugged itself onto the floor, quickly followed by his watch. His sleeves rolled up again, to the elbow. John settled his hands again about his machine. He looked up, to the back of the room, and met the proprietor's gaze eye for eye, glint for glint. He grinned, grim and sure, violent and ready.

John pulled the plunger, released.

Seven more games, seven more free games. The machine hummed beneath his hands, a purr of surrender and contentment at meeting a master of pinball. John paused, let forth a breath. The fear-sweat was gone, replaced with a sheen of effort, a cooling perspiration. The music thudded; he felt the pinball power pulse through him in time with the rock-and-roll.

Through the music, he heard a creak, a shifting of dark, massive bulk. He had been waiting for the sound without realizing what he had been waiting for. He looked up, through the smoke, dust, and music. The proprietor, Beezle, was rumbling slowly toward him from the far back of the room. His coal-red eyes gleamed.

John met his eyes only for a second. Grimly, he looked back to the machine. His next game, a free game, was waiting. The laser lights pulsed, flash and gone. He reached to the start button, punched. The machine was silent.

John jabbed at the start button again. Nothing. He glanced at the back glass, saw the "1" that indicated a game. He jabbed, punched, stroked the start button. Nothing, the machine said nothing. And Beezle approached.

"That machine's broke, sonny." Beezle's deep, thunderous, rumbling voice vibrated through the music, through the dust. A quarter, gleaming with the laser lights of the arcade, bounced on the top glass, pirouetted, spun and vibrated to a stop. "Try another." The voice of the proprietor echoed into itself, deep and thick with alcohol, cigarettes, metal, glass, neon death.

"It w-was working just a second ago," John replied, looking up but not able to meet the proprietor's blood-red gaze.

"Yeah, happens sometimes. Plays and plays like a dream and then *phffffffft*. Out she goes." He smiled. One of his upper left teeth glinted metallic in the sharp arcade light. "There's some great machines in the back," he said. "Classics." Beezle stepped to one side, between John and the outside. He beckoned with a huge, dark hand toward the rear of the arcade.

John stood back, with a vague fear holding him in place. He glanced at Beezle's smile, one tooth reflecting the bright light of the machines. He looked at the game he had been playing, the legend "1" tying him to the arcade. He looked down at the quarter resting on the top glass. He looked up. He could still feel the power behind his eyes, in his fingers. Fuck you, John thought, let's play some pinball.

He picked up the quarter, brushed past the grinning proprietor, and strode to the back of the arcade. He looked about him, walking in time to the pulsing music. The few who played at the other machines were beings of shadow, without solid form. The flashes of the games seemed to cut straight through their bodies, unhindered. John grinned, unafraid. He had the power. The world of neon, glass, metal, electricity embraced him. Beezle followed.

They passed a machine John had never seen before, a machine that was strangely different from all the others. Its arena was dark, smoky. The back glass was flat, unreflecting black. Red letters were inscribed across the top left corner, giving the machine a name. "Dante," it said in a bloodier, deeper scarlet than any of the scarlets of the other machines. John hesitated, then passed it by.

He found a machine he had played before, a classic, in the very rear of the arcade, near the counter that was Beezle's station. He glanced at the proprietor as he settled himself on his stool, and then at the game. He brought his quarter forth, deflowered the machine. "Gingebe——bing—bong," it said.

John played again, and won again. Today, on this machine, in this arcade, he couldn't lose. He smiled. His sweat was cool and without the stink of fear. The smoke and dust and alcohol was sweet, the music soothed and urged him to play and play. It was all part of him again.

Beezle was watching, his eyes aglow, his tooth agleam. "A great game, isn't it? Pinball." He creaked forward, watching. John glanced over.

"Yeah. I haven't played for quite a while."

"Well, you still got it. You're good. Nice to know that the stuff is still there, ain't it?" The deep voice rumbled below the music. It sounded hungry.

"Oh, yeah." John still played, caressing the machine, pounding the machine, shaking the machine.

Beezle grinned. "Don't you wish that you could just play pinball forever, not ever worry about going back to work or going home or eating or paying bills or listening to people you don't want to listen to or feeling lonely or horny? Just you and pinball, just keep playing. Do you ever wish that?"

John missed a flip, the ball drained. He looked up, shrugged. "Yeah, I guess so. Who doesn't . . . sometimes?" He met Beezle's stare, close up, for the first time. The pupils of the coal-red, blood-red eyes were skull shaped, and they glowed, not of reflected light, but of a red neon from within. "Who doesn't?"

Beezle smiled. "Friend, you're good at the game. Damn good. How'd you like to take on a machine that will break your balls? How'd you like to play a game that's never been beat?"

John felt the electric power within him. John felt the neon, laser, scarlet, metallic pinball power within him. "If it can't be beat, it ain't a pinball machine," he said as a cold, precise fact. "Any real pinball machine can be beat, if you're good enough."

Beezle straightened on his stool. "If you're good enough, you can beat it. Are you good enough?" He hung the challenge out in the thick air. Beezle swept his right hand out in a grand motion. John's eyes followed the arm, saw that it was indicating the deep darkness of Dante.

"Friend, John, if you win on that machine, you'll play and win forever." His grin narrowed, became solemn, deadly. "I guarantee it." John stared at the machine, considering his chances, testing his power.

He didn't ask the price of losing.

He wanted to walk out. He didn't like this craziness invading the sanity of the arcade. He turned and began to retreat toward the exit. He walked past Dante, the dark, unreflecting black pinball machine. Below the blood-red letters of the name he saw the number "1."

There was a game on the machine.

He turned, sighed, and stepped up to the machine. Beezle was behind him, looking over his shoulder. John called his power forth, and found it waiting for him. His eyes narrowed, and he laid his hands gently on the sides of the machine. He stared into the blackness of the back glass, he peered into the smoky darkness of the arena.

There was no start button, but John knew how to begin the game. He laid his left hand, palm down, onto the top glass. He felt a sharp sting.

He lifted his hand. A single drop of blood bubbled on the glass, sizzling. When it had all evaporated, the machine exploded in light: laser scarlet, neon violet, garish green. There was a rumbling creak, like heavy iron gates swinging open. There was a rolling thunder, the howling of a three-headed hound, the wails of the damned, the sharp gnashing of vampire teeth. Score: 000. To win: 666. Dante waited to play.

John touched the flipper buttons, testing responsiveness, tension, coordination. It felt good, the power felt good. He could tell, the machine was a classic. He pulled back the plunger, released.

The ball, white-gold, white-fire, shot into the playing field. It rolled and bounced off the far bumper, recoiled halfway back to the chute, touched on the bumper separating slot "Father" from slot "Holy Ghost." John tapped the side of the machine, bouncing it a fraction to the right. The ball responded, falling into "Father." Gongs sounded, lightning crashed. The ball shot out, danced across the arena and recoiled from the upper pin. Thunder rumbled, bells rang. Lights pulsed, laser strong, laser deadly.

John played well, as well as he ever had. He felt the pinball power growing in him, savage and strong, but different. He felt at odds with the machine. This was the first game that felt like an enemy, rather than a lover. But for all that, he was still playing well.

The gongs sounded through the music. The lights flashed through the smoke. The drop targets bounced. Vanity, Sloth, Anger fell. Greed, Lust, Gluttony dropped soon after. Light the Three Fates, double your bonus. Drop the Seven Virtues, win a free ball. Sin Mortal, when lit, gave 10 points. Sin Venial, 5. The white-fire ball rolled, danced, bounced, recoiled, slid, skipped, slammed. John fought the machine. John felt the power.

The gleaming ball bounced off the left bank, and John flick-stopped its motion with a quick flipper tap, caught it with the left flipper. He took aim at the remaining Deadly Sin drop target and flipped the ball upward. He was a fraction off and the ball touched the left side of the target too lightly. It dropped down, straight into the drain, into the Abyss. John looked at the back glass. Score: 245.

The second of three balls rested in the chute, white-fire. John pulled back the plunger, released.

As he played, John noticed that the hellish scene of the back glass shifted, changed. It moved, it showed a passion play, a grim tableau of . . . his life.

Every sin, each transgression, was displayed. Every

regretted act of doubt or weakness showed itself to him. Sin Venial, Sin Mortal, all on display. The machine passed judgment with each gong, the game foretold his doom with every laser flash.

Cold sweat broke upon John's forehead. His left hand slipped a fraction from the button, which caused the flipper to quiver at just the wrong instant. The ball looped and fell into the right-hand slot, into Hell. Score: 487.

John wiped his dripping forehead with a trembling wrist. The last ball waited, white-gold. He calculated silently the points he needed to win: 179. The music pulsed, thunder in his ears. Through the smoke and dust he could feel the cold-death breath of the proprietor upon his neck, waiting. "OK," John muttered to himself, "right on track. Right in the groove." He wiped both palms onto his pants, and then caressed the sides of the machine. He dropped his right hand down, fondled the plunger. He pulled it back and released.

The last ball shot out, and he played. He was taut with relaxation, calm with anxiety, fearless with fright. The gongs sounded, the lasers flashed, the targets bounced. The haunting scene of the backplate shifted, this time showing him all the others who had dared to challenge the machine, all failing and now wallowing in eternal damnation. They writhed in pain, reaching for him, asking for salvation. John riveted his eyes to the playing arena, desperately ignoring the shifting images, concentrating on his play.

Each passing second increased the difficulty of play. The ball spun harder, skipped faster. The targets fell only with a hard direct hit, each point had to be wrested from the game. The gongs crashed in John's ears, the

music had turned into an unworldly wail, a howl of bleak eternity. The lights flashed into his narrowed eyes, so bright that they threatened to blind him. John fought on, grim, tight. Every vestige of pinball skill, every erg of pinball power that he had ever possessed was called forth. He fought the machine, pounded the machine, shook the machine, wrestled with the machine for his life.

John caught the ball with his right flipper. He glanced up to the score on the backplate. 664.

He checked out his targets. Lust and Greed had dropped, giving him 20 bonus. He had won. He heard a hiss of disbelief from behind him as Beezle calculated the same outcome.

John felt a wave of salvation course through his soul, the confidence of his pinball power restored. He flicked the ball perfectly along the left side, up the side chute, to the very back of the playing field. It bounced off the far bumper, recoiled from the left side, and touched the pin separating Father from Son, and the machine pinged lightly. Score: 665.

John gently shoved the machine forward, to lightly bounce the ball straight up. Momentum would drop it into Father. Then the machine went dark, unreflecting black. John looked desperately at the back glass, horrified.

The upper left corner was inscribed "Dante" in scarlet letters. Below was his score, 665. And below his score in small, white, plain letters was the word *tilt*.

"Hmph," Beezle grunted behind him. "Sorry, Johnny. You bounced it a little hard that last time. That's the game."

John knew better than to protest. Tilting was part of the game. Pinball was pure that way. Shock began to set in. He paused, hands by his side, looking into the darkness of the arena. Then he looked around, met the proprietor eye for eye. "Mr. Beezle . . ." he murmured.

Beezle grinned, sneered. "Call me Stan," he said. "And now, Johnny, if you'll just step into the back room, you can pay for the game."

John allowed himself to be guided toward the back room. As he reached the dark-curtained entrance, he felt a blast of incredible heat from the other side. The same wails of despair he had heard from Dante filled his ears. He could feel Beezle's strong hand on his back, firmly urging him forward, through the curtain.

And then there was light in his mind. John straightened, stiffened, resisted Beezle's guiding hand. He whirled about, meeting the man's cold eyes with a chilling stare of his own. "Hey, wait a minute," he snapped. "What was the match?"

Beezle sneered. "What the hell you talking about? What match?"

"Shit, man, every machine's got a match point, a number to match with your score and win a free game. What was the match?" John returned Beezle's glare with equal ferocity, equal violence. The red light faded, the skull-eyes dimmed. If pinball was anything, it was fair. And you always, always, got a match point. "No match point, no deal, man," John snapped. "Pinball is pinball."

Beezle sputtered. Beezle snarled, and spit, and ranted. But John was right. Pinball was pinball, and everyone got a match point.

Beezle grabbed John with the grip of a triple-jowled Cerberus. He dragged him back to the front of Dante, slammed him into the front of the machine. "Find your match point," he sneered, "and let's get on with this."

John was sprawled over the top glass of Dante, the ball-buster, the only machine he'd never beat. He peered up into the unreflecting black of the back glass. He saw a glint of yellow light just to the left of the score. He reached out with a cold, trembling right hand.

He pressed his right thumb against the back glass. It burned. Slowly, painfully, he inscribed a small, bright cross on the black glass. The mark sizzled with a thick, green, foul smoke.

When the smoke cleared, the match point was revealed, glowing yellow against the black: "5."

Below the blood-red "Dante" John saw the number 1.

There was a game on the machine.

The music shuddered into sympathetic silence. With a werewolf howl, Beezle leaped at John, eyes afire, teeth bared and gleaming with poisonous saliva.

John rolled off the glass an instant before Beezle crashed onto the machine. Beezle's gnarled left hand ripped at him along his side, tearing through his shirt and cutting a shallow, burning gash below his ribs. John rolled forward, running half-crouched toward the front of the arcade. Beezle leaped to his feet, snarling with an unholy ferocity. John threw himself under the machine he had first played. He snatched his watch with one hand, his coat with the other, and rolled through. He scrambled to his feet and away from the machine, less than a second before Beezle slammed into the other side. The game crashed to the floor, spitting electricity, neon, glass and metal. Beezle was burned, blinded, staggered. John didn't look back as he ran to the exit.

The arcade exhaled, almost with a laugh. John found himself outside, running down the street.

Half a block away, he slowed to a brisk stride, watch on his wrist, coat over one arm. He almost felt like whistling.

After a few more steps, he stopped, cold in his tracks. He turned. "Shit," he muttered.

He had left a game on Dante. There was a game up on the machine.

He took one step toward the arcade. He felt the sting of his left palm, the burn of his right thumb, the gash of his side. He pirouetted, and strode away from Arcadus Arcane.

"Go now, and tilt no more," he nudged himself.

Recalling Cinderella
by
Karen Joy Fowler

About the Author

Karen Joy Fowler coaches girls' soccer, has a B.A. in political science, and an M.A. in North Asia Studies. She teaches ballet. As a schoolchild, she says, she wrote incessantly, and very well, quitting when she decided her contemporaries were catching up to her. Some years later—she's in her middle thirties—she thought she'd try again, and has been studying under Kim Stanley Robinson, himself one of the brightest new stars to appear in recent SF.

Her story here was a strong contender in the third-quarter contest, rewritten from an earlier draft for which she had received encouragement from Shawna McCarthy, editor of Isaac Asimov's Science Fiction Magazine. *We will be seeing other stories of hers in the science fiction magazines, soon and, we feel, over the years to come. There is a sureness and maturity in her handling of this story that leads us to make that prediction, and, though any writer's career is always perilously surrounded by imponderables, to make it with considerable confidence.*

Whatever befalls Ms. Fowler in the future, however, it begins here. And it begins well.

Illustrated by A. R. Conway

Raina . . . Raina . . . Raina. . . . **The name is like a heartbeat, the sound you hear inside your ear when everything is quiet, a** whisper in the dark. "Who named me?" I once asked Elaine.

"It was part of the package," she answered. "It was the first word you spoke. Don't you remember?"

I don't. And since I have no reason to believe that my memory is defective, and much evidence of the unreliability of hers, I doubt it happened that way. But if she were right, if I awoke saying "Raina," isn't it much more likely that I was calling to someone else? How often does a person say her own name?

This is what I remember: the sound of soft footsteps, three people walking on rubber-soled shoes. A rustling, from clothing, I suppose, and a loud inhalation of air. And then, a voice—Laura's voice, although of course I didn't know that then. "She gives me the creeps," Laura said.

"Nonsense." That was Dr. Margaret, Laura's mother. She picked up my hand and pulled the fingers back until the palm flattened. "She's just what we ordered. I'm very pleased." Her voice came closer to my face. "Raina . . . Raina . . . Raina . . . open your eyes."

I was in a white bed in a white room and a large woman was removing a tube from a vein in my wrist.

Her eyes were gray, her skin slick and oily looking. Quite unattractive, although of course I didn't notice at the time, having nothing to compare it to. Her jaw was so square it looked out of proportion to the rest of her face. It moved. "How do you feel?" she asked.

How did I feel? I didn't know. I began to explore, to search for feelings inside, but it was all emptiness and the one question. How did I feel?

Dr. Margaret had given me the question like a gift. Now she gave me the answer. She read a series of numbers from a screen beside the bed. Then she smiled at me. "Perfect," she said. "You'll be trained to help us here at the hospital. We have instructional tapes; Laura can show you how to use them." She gestured toward the door where two other women stood. One of them, the one with reddish hair and a jaw identical to Dr. Margaret's, grimaced slightly. That was Laura. The other was Elaine. No one had been introduced. I had to learn it all later. Dr. Margaret was still talking. "All we expect of you is the more routine work. I think you can be trained in, say—two weeks?"

As she spoke, Dr. Margaret examined my body. She felt for muscles along my arms, pressed her fingers into my skin, shined a small pinpoint of light into first one eye and then the other. "We catch breakfast and lunch as we can," she continued. "Laura will show you how to use the kitchen. But we make it a point to eat dinner together. It gives us a chance to go over the day's work and exchange ideas. Dinner is at the start of the third period. You won't be hungry today, but come anyway. Laura will show you where." She finished with a slight slap on the bottom of my left foot. "We'll leave you now to dress, Raina. Can you do that?"

And *these* were my first words. "Yes," I said. "I can."

The three women left then, first Elaine, then Laura, then Dr. Margaret. I saw the connection between them; I saw it most clearly then, when I had no memories to obscure my vision, but it was a thing I didn't understand. I concentrated on the physical features they shared—the jawline, certain facial expressions, the curve of their backs. A tenuous connection, but I was certain of it. Dr. Margaret and Laura were identically dressed in dark coveralls with scarves over their hair. Elaine was wearing coveralls, too, but hers were blue with a thin green stripe. They had left a pair of coveralls for me on a chair beside the bed.

The chair was a hard orange plastic with a curved seat, and the coveralls were bright green. I got up and put them on, and socks and rubber-soled shoes. I was filling myself inside with new colors, new textures, new thoughts, moving farther and farther away from the emptiness of my past. There was nothing to regret or miss in that whiteness, but there *was* something. Something irretrievable, something which had no shape and certainly no name, but which, over time, I began to think of as my family. My past.

I mentioned it once, and only once, to Elaine. We were having breakfast. Elaine had cut herself a large slice of spongy yellow bread, and told me it was impossible. "You don't have a family," she said. "You were grown on one of the farms. But you couldn't remember that—you wouldn't have any more memory of that than a baby has of the womb. Top of the line, though. State of the art. Nothing but the best for Mother. I don't imagine there was even a pattern for you; little bit of genetic engineering, I suppose. Language skills, manual skills. The basics. But no personality. You're really only capable of following simple instructions."

Laura joined us at the table, yawning and reaching for the bread. She watched Elaine spread her piece with purple jelly. "Haven't you had enough, Elaine?" she asked.

Elaine is very fat, so Laura continually nags her to restrict her diet. Yet, during our dinnertimes, Dr. Margaret frequently urges her to eat more. Dr. Margaret says that beauty is fleeting and ultimately trivial. She didn't select their fathers with beautiful daughters in mind. She gave them intelligence and money. What more do you need? Why shouldn't Elaine eat as she chooses?

Perhaps this is what Elaine believes. In any case, she looked defiantly at Laura and spooned more jelly onto her bread. "I may not get lunch," she said. "I've got a whole new group on their way to Athens. It'll take me all day to screen them. Mother says I caused the last flu there through carelessness."

"Who named me, then?" I asked, and Elaine and Laura turned to me.

"It was part of the package," Elaine answered. "It was the first word you spoke. Don't you remember?"

"Kind of a stupid name," said Laura.

It didn't take two weeks to train me. This prediction of Dr. Margaret's was merely the first instance of her tendency to underestimate me. I helped her in the lab, but my main duties concerned record-keeping and retrieval. It was not demanding work, but it was certainly important. In a hospital, access to information can be the difference between life and death. I worked hard, had little free time, and it occurred to me to wonder how they had gotten along without me.

The hospital is small, but it serves an entire sector,

five habitable planets with a total population of less than 5,000. "The Outback," Elaine calls it. "The outcasts" is what she calls us. Someday she plans to live in an older, more populous sector. Someday she plans to lose her excess weight.

If I understand the word "outcast" correctly, and it's one which I find difficult in any but the most literal sense, then I think it's a poor choice. Dr. Margaret is known and respected far beyond the sector. It was her work in immunology that had opened the outer sectors to settlement in the first place. Every year she receives another humanitarian award from some group or other, a tribute to her willingness to live and work out here with the miners. Dr. Margaret inherited money, and all her grants, awards, and patents have added to it considerably. She is rich enough to live wherever she wants. It follows that she wants to live here. Every year she gets requests from students and researchers anxious to come just for the privilege of working with her. But she chose me instead.

The truth is, Dr. Margaret doesn't care for people much. What Dr. Margaret likes is control. Elaine, Laura, me—everything in the hospital—we all do exactly what she tells us.

But once someone didn't. Elaine told me about it. It was the day I first entered her room. I had been at the hospital for two months then, two months and four days. Dr. Margaret had sent me to find Elaine, who had neglected to record her lab results from the previous day.

I looked for her first in the kitchen, then on the ward, using the monitor. I knew the location of her room from the tapes and it seemed logical to look there next.

I walked into the empty room, and I remember being

struck by the frivolity of the furniture. I imagined her mother fixing her room for her, though it did not seem the sort of furniture Dr. Margaret would choose. Certainly it was not like my room. Many of the larger pieces were actually wooden; I knew from the rings and whorls of the grain. There were pink curtains and a pink and white spread on the bed. A half-eaten box of wafers sat on the bureau and gave the room a pleasant, sweet smell.

I was curious about the curtains. We live several layers inside the hospital where Dr. Margaret can control temperatures and humidities precisely. I expected the curtains to hide a monitor, perhaps a communicator into Laura's or her mother's room. Instead, when I pulled it aside, I found a mirror—three mirrors, really, hinged together so they could be opened and shut.

Inside the mirror was my face, clear skin, even features and suddenly one side of the mirror swung in so there were several faces, all mine. At the sight of my faces, the thing buried inside me, past emptiness, gave a sudden cry. It stirred and struggled while I stared at the faces and tried to remember . . . tried to remember. . . .

"Raina!" Suddenly there were several Elaines behind me in the mirror, all looking annoyed. Her voice was shrill and aggressive. "Do you think you're pretty, Raina?" she asked.

I turned to her and I imagined what I could not see—that my mirror selves all turned their backs on me. "Your mother sent me to find you. She wants to know what your lab results were yesterday."

"Nothing," said Elaine. "What does she expect?"

"She wants you to record them."

Elaine waved a hand in annoyance. "Do you know," she said, "that on the other planets, the time period for one day is set at twenty-four hours? Not long enough for Mother, of course. She has to live here so she can add an extra work-hour." She looked at me closely. "Come here." Her expression was unreadable. "I'll show you a pretty face." She took a picture off her desk, an oval of a young woman from the waist up. She was dressed in the usual coveralls, but her hair was loose, black and very shiny. Her facial features were larger and less symmetrical than my own, but the effect of the whole was an appealing one. I looked at her closely to learn what a pretty face was.

"Mother could have made any of us this pretty," Elaine said. "If she'd wanted to. This is my oldest sister, Gwen. She left before you came. It destroyed Mother. Gwen went to live with a vehicle technician on Athens 4—not a real mechanic, you know. Strictly assembly-line. Mother hated him. He checked in here with one of those port diseases, if you know what I mean. But Laura would have gone with him if Gwen hadn't. You can't mention her to either of them, you understand? They don't want to hear about her."

Elaine took the frame back, careful not to touch me. "I don't want you in my room unless I've asked you," she said, every word unnecessarily distinct. But then she changed abruptly. She put one strand of her brown hair behind her ear—it was an artful gesture, done for timing—and she forced herself to smile at me.

"We couldn't manage the work without her," she told me. "On top of everything else. That's why we got you." She reached to me, moving a section of my hair in the way she had just touched her own. "I miss Gwen dread-fully," she said. "But don't tell anybody."

Gwen was my first secret, if you don't count the one I kept inside, the secret I kept even from myself. The hospital is full of secrets, and most I don't share. If anyone had asked me then what a family was, I would have answered that it was an elaborate arrangement of secrets. I don't see why it should be that way.

Laura enjoys her secrets. They make her absent-minded, they give her an adolescent dreaminess she is far too old for. Laura's secrets fill Dr. Margaret with disquiet. I remember one evening when we were washing for dinner. Dr. Margaret was scolding Laura for imprecise measurements in her lab work. "Now it will all have to be done again," she said.

Laura removed her coverall for sterilization. Her hair rested softly on her green shirt collar, curling under just slightly, softening her jawline. "Sorry," she said unapologetically. "I'm not feeling well. I'm about to start my monthlies." She looked at me, anticipating the question I would not have asked. "You don't need to know," she said, a curious lilt in her voice. "Lucky you."

"That's a ridiculous excuse," said Dr. Margaret, pouring a disinfectant into her palm. "I won't even respond to that."

"Why keep running the same tests, anyway? Look what can be done with domes and atmosphere control. Look at us. We *never* go outside. Why isn't that enough? Why tamper with people?"

Dr. Margaret exhaled impatiently. "You have no interest in the problem itself, then. You see nothing to be gained from the simple increase of human knowledge and the concomitant extension of human control. Really, Laura, you do exasperate me. You have a fine mind—I saw to that. If only I could convince you to use it."

"I like to work with the patients," said Laura. "Why can't Raina do the lab work?"

Dr. Margaret looked at Laura sharply. Laura was pulling her hair across her face and examining it with pleasure. It is very beautiful hair, Elaine tells me. "I'm thinking of doing just the opposite," said Dr. Margaret. "I'm wondering if Raina couldn't begin to handle a caseload."

In spite of being the only hospital in the sector we are never full. The different planets have their own first-aid stations, and most people handle their own low-level care. The only exceptions are the inoculations. We do them, because Dr. Margaret feels the immunizing agents might pose a danger if they were carelessly allowed into the environment.

Elaine told me there had once been a mining accident and they had had more than a hundred patients at once, but I have seen nothing like that. I had never been needed for patient care and had rarely gone onto the ward.

But shortly after this one of Laura's patients was reassigned to me. He was a young male, might even have been younger than I if I had known a way to count years for myself, an aging in the body without the usual passage of time. He was a geologist from the outermost station. Dr. Margaret came to my room to inform me of the reassignment. She entered before I had risen, entered without knocking although I believe she invariably knocks for admittance into Elaine or Laura's room. She looked tired. Laura had recently cut her hair for her— very short. She had slept on it and not combed it; pieces stuck up about the ears.

She was characteristically abrupt. "Raina, we are very close here, closer than most families, because we work together and are so isolated. There is no need for any of us to have secrets from the others."

It was my own thought. It gave me a peculiar feeling to hear someone else express it. It was sweet, this unexpected matching of something inside me to something outside. Very sweet. Then Dr. Margaret handed me a piece of paper. On it she had written two chains of prime numbers. "Here are the access codes that Elaine and Laura use. If you should see a message come in for either of them I want you to read it and to tell me about it. Memorize the access."

Always underestimating me. Having seen the numbers once I would never forget them. I handed the paper back. Dr. Margaret turned to leave the room, stopping briefly at the door. "I almost forgot what I came down for. You'll see you have a patient when you punch up your duties. An interesting case. Keep me informed." She left and I saw her neck receding from me, startlingly white where the hair had been cut away.

The geologist turned out to be one of those rare individuals who could not tolerate the inoculation. Instead, the introduction of passive immunities had caused an alarming agglutination of the red blood cells. He had required replacement of the entire blood supply; Laura had handled that and seen that he had no adverse reaction to the foreign blood. It was left to me to see if he could now tolerate and use the immunizing agents, a slow, tedious process, most of which could still be done in the lab. "Every single person is different," Dr. Margaret told me enthusiastically. "That's what makes medicine so fascinating. Just when you think you've got it all figured out, someone comes along who reacts differently."

The geologist persisted in calling for me. He couldn't wiggle his toes, he claimed. He had a headache. "I'm really quite busy," I told him, but he ignored this. Whenever I was in the room, he stared at me. Once, when I was withdrawing blood, I suddenly felt his hands attach themselves to my waist and begin to move upwards. I gave the needle an extra push and he released me.

"Ouch," he said, but he was laughing.

"Don't do that again." How did I feel? Before I could decide, choose and identify one of the feelings inside me, I turned, and saw Dr. Margaret watching from the doorway. I could see that she was pleased. "Bravo, Raina," she said. "I never thought you'd be so good with people."

I wondered what she meant, what anyone would mean if they said that. Did it mean I pleased the people around me? Did it mean I controlled them? Should I be trying to do either? These were new thoughts to me.

Two weeks later Laura came to my room at night. I could smell her coming—her shampoo floated through the door just ahead of her. Such a gentle smell.

Before it had even registered, Laura appeared. Her face was red about her eyes and I noticed suddenly that she had found a way to thin her eyebrows. She walked through the doorway and straight up to me, raising her hand. I heard and felt it hit my face. "You're even worse than Gwen," she said in a low voice that shook. "What do you know about loyalty? What do you care about love? You're Mother's perfect little daughter, aren't you?" She raised her hand to hit me a second time, but I had no trouble catching it.

"Don't do that again," I warned her. And then said "I don't want you in my room unless I've asked you." I tried to sound firm, but I felt sick inside, shredded. I can't bear disharmony. "Please go," I told her and, to my surprise, she did. She was crying and left the room almost doubled over. The last I saw of her was the exaggerated curve of her back.

Laura and Elaine argue with each other constantly, but it's different, somehow, from the way they argue with me. I never argue with anyone. It hurts to do it. Since Dr. Margaret oversees our dinners, they are peaceful and professionally oriented. Breakfast is often one long quarrel.

Laura tells Elaine she eats too much. "I say this because I'm your sister and I love you," she says, ostentatiously heaping her own plate.

Elaine tells Laura she frightens men away with the desperation in her approach. "It embarrasses me just to watch the way you throw yourself at them. I'm not saying this to hurt you. I only want to help."

They're happiest when they unite against me. I make all their differences disappear because I am so much more different. At breakfast yesterday, Laura was combing her hair. She was wearing yellow coveralls and trying to attach a clip, shaped like a bird, to the twist of her hair.

Elaine watched with annoyance, irritated because she thinks this preening at the table is unhygienic. But what she said was "Laura, do you really have the time to just be sitting here? Shouldn't you be in the lab? All the temperatures on those cultures need to be changed."

"It's not my day to work in the lab. I did it yesterday, *Elaine*."

"Yesterday you were paying me back for my working twice last week. You went out on call, remember?"

"I already paid that back. You're so dim. You think you can boss me around just because you're bigger." Laura smiled nastily. "Of course, you're bigger than just about anyone, aren't you?"

"Shut up, Laura. Why should I do your work on top of mine?"

"It's Laura's lab day," I said. I remembered Laura pleading to go on call in Elaine's place, offering to take the extra duty. I hoped to settle the dispute which, as always, was upsetting me. But I only annoyed them. They won't admit my memory is better than theirs. They both looked at me at once.

"Why don't you take the lab today, Raina? You like lab work." Elaine peeled the wax covering off an imported fruit.

"I think that's fairest," Laura agreed. "When we're not sure and all. Don't you, Elaine?"

"I really do."

"I'm supposed to help with the boosters," I said. "We've got a whole transport coming in from Athens 4."

"Then you'd better hurry," Elaine advised. I put down my knife, my breakfast unfinished. "Hurry up, Raina!"

I almost told her that I didn't have time. I looked at her and started to form the words and then didn't. I gathered up my dishes instead and as I was leaving the table I heard Laura whisper something to Elaine. "I thought for a moment she was going to argue with you," she said.

I looked back. Elaine and Laura were sitting with their heads very close together—the dark hair and the red hair almost touching. "No," Elaine answered. "Passivity is part of the program," then I was through the door, hurrying to the lab. I could have argued with her, though; could have chosen the words that would have been like a piece of myself, held outside me for Elaine and Laura to look at. Hadn't I told Laura to get out of my room? Hadn't I told my geologist patient not to touch me? Hadn't anyone noticed these things?

I wondered if they had noticed how much of the

hospital work I was now doing. Without extending my hours, I had become increasingly efficient. I now did more than any of them, even Dr. Margaret. I didn't mind this. At least when I had done something myself I knew it had been done well. Elaine is clumsy and Laura is forgetful. Each of them has contaminated entire experiments. And Dr. Margaret? Strange, with her reputation, but I'm beginning to think that she is unimaginative. Her approach to immunology is strictly a defensive one. I was beginning to wonder if we had to be so conservative. Not that it was up to me.

When I had finished Laura's lab work, I hurried to the patient hall. It was full and I was late. Dr. Margaret gave me an irritated glance. "Laura came in to help out when you didn't show," she said in an undertone the patients wouldn't hear. "I think you'd be ashamed to have her doing your work."

I began to punch up the records for the individual patients and came upon an anomaly which I called to Dr. Margaret's attention. There was a little boy in the Athens group on whom we had no record. He said he had been inoculated by his mother. It shouldn't have been possible, but a blood test bore him out. He wore yellow overalls and red boots and had shiny black hair. Elaine, Laura, and Dr. Margaret fussed over him and kept all the other patients waiting. "Isn't he sweet?" they cooed. "Isn't he the sweetest thing?"

Dr. Margaret gave him the booster personally, and a candy for being so brave. We stood together inside, listening to the ship leave. "You could still send a message to Gwen," said Elaine. "Please, Mother."

But Laura said, "No." I saw with surprise that she was crying; I hadn't heard it over the transport engine, but now she was having trouble speaking, her words lost

NO POSTAGE
NECESSARY
IF MAILED
IN THE
UNITED STATES

BUSINESS REPLY MAIL
FIRST CLASS PERMIT NO. 62688 LOS ANGELES, CA

POSTAGE WILL BE PAID BY ADDRESSEE

BRIDGE PUBLICATIONS, INC.

1414 North Catalina Street
Los Angeles, California 90027-9990

in great, gusting sobs. "She doesn't want us to have anything. She could have come here for the delivery. She knows how seldom we get babies." She said something else that was lost in her crying, then became audible again. "She could at least have informed us. We are the doctors, here, after all. Births and deaths all routinely logged. She could have let us share in this, but she didn't. She only sent him now to show us what we're missing."

Dr. Margaret spoke quietly. "Perhaps it's time for one of you to have a baby. I could arrange it. During the pregnancy we could get more help for the hospital like we got Raina."

"Another Raina," said Laura. "No thanks." She looked at me bitterly and left the hall.

Dr. Margaret put her arm around Elaine. "I loved her, you know. You know I did."

"Another Raina." Those were Laura's words and I remember them now as I remember everything else in this hospital, exactly, accurately. Why didn't I hear them? How could I listen so carefully and hear so little?

This morning I heard them again, as I sat at the console, reading in a patient history and was interrupted by a message coming over the screen—a printed message which meant it came from somewhere outside the sector. I couldn't access it with my own code, so I realized it was a secret message—something for Elaine, or Laura, or Dr. Margaret. A secret message for anyone but me. "There is no need for any of us to have secrets from the others," I told myself, and I punched in Laura's access.

The message came across the screen slowly. It was from a company called "Help Wanted." It read:

Regret to inform you RAINA

> has been found to have a
> flawed personality structure
> and may even be dangerous.
> Incidents in other sectors
> force recall of all units.
> Respond. . . .

I sat at the console a long time, looking at those words. "All units," I read. "Another Raina," I remembered. I could only make it mean one thing. I began to type the response.

> RAINA is like one of the family.
> We cannot think of . . .

Then I erased it and began again.

> Message received. Situation
> under control. Appropriate
> steps being taken.

And I sent it.

It was past time for me to be in the lab. I hurried there, anxious not to show Dr. Margaret another example of tardiness, afraid I might have to create an explanation for it. But the lab was empty. I began to update the logs and Dr. Margaret came in. She did not speak to me and I knew that if I didn't have to fabricate anything, if it were only a matter of withholding, then I could keep a secret. Dr. Margaret had taught me that herself; she and Elaine.

Dr. Margaret punched in a model of a new experiment she was designing and began to explain it to me. I concentrated on her instructions, pushing my secret down deeper inside me. I couldn't think about it now. I had to be alone. "It's a very cautious approach," I told Dr. Margaret. I hadn't even known I was going to say it. It was not a smart thing to say. I had not offered an opinion before and this one made her look up from the screen to my face with surprise and displeasure.

"I think that's best," she said and I felt that queer, unpleasant feeling inside me that meant I didn't agree. "You have a different idea?" Dr. Margaret asked coldly. "You have a better idea?"

"Your work is all parasite-specific," I said. "When the infecting organism changes, the agent is no longer effective. You've simply perfected the disease."

"I have had some small success with my methods." Dr. Margaret's voice was edged with sarcasm. "I've also seen what more radical approaches can come to—'the operation was a success, but the patient died.' That's quite an old joke, really, but I bet you've never heard it before." She turned away from me back to the screen, her back stiff with anger. "Just do the experiments I design." Soon she left for the patient ward.

My hands were shaking, but the sickened feeling inside me began to fade and was replaced with a kind of exultation. I had disagreed with Dr. Margaret and I had said so. How strong I was becoming! Stronger even than Laura. Strong enough.

I changed the temperatures on the cultures and saw what I would have to do. I did not make this decision easily. Some of the disharmony I had lived with had even moved inside of me so that I was all in parts— seeing what was required, yet still reluctant. I went to the lab shelves and selected a fatal disease, something airborne and quick. If Dr. Margaret hadn't been so limited in her vision she might have discovered an inoculation against it. Then I wouldn't have this option. It is her own weakness, after all, that condemns her. I left the disease still frozen and harmless in the lab until I could make my other arrangements. Before I defrost it, I must have a way out.

For I am not Gwen. Dr. Margaret would not be hurt by my defection, she would be outraged. She would come after me with all her influence and all her money and I would be destroyed. I thought all this as I sat in the lab among the glove boxes and test tubes. I laid my cheek on the black surface of the table and then lifted it up slightly. At a certain angle, the tabletop was so polished I could see a vague outline of my face. I covered it with my hand, pushing down the part of me which objected.

Then I went on with my work. I set up Dr. Margaret's experiment. I went to the ward to look at my patients. I saw the geologist last of all. "You'll be released soon," I told him. "Two or three days at the most."

He turned on his side, rested his head in the cup of his palm. His eyes and hair were an identical shade of brown; the hospital light reflected off them both. "So I'm cured," he said. "You've cured me of everything." His smile was broad and affected every part of his face.

I leaned toward him, lowering my voice. "Jim," I said. "Will you take me with you?"

His eyes opened in surprise. I spoke again, tremblingly. "Even if I need to leave the sector? Would you help me?" It was my first attempt to persuade anyone to do anything for me. I reached out and moved a piece of his hair back from his forehead. It was so easy. I am good with people.

Jim thought he could secure a vehicle within the two or three days I was willing to spare. Fuel, he said, would be the bigger problem, but he knew a man on Athens. . . . We agreed that I would use the time to erase him and myself from the data banks. I had planned to do this anyway, but he was quite insistent on the point. I wondered for the first time if he might not have some

secrets of his own.

There is so much I do not know. I have no memory of the time I spent outside the sector. In my own mind I have never even left the hospital. When I begin to think this way, I calm myself with what I *do* know: I can keep a secret; I am strong; I am good with people; I know nothing of loyalty and do not care about love. It is enough.

Now it is time for dinner. I will go in and sit and listen to the conversation. I will respond when I am spoken to and will otherwise say nothing.

I realize now that all of us have memories beyond our ability to retrieve them, memories we cannot remember. My life is all memory now, so much so that I can no longer distinguish between a recollection and a premonition. My past is my destination, after all. I am returning to what I left behind, to my family, to my sisters, endangered as I am now endangered, fighting as I am now fighting.

If I must sacrifice the flawed personality structures with whom I have worked—Dr. Margaret and her need to control, Elaine and her need to subvert, Laura and her need to escape—then I will do this for my sisters. I know they will be worth the sacrifice. They will, after all, be just like me.

And if they have been taught as I have been taught, then we will find each other. I do not doubt it—it has the solidity of memory. One day, in the darkness, I will whisper my name to someone else. One day, somewhere, I will look at someone else and see my own face.

The Ebbing
by
Leonard Carpenter

About the Author

Leonard Carpenter holds a degree from U.C. Berkeley in Conservation of Natural Resources. This fact is considerably reflected in The Ebbing. *His novelette is a literally haunting contemporary echo of the urban fantasy story first pioneered in* Unknown *magazine during the Golden Age, before Carpenter was born. Thirty-seven, married to a painter with whom he shares parentage of two young daughters, he is a backpacker, bicyclist and Frisbee enthusiast who works for a U.S. Government agency. Having taken journalism courses in college, he in 1981 began submitting fiction to various markets, apparently because born writers always find time sooner or later.*

As can happen, success has arrived in a cluster. Almost simultaneously with winning Second Prize in the first quarter's contest, Carpenter has placed several short stories, and gained a contract to write a new Conan the Barbarian novel. There are no strong-thewed sword-swingers in The Ebbing; *but there is barbarity. . . .*

Illustrated by Dave Simons

Promptly at 6:30 AM it began to rain in Isla Serena, California. The rain didn't fall from the sky; it sprayed out of green vinyl-padded sprinkler heads installed in lawns covering the common area around the lake. It was a healthy downpour, the equivalent of a brisk spring shower—in climates that knew such luxuries.

But here in the Orange County desert it didn't fit. The illusion of rain slanting down, sun-glinting, seemed alien against the backdrop of Camelback Peak's twin summits rising from a smoggy haze. Especially today, when there was a sullen restlessness in the air.

Dave Antelope, assistant gardener, wasn't taken by surprise that morning, and he wasn't drenched. He'd learned to wear a watch and keep his eye on it. When the whirring and chuffing of the spray began, he was already driving his mower along a paved path toward the maintenance yard. He sat feeling occasional windblown drops strike him, watching faint shivers in the leaves of young magnolia trees spaced beside the path—bad signs this early in the day. He kept his hand loose on the steering wheel, letting the machine almost guide itself back to its stable.

As he turned into the hedge-screened yard and swung the tractor up to the aluminum roller-door—already blinding in yellow eastern light—he saw Herm Farber standing in front of the office watching him. The chief gardener's hands were propped on the wide hips of his coveralls in a familiar pose of disapproval.

"You finish behind the golf links yet?" Farber called up to the younger man.

Dave stayed in the seat and kept the motor running so they'd both have to shout. "No. I was going to do shrubs and hedges now. I'll finish mowing tomorrow."

"Not good enough." Farber shook his head sharply. "The grass in the rough areas is too high. The golfers don't like wading ankle-deep when they're hunting for balls. Their games'll be off . . . and I'll hear about it from the club manager." He made a swirling motion with his extended hand to indicate turning the mower around. "Go back and finish it up."

"But Herm—Mr. Farber. Not much sense in cutting wet grass. And . . . ," He twisted in his saddle to look east, across the freeway's flitting car-silhouettes, toward the hills. "I think there'll be a Santa Ana wind kickin' up soon. Grass'll be blowing all over. Better to start the shrubs now."

"Antelope, if you don't mind, I'd rather be the judge of that. The radio didn't mention any Santa Ana wind. If your Indian lore tells you so, then you know more about it than the National Weather Service." The chief gardener's voice stayed more than loud enough to be heard over the sputtering motor. "Just do it, will you?" He glanced at his watch and turned impatiently away. "You should've had it finished up yesterday," he added over his shoulder.

Wordlessly, Dave engaged the mower's gears. He craned his neck and wheeled the wide-bladed undercarriage back until the end of the left blade-guard clashed against a post of the Cyclone fence. Then he jerked the wheel and putt-putted out of the yard.

The morning was clearer than usual. Even beyond the brown smudge of L.A. to the north, he could trace the faint, jagged outline of mountain peaks. He headed back toward the golf course by a different route, along the lake's edge.

The trapped water sparkled gold in the early light, with the ungainly reflection of the cantilevered foot-bridge scrawled across its center. The water took on subtly different shades and textures where stray breezes brushed it.

It reminded Dave of something else . . . a lake he'd seen in his childhood. Maybe the pond on the reservation.

Now, as he squinted at the everyday view, he had an odd sensation. Bridge, buildings, and Scotch-gardener landscape were softening and fading, to be replaced by a wash of yellow-brown: the folding curves of desert hills and mesas.

Then the lake zoom-lensed away from him, to become vast and still, remaking itself into a sea, the color of its waters deepening. The sky unfolded to an immense royal-blue gallery. He watched, rapt. At the new terrain's jagged eastern edge, a glowing full moon tugged free of the horizon.

Dave came back to awareness when he felt the mower's wheels riding up the grassy hill at the edge of the path. Instantly the hallucination faded; the tepid Orange County morning reasserted itself. He swerved back onto the pavement and rolled forward, shaking his head from side to side, while the clanking mower blades followed.

"Whoa!" he thought, "where did *that* come from?"

He pondered the question, but it was still unanswered

many minutes later. He watched the morning around him with a new caution.

Far to the north, another man approached a lake. His tracks descended for miles through an alkali desert shallowly layered by ancient surfs.

His tattered moccasins were as brown and wrinkled as the ankles they shielded. Across his naked, wizened back rode a thong-sewn goatskin pouch, its seams dark with moisture. A short leather cape covered his shoulders and rose in a tall peak to shade his head. His gait was a crook-kneed trot.

The ancient one ran like an insect across the sun-scorched flatness. He came to a place where the ground was frosted with salt rime, its clay smudging damply under his feet. Then the footing became uneven. Clear, still water puddled in a shallow depression that merged with other puddles to become a vast mirrorlike surface reflecting desert hills and pale sky.

He knelt. He unwound the water bag from his shoulder, unstoppered it, raised it, and dribbled a few drops into his mouth. The rest he sprayed into the lake before him, squeezing the goatskin until it was empty.

He leaned forward and stirred the water with his fingertips. Ripples spread, breaking up the desert pictures. He raised his dripping fingers to his lips, tasted, and spat in disgust. His curse was a single low, resonant syllable spoken in a language no living man shared.

Still kneeling, he swivelled his shoulders, ducked his head out of his cowl, and looked backward. His old face became even more pinched in the sunglare blazing off the snow and granite of immense mountain peaks standing close behind him. Amid the forest-green tresses of their upper slopes, mountain springs and waterfalls glinted.

He turned, bent low, and refilled his goatskin.

Kathy Middleton had a dream about dogs eating eggs. It was a vivid impression, but disconnected from any thought or story she knew. Pictures of the animals' yolk-stained, tongue-lapping muzzles faded slowly as she was drawn to awareness by morning light on the curtains and the racket of a mower somewhere outside.

Another morning in Isla Serena. She thought ahead to what the day might bring. At best, maybe a trip to the beach with Kyle. Hanging around here in her older sister's home didn't appeal to her much, in spite of Wendy's tolerance . . . or because of it. She felt out of place. This entire huge housing development was nothing but nuclear families—Jetsons. She giggled sleepily. It turned into a yawn.

She sat up in bed and looked around the room. It was pink—intensified by the muslin-filtered sunlight—and far too neat and rococo for her seven-year-old niece. Trish, poor kid, had actually seemed happy at the chance to sleep in her little brother's room for a while. This one was . . . cloying.

Kathy wished she were back in school. A tiny thrill of discomfort came with the thought, a hollow space under her heart. She'd screwed that up, all right. It might be a long while before she made it back there—or it might be forever. Her scholarship was forfeited, she couldn't expect financial help from Wendy and Charles, and Kyle was an unknown quantity.

She moved her shoulders to shake off the clinging weight of worry. A brisk shower would be good. She stood, took last night's jeans and sweatshirt under her arm, opened the hall door, and peeked out. Everybody was still asleep. She padded barefoot along the plush carpet. Maybe Wendy's way was best after all—security and quiet desperation in the suburbs. She snagged a towel from the linen shelf, went into the children's bathroom, closed the door and locked it.

After stripping off her extra-long T-shirt, Kathy examined herself in the full-length mirror. Her shape was slim as ever; the pregnancy hadn't lasted long enough to show. Good. She raised her arms and rotated her body. Now she was starting to have tan lines that highlighted her breasts and pelvis; time to use a lower-numbered bottle of sunscreen.

She knew how to build a good suntan, anyway, if not a life.

She bent over the tub, and worked the ball-jointed lever that controlled hot and cold, intending to set the water temperature before turning on the shower. But no water came gushing out. Instead, there was a dry rattle in the pipes.

As Kathy watched, grains of sand trickled out of the spigot, forming a little pile in the tub.

"Morning, Darryl. Want any help?" Mal closed the front door of the condo behind him and cut across the sloping lawn toward his cousin, who was playing a stream of water over the white car at the curb.

"No, that's okay. Don't get your clothes wet." Darryl was dressed in tennis shorts and zoris; his round, hairy abdomen was bare. "Just save your energy. If you're going to spend the day at Disneyland with your kids, you'll need it." He tossed his hose aside, grabbed a sponge from a yellow plastic bucket, and sloshed suds over the car's roof.

Mal settled his thin frame gingerly on the lawn. "Frankly, from looking at it yesterday, I wouldn't have thought your car needed washing."

Darryl blinked at him. "Oh, yeah." He shrugged. "Well, white paint jobs need more care." He ran a hand lovingly over the dripping flank of his machine—the latest Japanese Q-car, looking like a beveled Mercedes. Its denture-ivory finish made its polarized windows seem black. "Besides, it's fun being out like this, in the sun, getting wet." He dashed the remaining contents of the bucket over the white carapace and continued scrubbing. "It's my way of communing with Nature."

Mal shook his head, smiling. "California's certainly . . . different." He propped his arms behind him in the grass and leaned back on them. "It's funny: I feel like I'm at Disneyland already."

"Really!" Darryl nodded. "With all the weird characters running around." He bent down to groom the car's chrome-plastic grille. "Cartoon-land."

"No, I didn't mean that." Mal paused, as if formulating an elusive thought. "It's more . . . the buildings. Not the architecture." He glanced over his shoulder to the stucco mansion, frosted with adobe roof-tiles and brick chimneys, that housed his cousin's condo and two others. "It's the scale of things. Taking a piece of blank real estate and putting up whatever strikes your fancy. Like putting London Bridge in the middle of the Mojave Desert."

"That's the modern way." Darryl was kneeling to work on the mag wheels, the hose streaming into the grass beside him unheeded. "Gets us clear of the crime and the urban problems."

"Yes—well, you're in a much better position to do that, out here. Back East, everything is locked in by history. But here out West, you're free of all that. You don't have to worry——"

"Arrh!" Darryl's cry, as he jumped back from the car, cut Mal short. "What the hell? Look at this!"

"What's the matter?"

"It's the water!" Darryl pointed to where a translucent, gritty, rust-red fluid was spreading down the gleaming enamel of his car. "It's crudded up all of a sudden." He held the red-streaming hose away from him, then dropped it. "Oh, cripes, look at that!"

Mal came to the edge of the lawn and leaned down to stare at the hose that was now discharging onto the sidewalk. The puddle where it lay was red and silty, and the water gouting from it was thick with tiny, translucent, grublike creatures, swimming and wriggling in a pale surf along the concrete. As the two men watched, the hose sputtered, spat, and twisted on the ground like an angry snake, spouting living things into the air; they both jumped away with startled exclamations.

Amazement held them silent for a moment. Then Darryl turned and stamped up the walk toward the house.

"Where—where are you going?" asked Mal.

"To call the freaking water company, that's where! Do me a favor, Mal, and go turn the hose off." He banged through his front door.

Mal glanced at the rust-colored puddle spreading along the sidewalk and swallowed, feeling a little nauseous. He started across the lawn toward the corner of the building, where the green textured hose wound out of sight.

Tom Boster awoke slowly and pleasantly, as he always had on Saturdays, ever since his boyhood. Letting the murky tide of sleep retreat, he lay purposely still. He felt his body gradually firming and his circulation increasing, bringing a growing sense of well-being. Then he started methodically flexing his legs and shoulders where he lay on the soft mattress. He took some deep breaths. Who said that retirement had to be a time of worry and ill health? Right now his sixties felt better to him than his thirties had.

When he was ready, he slipped out from beside the slack figure of his wife and stood by the bed, clad only in the pastel-colored briefs that he'd taken to wearing on hot Isla Serena nights.

He didn't stop to rummage on the nightstand for his glasses, but headed straight for the sliding patio door. His bare feet knew the way so well that he scarcely had to open his eyes. He moved the door back silently on nylon rollers, slipped past the curtain, and jogged to the head of the pool.

His skin was braced more by the sun's heat than by the cool motion of air across his back. Today would be a scorcher, but he'd get the jump on it. He mounted the diving board and stood a moment, squinting along its sun-bleached fiberglass length, feeling the rough tread against his soles. Then he paced forward, bounded, and sprang.

A few moments later his wife came groping through the patio door, rubbing her sleep-fogged eyes. She stopped with both hands against her face, staring down at what lay in the bottom of the dry pool.

"Here, Muffer! Breakfast." Trish pushed backward through the kitchen door, carrying in one hand a heaping dish of kibble, and in the other a stainless-steel mixing bowl of water so heavy it strained her arm. "Muffer! C'mon!"

She set her offerings on the patio bricks next to the

house and looked around the yard, shading her eyes. There was the dog—a glossy black hunting creature in the strip of green shade near the fence. The Labrador was trotting back and forth with a restless, loping motion that Trish didn't remember ever seeing before; then suddenly he darted straight past her to the water dish and drank greedily, surging the water up and down in the bowl with his muzzle and swirling it all around. He looked like some kind of machine-dog instead of the playful friend she knew.

Trish didn't know why he was so thirsty—unless it was the weather. It was hot and dry, and the wind lashed the trees at the sides of the yard and rattled the patio-cover, making it feel even drier.

When he finished drinking, the dog didn't dive for the kibble. He just shook water drops from his head and stood still in front of the bowl. "C'mon, Muffer, eat some breakfast." Trish stepped forward to pet him and coax him toward his dish. But she became aware of a low, grating noise. When she realized it was coming from the dog's muzzle, she stopped dead. As she stared, the sleek head jerked to the side, and his near lip curled back from yellow-white teeth. His fitful, nervous growling grew louder.

"Muffer, what's the matter?" Trish watched the dog a moment, then decided she'd better tell Dad. She backed away from the watching animal and slipped through the kitchen door into the house.

Dave Antelope put the tractor into neutral and killed the motor. He removed his long-visored cap and mopped his brow with the back of one hand, pausing to pick bits of windblown grass clippings off his damp forehead. He silently cursed Farber for sending him to work in such an exposed area.

It'd turned into one hellcat of a day, too gusty and fierce for any golfer. And that was just considering the weather, without even thinking about the other, stranger things.

The absence of mower's noise made new sounds audible . . . the rustle of windblown hedges, a distant siren's wail, the lap of waves against the concrete curb of the lake, and wind-snatched verses of the endless song of tires slapping the Santa Ana Freeway. That was a sound Dave usually heard only in the evenings, on the land breeze. Most days it was a westerly wind, and Long Beach Freeway tires, rushing to and from the junction of the two steel rivers south of town.

Dave reached under his seat and took a pull from his can of ginger ale. It was warm and flat. He felt no livelier himself. The subtle things he'd been sensing all day, the odd glimpses out of the corner of his eye; there was no way to explain them. In his drinking days, maybe, or if he'd ever taken hard stuff that might cause flashbacks. But he hadn't. The only thing he could say for sure about his visions was there was something hauntingly familiar about them. Something elemental, like the campfire legends from his childhood.

He shifted in his seat to watch the lake's torment. Sheets of hot, desiccating wind drove ranks of ragged waves before them, tearing droplets from the very surface of the water and carrying them far. Waves washed the asphalt of the jogging path, and Dave could feel cool pinpricks of moisture in the air. He wondered how much water was being lost to evaporation. There'd been a controversy about water use when the tract was being planned, he recalled, but the engineers had deepened the lake, changed the composition of its bed, and quieted the complaints.

The view of the Camelback was obscured by wind-blown dust, some of it rising from graded vacant land across the lake's narrow tip. As Dave watched, a dust devil drew a tan-colored cloud high into the air and swept it across lawns and water toward him. He closed his eyes and averted his face while grit struck his hands and neck and rang faintly on the tractor cowling. When it let up, he opened his eyes in cautious slits.

The dust had become denser, and whitish in color. For the moment it was hard to make out even nearby shapes, and a new dust cloud towered high enough to darken the sun. Its substance smote his tearing eyes and his nostrils with alkaline sting.

He ducked his head. When he looked again, the gray curtains shifted and parted a little.

The lake was dry and vast, its chalky bed fissured crazily, swept by salt tempests. No trees or buildings stood on any side—only the dim outlines of white, jagged towers rising from salt-encrusted boulders some-where in front of the tractor's hood. He dared to look to windward, where horizon and sky were merged to a continuous gray mass; a mass that suddenly smote Dave, sandpapering his skin and driving him almost out of his seat.

When he dared to breathe and look up, Isla Serena was back. The hot harpy wind felt almost welcome. He looked around warily a moment for any fleeting trace of the desert; then he climbed down from the gritty tractor seat, pocketed the keys, and walked straight away across the lawn.

Charles Vonzell did a double take as he saw the chopped VW pull into his driveway. The disreputable, noise-blatting vehicle was as alien on Smoketree Esplanade as the tumbleweed that had come bounding down the street moments before.

Then he remembered his young sister-in-law. He called, "You must be here for Kathy," and put one foot down from his step-stool, but the car's youthful driver just nodded and hit the machine's falsetto horn twice. Vonzell shrugged and turned back to his job of untangling the wind chimes from the hanging geranium.

Still, he couldn't help wondering about the boy sitting stoically in the sun and in the hot gusts with no protection but a dirty windshield and a roll bar. He sneaked another glance over his shoulder. The derangement of the younger man's hair seemed more than just an accident of the wind; its cut was punkish, substantially shorter on the sides than on top.

The company Kathy kept was her own business—but she had, after all, come to them for help. He took the ceramic bells down, furling them carefully. He hopped from his stool and walked from the porch toward the driveway. "Care to come inside? Hot day to be waiting out here."

The youth sat picking with one finger at a scabrous area of the padded dash. He looked around, his eyes following a dust devil that whirled leaves and a single clattering soft-drink can along the street. "Right," he conceded. He climbed out of the jalopy and followed Charles to the house.

Just inside the front door, Wendy, in a long, ruffled gingham dress, greeted them and handed each a glass of lemonade. "I'm Kathy's sister," she said to their visitor. "I heard you coming."

"Mmm." Vonzell tilted his glass. "Have a seat," he said, settling to the edge of the chintz-covered colonial sofa.

The youth squatted on the hassock of the reclining chair. "Is Kath up yet?"

Wendy sat at the other end of the sofa. "Yes. She told us at breakfast that she was expecting you. . . . Kyle, is it?"

The youth nodded once.

"Where're you thinking of going?" Charles looked through the picture window at the waving trees. "Someplace indoors, I hope. Hell of a day to be outside."

Kyle stared straight ahead. "We were thinking, maybe, the beach."

Charles winced. "I don't know about that. Sounds like a good way to get yourselves sandblasted."

Kyle shrugged. "Might be cooler there."

Kathy entered from the hallway. "Hi, Kyle." She came forward and stood near him, hands clasped over the strap of a canvas beachbag. "You've already met? Charlie, Kyle's studying art at S.C." She was wearing sandals, jeans pegged to her mid-calf, and an old, faded lavender Save Something-Or-Other sweatshirt torn stylishly at the neck. "Charlie's into city planning."

"Oh, Kyle, what medium of art are you in?" Wendy inclined her head toward him. "I used to do macramé."

"I'm working with dada."

"Oh, really? I think I've heard of him."

Charles interjected, "Say, Kyle, be sure and take a course in computer graphics. Fascinating field—and there are lots of jobs opening up. I even use it in my work."

"I could tell." Kyle finally took up the gauntlet and looked at Charles. "Instant art, instant cities." He set his glass of ice on the coffee table, ignoring the Early American coaster-caddy. "Like this suburb of yours; it looks like it was built by Pac-men."

In the beat that followed, the women stayed silent—Wendy looking startled, Kathy interested. Then Vonzell said, "Don't be too quick to knock it. Out here we've solved a lot of problems. People have the same values here, so they stay civilized." He reached forward and set Kyle's glass on a coaster. "And it's planned growth, not just a hodgepodge."

The younger man's long face, rather vulnerable-looking when viewed straight on, made a slight, impatient jerk to one side. "Marvy! But why is it that the more of these wonderful places you make, the worse of a scumhole my part of town gets to be?"

"Maybe it's because the best people move out here." Charles shrugged. "I certainly wouldn't want to live in a flaky area where my life was disrupted by crazies every other day. What's wrong with living comfortably, the way you want, if you're not bothering anyone else?"

"Great—but how many of you? This city keeps spreading like a blight." Kyle's face ticked again. "I mean—it's not just another blank computer screen out there, you dig? It's a country. The lumber has to be chopped down, the water has to be ripped off from somewhere. Art is limitation." He turned his gaze back toward the corner of the floor. "Somebody pays the bill. I have the feeling it's gonna be me."

Charles opened his mouth, then closed it on silence. Nobody seemed to have a reply.

Finally Kathy broke the stalemate. "Well, we'd better get going, if we're going to go." She moved forward past Kyle and swept him along with her. "See you folks later," she waved back as she held the door for him. The wind slammed it after them.

The chief gardener looked over the expanse of lawn

as broadly as the wind allowed. When the most violent gusts pummelled him, Farber pulled the bill of his cap down over his eyes with one thick hand. There was nobody in sight; no sign of David Antelope.

As he drew near the abandoned tractor, he couldn't see anything wrong with it, although its paint was filmed with dust and trash had accumulated in the scant shelter of its tires and mower blades. He shook his head angrily. It shouldn't have been left untended, today or any day. The risk of liability from accident alone was tremendous, not to mention theft or vandalism. He'd been waiting for something of the sort from Antelope. The explanation had better be a good one.

Farber hauled himself up into the tractor seat, groped under the dash for the spare key, and inserted it. After a few pumps on the gas pedal, the machine started easily. Damn that guy! He threw it into gear and hauled the steering wheel around, heading for the yard.

The horizon was a fringe of soughing fences and wind-whipped trees. The grass, short as it was, was driven in waves broader than those on the lake. Yet there were moments of hot, deceptive stillness. In such moments the air would seem intensely clear, though the light was colored by yellowish dust blown aloft. Then suddenly a new rush of air would smite Farber like a club, tearing at his shirt-lapels and noticeably slowing the tractor as it labored forward.

After one such blow, Farber felt a shadow fall over him; he looked up to see a cyclone-sized dust cloud rising from the raw land across the lake. Its center was a tan swirl that threatened momentarily to draw into a funnel; its top was sharp-edged against blue sky. He shut his eyes as the dust descended and rang on the tractor hood. He was forced to cover his face so long that he began to doubt his memory of the tractor's course across clear grass. His foot faltered on the accelerator.

Then the tractor's wheel rode over some obstacle. Startled, he hit the brake and opened his eyes, but was forced to close them at once by the pelting sting of the grit-storm. It continued while he struggled to recall what he'd glimpsed. Not grass; instead, a desolate surface with dark, jagged, volcanic rocks, some stained white on top. Debris on the ground—bones and matted feathers. What the hell!?

When once again he felt the wind diminish, he opened his eyes cautiously . . . on a landscape that seemed as dreadful to him as the surface of the Moon. Naked, furrowed rock strewn with boulders and scattered bones stretched away endlessly . . . but the distances were obscured by blown dust. And there, across the dry lake bed, came a cloud with a special glinting whiteness. It roiled and swirled in a curving course toward him, casting its own deep shadow.

Farber felt a terror of it without knowing why. He gunned the tractor, turning the wheels away from the sweep of the cloud. The machine lurched forward, crunching over pumice, bones and broken eggshells. But it didn't move fast enough. And the white cloud seemed to shift its course accordingly.

As it bore down on him, Farber could see sun flashing on myriad white wings and beaks. But not all the creatures were birds. There were gray, leathery-skinned things with tooth-fringed jaws, wheeling close with the others. Farber hit the accelerator in breathless panic with no noticeable result.

Then the flock closed over him, beaks stabbing, teeth slashing. He felt his heart falter in his chest and clench painfully. Then it burst.

Vonzell sat listening to the hard, annoying throb of Kyle's engine receding down the street. Even after it faded far away, the noise was renewed fitfully by stray gusts of wind.

Trish pushed hastily into the living room through the door from the garage.

"Oh, Daddy, here you are! Daddy, Muffer's acting funny!"

He leaned forward, resting his elbows on his knees, and said in a tone of mock gravity: "Well, now . . . funny. Do you mean funny-funny, or strange-funny?"

"Strange, Daddy!" The child twisted her thin body impatiently. "He won't eat. And he growled at me."

"Well." Vonzell rose to his feet almost involuntarily, with an odd sense of lightness. He must be scared, he realized. "We'd better go take a look at him, hadn't we. Where's Troy? Is he outside now?"

"He wasn't a few minutes ago. . . . I don't know. He was in his room." Trish followed her father through the kitchen.

Vonzell pulled open the back door and unlatched the screen, standing for a moment with his hand on each door to keep the wind from controlling them. Over the lashing of tree limbs and the rattle of the patio roof, he could hear growling and scuffling behind the shed. He turned and bent to his daughter. "You stay here, Trish." He pulled the door to and shut the screen quietly behind him.

As he rounded the shed he walked into a nightmare. There was the dog, its fur glinting metal-blue in the sunlight. Its black jaws were clamped around Troy's throat.

The five-year-old was on one knee and one foot,

stretched backward by the attack. The dog pressed its body into the struggle like a winning wrestler, growling deeply and tossing its head at intervals to work its grip tighter. Troy's hands beat at Muffer's sides weakly; his face was pale blue with asphyxiation.

Vonzell's initial moment of faintness was followed by a mighty surge of adrenaline. He ran up astride the dog and seized its muzzle.

He tried to work his hands between the slavering jaws, but they were clamped tight against the child's bruised and broken skin. The incisors had torn deep punctures that oozed slippery blood. Vonzell's wrenching, prying fingertips couldn't get a grip.

The dog chuffed and snorted. Its eyeballs rolled back in its head to glimpse its attacker, but all the while it held on to its prey with doubled energy.

Vonzell shifted his grip ineffectually. To pull the child away from the dog would only help to tear out Troy's throat. He could get an arm around the beast's neck, but the corded muscles covered by thick, loose skin were too tough to strangle. Panting, desperate, he kept his thighs clamped on the glossy back.

His vision swam and discolored, sweat stinging his eyes. Hot winds smote his back and dead leaves flurried past. Then the bristling hide under him seemed to turn tawny and sparse, like a coyote's.

With a sudden scream of rage he thrust his forehead down, feeling the crack of skull against skull. His face pressed into sour-smelling fur and nuzzled in it until he found the base of the dog's ear; then, grunting, he bit down hard. He heard a stifled yelp. He felt the drooling jaws loosen an instant—just enough for him to work his fingertips slightly inward between them.

Saw-edged teeth cut his finger-pads. He gloried in the

feeling. He wrenched with his back and shoulders, and his fingers inched further into the cruel trap of the mouth, while his own snarling mouth burrowed, gnawing at the dog's head. He kneed and scissored the animal's haunches between his thighs, forcing the brute to the ground, and tried to bite its eye, but because of the protecting ridge of bone his teeth only sank into the bristly brow.

Then the dog was rolling on its back and Vonzell was screaming in exultation. Wrenching the scrabbling paws aside, he dove for the throat—and felt, under dusty fur, tendons and arteries pulsing and straining between his clamped teeth.

"Charles! What are you doing?" a voice cried. He lifted his head, spitting out coarse hairs, and looked around. Wendy was kneeling over Troy, who lay on his back on the grass, wheezing brokenly. She looked from the child to Vonzell with anguish.

Then there was a flurry of paws under him. Teeth snapped next to his ear. He threw his weight back on the still-frenzied dog, seized it in a narrow, tight hammerlock, and dragged it toward the shed. He kicked aside one of the sliding tin doors and hurled the beast inside atop clattering bicycles and barbecue. It took him long moments to bind the handles of the flimsy aluminum doors together with his belt. All the while the structure clattered and bounced from the dog's assaults.

Vonzell turned. Wendy was gathering Troy up in her arms; the boy was breathing more now, and bleeding less. "You stay here . . . with the dog. I'll take Troy to the hospital," Wendy said.

Both she and Trish, who was standing some distance behind her, watched Vonzel a little fearfully.

In the mountains, the last drops from the goatskin bag dribbled into the frothing stream. Their substance was instantly lost to the numberless currents twining and leaping over the boulders of its bed.

The cataract shouted with throngs of voices, like all the nations of history milling in loud confusion. The babel was thrown back from the immense granite cliff that rose on the opposite bank, doubling the sound in the old man's ears and adding a hissing overtone.

When the mingling of waters was complete, he turned from his ritual. He cast the goatskin away. His still-brisk stride carried him upslope. His moccasins found a trail so faint and fragile that a hare might have doubted it. It wound over and under rock outcrops, along bases and brinks of sheer granite faces, to a quartz-speckled rock promontory jutting from the canyon wall.

Beyond spread a view that stunned even eyes meeting it for the ten thousandth time: amid vasty desert, a lake. It was of intense blue and ringed by blazing white. All around it lay low peaks and barren tracts, some cratered and scorched to red or deep brown by Earth's fires. In the lake's center were two islands—one large and one small, one white and one black—the smaller one now only half-circled by blue, really a peninsula of the bone-bleached shoreline. Bristle-haired coyotes slunk out to eat the eggs of the white birds nesting there.

Standing pine-straight, his arms clasped across his chest, the old man's mouth slowly formed a sound. He spoke the very last word of his people's tongue that any living person might know. "Mono." Carried quickly away by warm, rising mountain gusts, his intonation was more like a sound of anguish than a name. And none heard it.

He turned and moved toward the canyon slope.

While passing alongside looming slabs of gray stone, he sidestepped and seemed to melt into the rock, so narrow and concealed was the fissure he entered.

Inside were dim light and dry dust. Ancient pigments flaked from a now-indistinguishable painting on one arching wall. A few shaped stones and collapsed earthen vessels littered the chamber's edges. The old man sank stiffly down on a rectangular space in one corner, laid his scrawny body flat, and, with a long, sighing exhalation, went back to sleep.

Dirk ran recklessly, letting wind hurl him along the curving path by the lake. What a day! He'd even wondered whether to come out, because of the wind, but damned if he hadn't done five miles every day this year; he'd needed his fix.

And it'd turned out to be a heady, exhilarating thing. The levity of the air practically demanded violent physical exertion; his race became a two-step dance with a crazed elemental force. The hot wind seemed to charge every square centimeter of his skin with static energy.

True, the gusts did try to hustle him into the water from time to time. And soon, when he rounded the toe of the lake, he'd be running against the wind; then it might become more of a fight than a dance. But he knew he'd enjoy it. He couldn't remember ever feeling so alive—a far cry from yesterday's Dirk Murdock, the disgruntled desk-jockey who lived alone in a dreary suburb.

He came up to his usual cat-corner across the beach, the shortcut that kept him away from the monoxide-spewing street at the lake's end. He sprang off the path. Through habit, he changed the set of his legs and feet for a heavier impact on loose sand.

At that instant, a wall-like gust of air struck him from one side. Simultaneously there was an unexpected give to the ground surface, and he was thrown off balance. He dove into a practiced shoulder-roll and prepared to come up in a half-second, still running, as he'd done many times.

Instead, his roll turned into a slide. He found himself sprawling in a wet, sticky substance—a substance other than sand. He opened his eyes to find himself plastered with muddy slime.

How could the lake have done this . . . ? He looked around and saw—not playground equipment, but angular pillars of rough white stone. No lake, only mud flats. Not city, but desert.

Dirk heard himself scream: a yelping, quavering cry.

He clamped his mouth shut to stop the sound. Closing his eyes and reopening them didn't help. Nor did shaking his head. The reality of the mud was undeniable; he could barely drag himself to his knees in it. It was light tan and silty on his body and shorts, but its surface around him had darker patches.

He extended his hand toward one dark place just in front of him—and saw a living carpet of flies swirl up. He flinched, uttering another, sharper cry.

The flies settled back to the surface of a clear, oily-looking puddle. Then he heard his cries answered— nightmarishly, by a tremendous bellowing and thrashing somewhere nearby. Feeling new alarm, he swivelled his head looking for the source . . . and saw mud splashing from behind a thick, rococo formation of the salt-white stone.

He watched a monster lurch into view—huge, four-legged, and bristle-haired where it wasn't caked with mud. It looked like a cross between elephant and moose, with multiple horns on its bulging head, and a tusked mouth that blatted out cries of rage. Half-mired as it was, Dirk couldn't tell whether its mighty legs ended in hooves or claws.

Still it made plunging, wallowing progress, its dense-muscled body arching for each leap. It looked like a plant-eater, but even so it was murderously frenzied by its imprisonment. Dirk realized that its motion, and the wild orbits of its red-tinted eyes, were directed at him.

He tried to get his legs under him and rise. He sprawled once, then felt his feet tunneling deeper, endlessly deeper, into the slime. At last, when the mud was to knee depth, it took his weight. He tried to run—but found that his feet were trapped firmly by the flared soles of his running shoes. He pulled and twisted at his leg, and finally felt his foot suck free of the tight-laced shoe.

One plunging step forward; then the other foot had to be freed of its shoe. As he tugged, he looked over his shoulder at the animal. It was meters nearer and still charging with unabated, slow-motion fury. The sight of it brought to mind a picture from one of his childhood books, an artist's conception of a prehistoric mammal . . . baluchitherium?

When at last he was running, his movements were agonizingly slow. A long, leaden pull and a lurch forward, followed by a new downward slip that gave back most of what he'd gained. He lunged for the nearest of the stone pillars. A steep one—but climbable with luck. Behind him he could hear the thrashing of trunklike limbs and the rhythmic, metallic rasp of the great snout pumping air. It outpaced him slowly but steadily.

But the footing became firmer near the rock. He heaved himself forward, grasped the rough, white surface, and began to clamber up.

His slimy limbs slithered against stone. Sharp crystals scored the skin of his arms and legs. Still he managed to crawl upward. His goal was a high rock shelf that stood well out of the chuffing monster's reach.

He pulled himself over the edge, and was struck full in the face by a keening, flapping white bird. He lost first his grip, then his balance, to topple backward under flailing hooves, horns and tusks.

"Don't mind my relatives." Kathy put her hand to the side of her head to keep the wind from ravishing her hair. She leaned forward into the shelter of the windshield. "They're just . . . limited."

"Aaa, they're primates." Kyle palmed the tiny steering wheel with exaggerated effect as wind buffeted the Bug. "Show 'em your tailpipe." He sneered at her, twisting his face into the deliberate ugliness of a punk performer.

She smiled at the side of his head. "Anyway, you told 'em something. I can really go along with that—about caring for nature, and taking responsibility, and everything. I've never been able to talk to them that way."

"Aaa." Kyle's face twitched to the side. "I was just pulling old Charlie's chain. I said anything that came into my head." He downshifted and rolled through a stop sign onto Barrientos Drive, then gunned the motor. "I don't really give a puke about any of that."

"Oh." Disappointed, Kathy leaned her elbow on the dash and looked out the windshield. She picked up a crumpled napkin from the floor, spat on it, and tried to rub some of the grime off the glass; then she gave up and threw the napkin back down.

"Oh, Kyle, the weirdest thing happened this morning

with the water at my sister's." She faced the driver again. "I turned on the faucet to take a shower . . . and nothing came out but sand!" She waited a few moments, but he said nothing. "It was creepy! And some of the other faucets in the house were still working." She shivered her shoulders slightly. "They couldn't get anybody to fix it, because the water company and the plumbers have gotten about nine million calls today. Really strange!"

Kathy reached down into her bag, took out a scarf, and put it over her head. She knotted it under her chin. "This wind is grody-and-a-half! It's sure to be worse at the beach. Maybe we should go to a show instead."

Kyle steered into the curve around the lake, bearing rightward to compensate for the stiffer wind. "Not unless you've got the bread. 'Cause I don't." He swerved tighter. "No? Then I guess it'll have to be either the beach or my place. . . . Say, would you look at that!"

Kathy peered through the windshield. "Oh!" A white RX-10 had smashed into the base of a street light. The tubular aluminum pole was buckled, and the curving, oval-headed light standard leaned down over the street at a dizzy angle, swaying from side to side in the gusts. She flashed a look at Kyle. "Better slow down."

But Kyle wasn't slowing down. He was gaping in fear and disbelief.

For what he saw overhanging the road was something other than a broken light standard. It was the titanic head of some kind of dinosaur, whose long, curving neck was arching out of the wave-tossed lake. It had wrecked one car already; now it was swinging toward his.

Grim-lipped, he twisted the wheel and sent the little buggy screeching on two tires across the traffic lanes.

Kathy screamed and clung to the dash to keep from

being thrown out. Kyle held on to the wheel and headed off-road.

When the car hit the curb and flipped, he was lifted partway out of his seat by centrifugal force. He felt the roll bar pressing the back of his neck, saw the ground rushing up—and nothing more.

Kathy was unconscious by then, already thrown clear. She didn't have to watch his severed head bounding toward the lake.

The morsel was snapped up in mid-bounce by crazy-toothed reptilian jaws.

When Kathy came to, with her vision blurred and her neck aching, she was lying on her side in deep mud. Kyle was nowhere to be seen, nor was the car, nor the street.

Instead there were ragged white pillars looming near her. She propped herself up on an elbow and looked around as much as her damaged neck would allow, trying to understand. Then she heard and saw the horned behemoth plunging toward her. She screamed and clawed the mud vainly, trying to drag herself away, but slipped back into unconsciousness.

Stan Kelsey glimpsed an emergency vehicle at a condo complex down a side street—Larksong Terrace—and spun toward it. He pulled up to the curb across the street from the orange van, grabbed his tape recorder, squeezed his portly body out of his seat, and slammed the door that bore the logo of KIVA Radio News.

A paramedic Kelsey knew was working efficiently at the back of the ambulance, getting ready to receive a patient.

"Hey, Frank." Kelsey let the recorder hang from the strap over his shoulder and tucked the mike into his coat pocket. "Say, off the record—what the hell's going on?"

Frank looked up and gave a nod that was curt from weariness. "Oh, hi, Stan. They've got us workin'." He brushed his brow against the shoulder of his short-sleeved shirt. "Serena's a real disaster area today."

Kelsey nodded. "So I've heard. But I haven't been able to tell exactly what the problem is. It's not just the wind . . . ?" He left the question hanging.

"No way. Things get crazy when the Santa Ana blows, but this time, you name it." Frank shrugged. "Vehicle accidents, pool drownings, mad dogs. The guy we're picking up now ran through a plate glass window.

"We just had one guy, a tourist from Cleveland or someplace, all tangled up in a garden hose beside his friend's house. Out of his mind—thought the hose was a giant snake attacking him!" He shook his head. "Can you believe it? I'm used to all the blood, but things like that, crazy things, still get to me."

Kelsey was scribbling on a notepad. "But the cause hasn't been nailed down yet?"

Frank resumed stowing the cardiac arrest kit. "Not that I've heard. Public health teams are down here. It could be something in the water." He glanced up. "A lot of the weirdness seems to be related to water, or to the lake."

A gurney nosed around the side of the house. It was pushed briskly by an orange-coated medic, with another attendant hurrying alongside and holding up a plasma bottle. The face of their patient was nearly as white as the sheet tucked up to his chin. Kelsey stepped back as they lifted the stretcher into the van.

At that moment a police car stopped at the curb. A uniformed officer got out, walked up to the ambulance, and exchanged a few words with the medic in the driver's seat. Then he nodded and waved it on.

Doors slammed. The ambulance pulled out, and Kelsey scurried behind it, catching up with the policeman near his car. "Excuse me. May I ask a couple of questions, Officer . . . ?"

"Dominguez, Pete Dominguez. Okay, but make it fast; there's a lot happening right now."

"Is it true that these mishaps may constitute a public health problem?"

"Yeah—a mass poisoning. It's been traced to bad alkaloids in the water."

Kelsey whipped his mike out of his pocket. "How widespread is it? Is it limited to the municipal water supply in this tract alone?"

Dominguez shook his head. "It isn't the city water. Nobody around here drinks that. It's the bottled stuff." He pulled a limp handkerchief from his pocket and wiped his forehead.

"An illegal PCP lab up in Pasadena got its drainpipe tied in with the Eldorado Spring Water Company—they get their so-called spring water right out of the L.A. aqueduct from the Owens Valley, like everybody else up there. But they must've delivered one hell of a bad batch to the houses around here." Dominguez held up his hand. "But don't quote me! There should be an official statement coming out in a few minutes." He paused to listen to the radio squawk inside his patrol car. "I gotta go."

"Thanks." Kelsey turned and jogged heavily for his car phone, as fast as he could.

Dave Antelope walked out of the shelter of a concrete wall and across the field, trying not to blink. He kept one hand to his face, screening his eyes against the wind;

from time to time, when they began to feel like dry pebbles in his face, he would clap his hand over them and pause, or take a sidewise, uneven step, then continue on his way.

He couldn't say exactly why he'd turned back. The odor of magic was intense here. It was like walking close to one of the towering black speakers at a rock concert; moving through palpable waves of sound. Yet it was nothing that the front of his mind could grasp clearly; more a dreamlike memory of his childhood feelings while listening to Grandfather's stories on the stoop at night.

He'd come back out of pure wonder, and also a nagging sense of something left unfinished. At the lake. Had he really set some menacing process in motion? If so, he knew that he could deal with it better than any of the locals—wet-nursed by television, numb to nature and real magic. Some of the sounds he'd heard in the last hour—sirens, brake-squeals, frenzied shouts—told him that things weren't going well for them in their planned community.

Again he inclined his head forward and raised his hand, feeling muscles convulse around his watering eyes. He tried to compose his thoughts and subdue his fear.

Blink twice, he reminded himself, always twice!

For an instant he was reeling in a white waste, but the delusion failed to take hold; his foot settled again into cropped grass. He glanced around. There were no other walkers or moving cars in view. He walked forward toward the lake.

As he topped the last rise, the tractor-sound was explained. There was the mower, jammed up against the kiddie-slide on the beach, still sputtering, its wheels churning in wet sand. A form was slumped in the seat; a familiar, stout form in coveralls. One big hand dangled limp at the end of an arm thrust through the steering wheel.

Dave kept his pace steady, working to quell his heart as he took in the scene. Near the tractor was an overturned car—a beat-up dune buggy. A few yards from it, a young woman lay crumpled on the ground. The tractor, chuffing and shuddering, was caught against the base of the playground slide only by the end of its bumper. The grinding of one heavy-treaded rear tire in the wet sand was gradually working the rogue machine free. At any moment it would drive forward directly over the unconscious girl.

Dave had to break from a walk to a trot, and it hurt his control. As he drew near the tractor, his vision flickered. One more of the onion-layered worlds that seemed to lie just under the surface of reality began to press through. He felt his feet drag in clinging mud— saw the hairy, tentlike flank of the gigantic beast, its red eye rolling toward him, its mighty neck and horn-crowned head just starting to swing.

He escaped open-mouthed and blinking, his eyes streaming. Before him, instead of a heaving, mud-spattered hide, he saw the dusty green enamel of the tractor. He set his foot on the worn step and drew himself up next to Farber's cold, inert body. He twisted the ignition key and jerked it out. While the motor dieselled and died, Dave's stomach convulsed at the other human remains he saw, clad in jogging shorts, tangled in the mower blades on the far side of the machine.

It seemed easier to keep mental control after the noise had ceased. Dave stepped down, walked under the slide, and knelt beside the young woman. She was breathing and semiconscious, making faint, uneasy sounds at whatever it was that her delirium showed her.

When he touched her face, her eyes opened and focused on him. She quieted then. She wasn't losing any blood . . . which was more than could be said for the third corpse, lying incomplete under the dune buggy. He saw her head turning that way, and he spoke abruptly to keep her from looking.

"Are you in any pain?"

"I . . ." She blinked and gazed into his face. "My neck is a little sore."

He put his hand to her forehead, then ran it gently along her spine. "Do you have feeling in your arms and legs?"

"Yes. . . . I don't think I'm badly hurt." Her voice was thin and unsteady, but she gathered her arms under her and pushed herself up to a sitting position. "But I've been seeing . . . strange things. . . ."

"Really? What kind of things?"

"Well——" She put a hand to her eyes. "When I started to wake up, things seemed different . . . like another world. There were weird rocks . . . and this huge animal charging at me. . . ." Her voice quavered and trailed off.

He smiled and tried to look reassuring. "Don't worry. That's been happening to everybody today. Even to me." He took off his jacket and draped it over the torn sweatshirt that left her shoulders nearly bare. "What's your name? I'm Dave."

"Kathy." Her look into his face regained some focus.

"Well, Kathy, we should get you away from here. Into shelter." The wind had lulled a little, but from moment to moment it still fretted at his hair or cuffed the side of his face.

"What was it, anyway?" Kathy raised a hand to brush hair out of her eyes. "It seemed so real!"

"Magic." He slipped a hand around her back. "Here, can you stand up? I'll help you." He rose from his kneeling position and pulled her with him.

"You mean, real magic?" She was unsteady on her feet and had to cling to his shoulder. She kept her neck immobile and didn't look to either side. "You believe in that?"

"Yes." He supported her with one arm and steered her quickly away from the wreck and the corpses. "I'm Native American. I believe in a lot of things you'd probably call magic or superstition."

She twisted her body so as to look him in the face. "So what's the magic that's been out to get us today? A spell cast by an evil sorcerer?"

"Not likely." Dave shook his head. "Magic is based on nature. Everything in nature has a spirit, and sometimes spirits speak to us or give us visions. A human magician can call on these forces, and maybe focus them—but the real power comes from the Earth."

Kathy glanced skeptically at him from the corner of her eye. "Sounds pretty vague. You might as well say it's due to the wind, or a virus, or something."

"No." Dave smiled. "Magic always provides us with an obvious cause, along with the real one. So that believing in it will always be a matter of faith." He glanced up and down the lakeside road, amazingly free of traffic for a Saturday afternoon, and led Kathy off the curb. "But what we're seeing now is the passing of a very great spirit. Giving up its power and its memories, in a kind of death-gasp—but seeking revenge, too."

He raised his eyes from the pavement and squinted ahead in an effort of concentration. "I sense that a mighty clash of forces or beliefs is happening in the world. One side is winning, but the other side won't surrender and die very easily. There's a lot of fighting still to come." He frowned. "And a lot of haunting."

It was then, as they were stepping across the road's center median, that Dave stumbled and the ground began to shake. They both staggered into the fast lane clinging together. Dave steadied Kathy by clutching her shoulders, but she was staring past him. She raised an arm to point, and her mouth formed almost soundless words. "Look, look—the wave!"

He turned and saw it sweeping toward them across a field of quaking, grass-tufted clay . . . an endless wall of muddy water cresting high up against a black-clouded, lightning-seamed sky. He blinked at the vision, peered into its contours, tried to make it change. But its thunderous noise, its spray-steaming crest, and its sheer massiveness overwhelmed all his reasoned defenses. He seized Kathy's arm and began to run straight away toward sage-dotted slopes that seemed impossibly remote.

"No, Dave! This way!" Kathy's voice broke through his panic. She was holding him, dragging at his arm with both of hers, pulling him to one side. For a moment he tried to fight her off, but there was something in her touch that calmed his fear, and he let himself be drawn along with her.

The wave broke in his vision, melted, and transformed into the blurred shapes of two speeding automobiles that roared past him practically abreast, the nearer one only inches from his staggering legs. Buffeted by the wind of its passing, Dave stumbled over the curb and sprawled onto the sidewalk beside Kathy.

"You escaped from the vision first," he told her, his eyes searching her face.

"I know." She lay panting on the concrete, speaking between gasps. "It was easier, somehow, because I was holding on to you."

Around the curve of the road, in the wake of the hell-bent cars, came a siren-shrilling ambulance followed by a police cruiser. At Dave's signal the police car slowed sharply and pulled up to the curb.

"Please, there's been an accident," Dave said to the officer. "We need help."

At 2:33 PM, the ancient lake died.

With its mountain tributaries diverted far southward to the water-hungry city, the inland sea had become too brackish even for brine shrimp to survive. The last of the California gulls departed, their hatchlings long since starved and their island nests laid open to predators by the inexorable retreat of the waters.

That afternoon the hot, wailing winds tore at vast fields of baking alkali that once had been the Mono Lake bed. The desert basin was obscured by a shroud of acrid dust.

High in the mountain gorge, the granite cave remained dark and silent. The old medicine man still lay on his pallet, but any living person venturing inside would have found only crumbling rags and bones.

Theodore Sturgeon Answers the Question "What Are You Doing Here?"

About the Author

Contest judge Theodore Sturgeon began his professional writing career while still in his teens, and had become a major, brilliant contributor to the Golden Age of science fiction by 1939. His career embraces fantasy as well as science fiction, and many other kinds of writing. There is no form of speculative fiction that he hasn't done superbly well, winning multiple awards for his short stories and novels over a span of six decades. More important—he would agree—is his facility for inspiring generations of successors who may be chronologically younger but would be hard-pressed to exhibit even a fraction of his boundless joy in life and his informed delight in creativity.

Why, you came to be amused, of course. Entertained. Amazed, astonished, perplexed, perhaps. Two more things: Relieved. Inspired.

You're here, 'way down deep, because you need space. Spell that Space if you want to. There's something you can get in science fiction that just isn't around very much anywhere else. (Same with fantasy, of course. The late Fletcher Pratt once cried out, during a seminar dedicated to the impossible chore of defining science fiction: "*All* fiction is fantasy!" I see fantasy as the great mosaic, with science fiction a hot tile in the middle of it.) But what you came for is escape from what They Say is So—from what They Say are parameters and horizons; for these things are confining, and here the sky is not the limit, nor is time. Here is the gateway to all the space you need—and for you, it is a need.

You see, I know you.

So much for relief—your deep need to breathe freely outside Earth's atmosphere. And that ties into inspiration—itself a breathing word.

A while back somebody—I think it was the Chrysler Corporation—coined a word, "Imagineering," in their ad copy. I like it. Imagination comes before invention as hypothesis comes before theory. Isaac Asimov once wrote that there are basically three kinds of science fiction—all containing "if": *if only; what if; and if this goes on.* Any or all of these might be present in a science fiction story, but there is no doubt that the "if" appears in all, that "if" is shorthand for "imagination," and that it describes the inhalation of wonder called "inspiration." It is said of Albert Einstein that he lay on a sunny hillside and let his mind take a trip around the universe, and found himself right back where he started. From that concept began his theory of relativity. That trip was certainly fantastic at the time, and his experience of it an inspiration.

My deepest conviction is that there is no upper limit to the capabilities of the human mind, and that your coming here to these pages is a result of your need to move toward that limitless "up."

I've expressed almost all these thoughts in terms of "up" and "out." Paradoxically, to stick rigidly by that, and claim that it was all of the "about" of such a publication as this, would be a confinement! We have to look at what I like to call "inner space" as well as outer space. Some of the finest stories ever written—perhaps *all* of the finest—derive from, deal with, affect and inspire that "inner space" quantum. Here are dreams, tears, anguish, loss, laughter, loneliness. Get out your scalpels if you like, and anatomize some of the most memorable and moving prose you know of. Seldom does a truly gifted writer kill a character unless he/she made you care about the victim. Seldom do characters, so well sculpted that you can, as you read, identify with them, fall in love without your falling a little in love too. Sometimes this feature of good writing is called "attention to the human element." Whatever it's called, it is that struck chord in the writer's words which resonates in the reader's own inner space.

There are immensities in inner space too. There are stars in inner space.

Let's go there.

Welcome.

—Theodore Sturgeon

The Land of the Leaves
by
Norma Hutman

About the Author

Norma L. Hutman is a New York State teacher, and also a flight instructor. In addition, she wants to be a published author. The intensity of that want is expressed as follows: "I write because my soul demands it." The nature of her attitude toward life is indicated by expressions such as: "I'm also a flight instructor because flight is life's grandest experience: a gift stolen from the gods, like fire. I understand poor Icarus perfectly."

A second-quarter finalist, Ms. Hutman thus joins a long and striking tradition of aviator-writers, although The Land of the Leaves *at first seems very far removed from the world of engines and airfoils. It's not until one remembers that Antoine de Saint-Exupéry wrote not only his factual sagas of pioneering flight in the Andes and the Sahara but also* The Little Prince, *and that Richard Bach wrote not only* Stranger to the Ground *but* Jonathan Livingston Seagull, *that the correlation begins to come clearer. She might just as readily have said: "I write because I fly," or "I fly because I write," and Icarus would have understood her.*

Her windows opened above the tops **of the trees. The last golden leaves reached almost to the edges of her draperies when on a** windy spring afternoon they flew free through the open casements, just as they reached, almost, the lowest terraces of the palace. When she leaned out she could see where the slender, final branches joined sturdier reed-like branches, golden too, far below her casements. And farther still, hundreds of feet beneath her balcony these golden branches disappeared into a golden mass, the thick tangle of the forest which lay at the kingdom's feet, stretching westward from the palace, a sea of gold churned to golden waves in the wind, and beyond to where the shadow of the mountain lay eternally on the black forest, roofed perhaps with black leaves, a dark distant sea beyond the shimmering ridges of gold.

No one had ever been there, of course. From the terraces of the palace where the ladies walked in cool summer shade, the darkness beyond the leaves was a matter of speculation. "Doubtless there are black leaves, strange as the trees which lie at our feet," they said. No one had ever been *there,* of course.

From the highest battlements which stood in the center of the palace the knights could see, if they turned their eyes westward, whence no enemy ever came, the black horizon after the undulating gold and they said,

"Stunted trees perhaps, which never get any sun." They had never been there.·

No one had ever been in the golden forest which lay at the kingdom's western feet; unmeasured feet, meters, miles perhaps, below. The palace rose on rock over the kingdom which squatted pleasantly at its feet, colorful as scarves on market day, noisy and aromatic with puddings and friendships, comfortable and cobblestoned, with its back turned on the strange golden sea that swam behind its back, somewhere far below the guardian fortress and the cool terraces of the kingdom, somewhere below her casements which almost touched the last golden fingers reaching up out of their strangeness.

There was a tale of a young man who, having looked seven years for a path that would lead from the base of the palace round back and perhaps down into the wood, unblessed by success had in his obsession hurled himself from the lowest terrace into the golden forest. The leaves had parted to admit him. Those who stood in helpless horror as he fell reported seeing him sink soundlessly a long, long time. Of his final impact they heard nothing. Afterwards the leaves closed together again, the branches unbroken, the surface as unaltered as when a man plunges into the sea and the water folds over him again, forgetting him. So had the kingdom for the most part forgotten.

But she heard the tale and because she was young and a princess, idle and intelligent, proud and a dreamer, she remembered the story and stood watching the implacable golden sea which lay, offering her no answers, just beyond the measured, satin and tapestried world of her comfortable kingdom.

She did more indeed than look; she searched for the path which had so long eluded the young knight of the tale. She had no more success than he. She searched about the base of the castle, followed garden paths, explored the casements, the kitchens and the stables, everything which might conceal a secret door, an unnoticed gap between stones, a cave, even a large hole in the ground. She found nothing.

And she stood dreaming over the golden leaves, for though she loved dancing and was frivolous and young and wore skirts of silver thread and capes of ermine, still she was a dreamer and she skimmed the gold horizon and fastened on the far black shore and shuddered and wondered and searched.

Then one warm evening while she stood in the shade of the terrace which hovered closest to the tips of the golden leaves, suddenly she heard a sound. She had been alone. Turning she watched him just as he swung his left leg over the railing and arrived—out of the air, out of space, out of the golden forest—beside her.

"Good evening. Lovely spring we are having, isn't it?"

"Who are you?" she asked, caught between terror and curiosity.

"Did I say the wrong thing?" he asked. He was tall and handsome, and had it not been that his eyes were pointed and his eyelashes, his toes and his ears as well, she would have taken him for a prince, one of the many who came to seek her hand.

They did not come, however, from thin air and magic forests.

She was not long in identifying him, "You are an elf."

"Nice of you to notice," he said, bowing. "I've been practicing introductions. Did I get it wrong?"

"Oh, no. Not at all."

"But you're frightened."

"You're an elf."

He lifted a pointed finger to a pointed ear and scratched it. "I know that. What has that to do . . . you're not afraid of elves, are you?" he asked in sudden inspiration.

"Well, I've never met an elf before."

He blushed.

"And you came, didn't you, from the golden leaves?"

"I should think so! A devil of a long climb. Where else do you think elves live, but in the golden forest?"

"Ah!" she said, forgetting her fear and drawing closer to him. "I have always wanted to go there. Will you take me?"

"Oh, dear. I should have listened. I should have taken their advice, oh dear," he began to lament.

"What is it?" the princess asked the elf.

"I was warned you would ask to go. They—the older elves—they told me that you would want that, because you are as you are, because I couldn't have fallen in love . . . oops." He turned bright gold, which is the color of the elfin blush.

"How could you fall in love with me?"

"I have been watching you from the leaves for a long time, for as long as you have lived."

"But you're younger than I," she said, considering him.

"Elves are very old. I have been younger than you since before your great-great-great-grandmother was as young as you are."

"Oh. And because you love me you will show me how to go to the golden forest?"

"Yes. I will show you. But you cannot go."

"I don't understand."

"Any mortal who enters the land of the leaves must journey until he comes to its farthest shore where darkness is. And for that journey the price is itself mortal."

"And there is no other way?"

"None known. Perhaps there is one. To risk finding it were a great quest. I do not know for what reason any mortal would undertake that quest."

"Nor I," she said and she saw with wonder that he wept.

"At least," he said, "I can show you the way into that world. Come, we must go to the foundations of your palace."

"But I have looked there," she insisted.

"Not with an elf," he said and his voice was sad. But she trusted him and they went by the light which his fingers gave off through dark passages to a remote corner of a remote wine cellar, where the elf struck a stone and it swung back revealing a dark passage.

"Come," said the elf.

"But you said I couldn't go."

"This far, yes. To the edge of the forest."

So she went with him, down halls and endless staircases, numberless staircases, staircases after staircases until the passageway was suddenly filled with a golden light which surged up from beneath them and they arrived at the door which stood open to the golden land, the land of the leaves.

"I dreamed," said the elf, "that you would love me. I see I am wrong."

"I am sorry," said the princess.

"No," he said, "you are mortal." And he began to step through the door.

"Wait, tell me your name."

"Yes, I am sorry. I had forgotten my manners. And I was so many years learning them so that I might speak to you. Your name I know, Princess Aminta, so it is

Illustrated by J. R. Rockwell

right you should know mine. I am called Tarl. Go back now, up to your land, your palace and your windows over the leaves. I shall watch you."

Then he was gone and the door closed and she was in darkness. And in darkness she made her way back up the numberless staircases. But when she came to the palace she found she had been gone only an hour and no one had missed her.

After she had closed the stone door on the stairway she closed that other door, the one in her mind, on the world which lay under the layer of leaves. She still stood in the moonlight on her balcony and watched the leaves swim in summer wind, but when the light deceived her, conjuring up the Elf Tarl out of fragments of moonbeam and recollection, then she went in from her balcony and on the morning after one such recollection, she told her father she would accept suitors and choose a husband.

Thus the year was one of joy, for the marriage of the king's only child promised the succession of the kingdom and the land was bright with princes, streaming banners and gifts and protestations of love.

They came from north and south and east. From the west no one came, for west of the kingdom lay the golden forest and beyond it, night.

They came singing and boistful, modest and rich, resplendent and valorous and always hopeful. From east and south and north they came.

The dragon came from the west.

It came in fire and suddenness, September's rude gift after the gentle summer. It came and sat upon the fringe of the kingdom and gobbled up its prosperity, children and cows, corn and cottontails, deer and daisies and herdsmen and hunters. It scorched the villages, singed the pride of the people, incinerated the harvest, and sat fat, scaly and secure, grinning with malevolent delight at the misery set in motion by the scantiest switch of its tail, the merest bellow of its sulfuric breath.

Heroes came and fought and died.

Prophets considered; omens were read. One bent, wise man said, "The answer must come like the problem from the west and there only those may go who know the way."

And the princess heard this and Winter came to her heart, for she knew the way and she would not go.

The kingdom slid sullenly into Winter, dying slowly with the year. The princess considered the kingdom which was her father's and would be hers and she did not go.

The king and the queen wept all the long white vigil through, for their perishing people. The princess told herself that she loved her parents and she did not go.

Princes came to save her, clattered over the frozen cobbles and slithered on the hoarfrost and went forth to win her hand and to be bested. The princess wept and still she did not go down the endless staircases to the gate upon the land of the leaves.

And then one prince came, handsomer than the rest, strange of countenance and untouched by fear. He came on a white stallion which seemed sired and shod in another age. He came hooded and quiet, stern and proud and he said, "I shall slay the dragon."

And the king said, "If you do this, you shall have all such rewards as I may give."

And the prince said, "I wish no rewards."

And Princess Aminta said, "If you do this, I shall wed you."

And the prince replied, "This indeed do I wish."

So he went to fight the dragon and they met in deadly

combat and the dragon fell in its own smoke and died and lay still and the kingdom was delivered.

But in his victory the prince suffered a fell wound, so that he lay dying in the palace. And all the doctors of the land came and said, "He must die, for in this land there is no cure for him." But the magician said, "There is a cure for all such wounds, but it lies where the dragon dwelt, in the darkness beyond the golden forest."

Then when she heard this, the princess, clad all in mourning, put on a black cloak and went down the stairs to the bottom of the world and stepped into the land of the leaves and said, "Cost what it cost, this I shall do. For I love this man who has come, being not one of my people and having no oath to us, and has delivered us. And he has taught me to love without reason or fear or measure and in this lesson will I study me and go into the darkness, cost what it cost."

And she went through the forest and it was hostile to her. The trees cried, "She would not go for her people and she is a queen; she will not find the way." And the animals said, "Shame shame, she would not risk anything for her mother and father and they have loved her; she will not find the way." And the toadstools piped, "Shame." And the gnomes of the forest made faces at her and said, "You would not weep for the deaths of others; now you will weep."

And she wept and cried, "I shall endure any penalty, but that I may find the cure and the prince may live."

Then as the golden leaves grew thin and she saw the first black and blasted branches of the forest of eternal shadow, a wizard stepped from the trunk of a great oak and stood in her path.

"What will you give for the boon you seek?" he asked.

"Life," she said.

And he knew she loved life, for she was young and fair and golden, as young and fair and golden as the land of the leaves. And he said in his Winter voice, "So shall it be. Go with courage to the end of darkness. Let no tree hinder you, for they are the spirits of those who have failed the quest. Take the silver cup you shall see by a fountain and fill it at that fountain and bear it back through the perils of darkness. And if you can master these, then the water of life will give your prince life and health again."

And she cried for joy.

But the Winter voice continued. "Then when he is risen from the shadow of death, must you hurl yourself from the balcony into the golden forest."

"This I shall do," she said. And she did not weep.

And the wizard saw that she did not weep. And after she had gone on, he smiled, but it was a cold smile.

Then she entered the darkness. The trees grasped at her; they had no voices, dead voices, echoes without voices and they said, "Stay with us. Rest here. Lie down and sleep a bit. Later you may go on." When she did not halt, they clutched at her and the echoes became shrill and they cried, "Despair, despair. You cannot have the boon and life. Go back. Save yourself. Forget the prince. Save your own life."

But struggling free she burst finally into a clearing white with moonlight where there was a fountain lit within by silver candles. And she took up the silver cup beside it, filled it at the fountain and she started back.

Then when the black trees closed upon her she held up the cup and their power was broken. And she saw the water held power over death. And she entered the golden forest where the animals and the gnomes and the trees and the air itself called, "You will die, you will die." And she held up the cup and they fell silent. And she saw that the water had power over fear. And the wizard spoke in his Winter voice and said, "Drink the water yourself, child, and you shall have eternal life." Then she laughed and said, "What I have pledged, I have pledged. You have no power over me."

Then she came to the door and the numberless staircases and she ascended through time with the light of the silver cup to guide her feet and she ascended to the chamber where the prince lay dying. And the doctors said, "Now he dies." But she gave him the water and he rose up and was well. Then all rejoiced and sang for happiness, but the Princess Aminta went to her chamber and out onto the balcony and looked again on the golden leaves, shining in the spring sun and she mounted the rail of her balcony and hurled herself into the gold.

Then the leaves parted and fell and vanished and opened and vanished and she fell numberless miles to a golden down which caught her and settled her unharmed upon the earth, which was a meadow scented violet and lilac. The trees were gone and all their ages. Instead the land was new, plowed for seeding and the voices which sang were strange voices but joyful.

And her prince came to her, healed and smiling, his clothes silver and gold and his hood thrown back, so that she knew him.

"You are the elf," she cried.

"Actually, yes," he said, "I hope you don't mind."

"You knew all this."

"Yes. I came to give you your freedom. Will you wed me? You owe me nothing now. You have given me life."

"Did you risk your long life for love of me?"

"Silly, I suppose, but yes, I did. One doesn't give up

dreams easily."

"I shall wed you willingly," she said, "for I love you, more than myself."

"I know," he answered.

"May a mortal marry an elf truly?" she asked, and he promised her, "As dream may marry life, my princess. And our people shall live here together. And our children will be the children of your palace and my wood, of your time and my timelessness, of your balcony and my forest, of your waking and my dream. This may be; you have made it so."

Then they were wed in the palace of tall battlements and the new wood at the beginning of time. And after the kingdoms prospered as one, elves and men, in the space between dream and waking. And indeed they dwell there still, in the hollow curve of dream, sheltered at the center of the world.

Anthony's Wives
by
Randell Crump

About the Author

Speculative fiction sometimes takes forms so subtle that they cannot be readily defined as either science fiction or fantasy. They are a little of each, a little of neither. Yet this is a sign not of fragility but of unique power; the power to suppose situations that strike home to the emotions while remaining unencumbered by formal credentials; the power to be individual.

The names usually invoked in connection with this sort of creativity are Franz Kafka or Jorge Luis Borges, two quite different talents. Here's another: second-quarter third-place winner Randell Crump, who has been composing stories since early childhood and began writing them down in high school. In 1981 he dropped out of college to devote his time to writing, and now supports himself by working as a laboratory technician. He has had one story published, in a small magazine, and has completed a novel that is looking for a publisher. He is a 1983 graduate of the Clarion Writing Workshop.

Like most other contest entrants, he hoped for both the prize money and the satisfaction of seeing his work in print; the two things together mean that someone has heard his voice and wants him to speak again in the future.

With a writer as individual as Crump, however, such encouragement can be scarce at first . . . as rare as the quality of this unforgettable story. . . .

THE L. RON HUBBARD AWARD

A sterling silver quill and star, set in a lucite obelisk, recapitulate the design theme of the Writers of The Future anthology. This prestigious new award was presented to the top winners at ceremonies in February, 1985, and will henceforth be conferred annually on the author of the best story as selected by a blue-ribbon jury.

1984 WRITERS OF THI

At a ceremony marking the release of the first Writers of The Future volume, more than 250 SF and show business personalities gathered at Chasen's famous restaurant in Beverly Hills. They saw the presentation of award certificates and trophies by a stellar panel.

UTURE AWARD WINNERS

Shown here with their First-Place L. RON HUBBARD trophies are (left to right) David Zindell, Dennis J. Pimple, and Jor Jennings. Behind them are judges Roger Zelazny, Algis Budrys, Robert Silverberg, Jack Williamson, and Gregory Benford.

SCIENCE FICTION GIANTS CELEBRATE THE WRITERS OF THE FUTURE

Photo by Alan Berliner

PHOTO: Blue-ribbon panel judges (left to right) Jack Williamson, Robert Silverberg, Roger Zelazny and contest administrator Fred Harris at the Writers of The Future celebration. In the background (center left) is blue-ribbon judge Gregory Benford.

JACK WILLIAMSON—"This represents a remarkable opportunity for talented newcomers. I don't believe there's ever been anything like it in publishing history, and I'm proud to have been part of it. I congratulate L. Ron Hubbard on making this all possible and these new writers on their fine stories."

GREGORY BENFORD—"Young writers need help more than in any other craft and this is a unique spur to a whole generation of top-notch science fiction writers."

FRED HARRIS—Author Services Inc.—"With the institution of the contest and the L. Ron Hubbard Award, Mr. Hubbard has begun a tradition that will continue year after year. We look forward to seeing an ever increasing number of new writers submitting their stories and wish them all good luck."

She wasn't dead. Yet.

But for Anthony it was as if she had already died. They had been married almost forty-nine years ago, both twenty—born on the same day, as it happened. So they wed on their birthday. During the forty-nine years innumerable accommodations and adjustments had been made. They had developed a peculiar style of holding hands; he had learned to interpret her sometimes cryptic and elliptical speech; he had been able to ascertain her mood by the way she combed her hair. His personality and behavior had molded to her like the cushions of a couch to a person's body.

But now there was an empty space where there had once been a person, and as when one removes a cushion he has been sitting on, Anthony couldn't get comfortable.

He still watched the television at a high volume so that she might hear. Often he would begin to speak to her, shouting over the noise of the TV. Then he would remember: she lay in the other room.

Cynthia had absolutely refused a doctor. Wanted to die in peace, she had said. Didn't want to dillydally. So no one had come to Anthony's small house near the foot of the mountains (this was just as well; Anthony's pension was not generous), and because Anthony rarely went into town, no one even knew his wife was sick. He would take care of this himself.

Anthony lay in bed, not willing to get up, postponing the first examination of the day. Was she still alive? Had she died during the night? He didn't sleep in the same bed with her. She had long ago begun to smell as if she were dead, the odor so strong that even with her lying in the other room, Anthony would often be awakened by the stench, a dream of death gradually lightening into open-eyed consciousness.

But it wasn't only the smell that forced Anthony to move the sleeping quarters of his beloved. It was an irrational fear that he might be taken by mistake. Who could trust the eyesight of Death? Or perhaps Death would take both of them: *As long as I'm here anyway* . . .

Death was something Anthony would just as soon not court.

He rolled out of bed, slipped his robe on, and wandered into the other room. He closed his eyes in a tight grimace and paused at the door, and at that moment, he wanted her to die, wanted to be rid of this daily trial, wanted to go on with his life, as empty and hopeless as it might be.

And when he looked at the woman, lying still under the sheets, exactly as he had left her on the previous night after tucking her in and kissing her dry forehead, he knew that all of his waiting had ended. Her skin was drawn tightly over the bones of her face (had he once thought she was beautiful?); the mouth was open slightly (he had kissed *that?*); the odor was overwhelming and tangible, as if he had to push it aside in order to see his once-wife.

There was relief mixed with sorrow. It was finally over, but it was over finally. There had been many nights when he had wished for some sort of miracle, something

Illustrated by David Dees

to bring his wife back to him, whole and sound. But miracles were the stuff of cheap movies. Real life held no unexpected happiness.

Since Anthony was poor, he could not afford a proper burial. But that only meant that Anthony could not pay for that which someone somewhere had decided was a decent funeral. He was perfectly capable of burying his wife in the woods behind his house, and no one would be hurt except the funeral home. And Anthony didn't give a damn about those half-dead people in their new clothes and formaldehyde cologne.

He uncovered his wife and took out the flour sacks *(How am I going to eat? I don't know how to cook.)* he had crudely sewn together, and used them to wrap her body. She was stiff and cold and it was hard to touch her because all he could think about was how she used to be and even when she got old her skin was still soft and he had loved her so much and now she was gone gone gone.

(But hadn't he, at least once or twice, wished for this moment?)

He carried his wife, cradled in his arms, out the back door. He looked down for a moment at the wheelbarrow but thought that it would be undignified. And, besides, he felt the need to aggravate his suffering.

He had to stop and rest frequently. Later he would think that it had been a mistake to disdain the wheelbarrow: he could have had a heart attack. But for the moment he was content to take a couple of dozen steps then sit on a rock or a tree stump and pant heavily.

When he arrived at the clearing, which he had already selected, he laid Cynthia down gently then returned to his house and brought back the tools. He should have taken the tools out first, but he wasn't thinking; when he returned with the pick and the spade, he saw a fox sniffing the body. He screamed, his voice shattering the stillness and rasping his throat. The curious animal fled, scrambling over the body in order to take the most direct route to the opposite end of the Earth as this mad approaching creature.

Anthony dug silently, his tears softening the ground in tiny spots. He had known for a long time that this moment was coming, and yet he wasn't prepared for it at all. It was only now that he began to think about everything the death of his wife meant. But he only began to think about it. He quickly blocked out all thought and concentrated only on the swing of the pick and the soft crunch as the shovel entered the dirt.

That night, as he finished off some of the canned peaches Cynthia had put up, he began to think that maybe it wouldn't be so bad, maybe he would be able to make it. He had already learned a little about cooking since Cynthia had taken ill, and he still had his gardening to keep him busy (although he would have to take a few days off; his arms and shoulders felt as though he'd been standing at the wrong end of a bucking horse). And now his pension would go farther: he only had one mouth to feed. Maybe he'd be able to have meat more often. That would be nice.

He stared at the ceiling, with its chipped paint and water stains, and thought about his wife. There were times when he could only remember the bad, and there were times when he could remember nothing but the good. This was one of those latter times. And knowing that all that good was gone forever made Anthony break into tears once again. He hoped it would be the last time.

But it wasn't.

Anthony raised up out of bed, clamping his eyes shut as the sunlight leaped in through the parted muslin curtains. He was all the way to the door before he remembered that there was nothing to check anymore.

He turned away, thinking that he would have to air the house out, because the smell had soaked into the boards and cloth. But turning away made him feel incomplete, as though he had started something and failed to finish it, as when a pheasant breaks cover and the gun is jerked to the shoulder a bit too slow, sometimes a person will shoot anyway, even though he knows he can't hit the bird.

Anthony opened the door.

She lay covered with the sheet. Tight skin, opened mouth, the smell.

Anthony shook his head, slapped himself, pinched himself, then crumpled to the ground. It couldn't be, it couldn't be, but it was.

He had it all to do again.

"Cynthia, I told you I was going over to Albert's to help with his car. It's hardly my fault if you can't remember anything."

"So now you're saying I'm getting senile, is that it? Well let me tell you something, mister. Did you ever consider the possibility that you never told me, that you only thought you told me, that *you* are losing *your* mind? Did that ever occur to you? Huh?"

"I like it out here with you. The waves sound so soothing. I can almost feel them. I'm falling in love with you, Anthony. I really am."

The clothes, hanging in the bright summer sun, wafting gently in the breeze; the hay, jabbing his hand in a hundred places as he fed the horses. Quiet. Quiet and beautiful. Off in the distance a dog barking, the noise comforting. Cynthia sitting in a lawn chair, her bikini top rolled down as far as she dared (neurotic modesty), thumbing through a magazine, her feet so soft and small, one on top of the other, with the toes of the upper curling around, grabbing at the other foot, playfully, unconsciously. Her feet.

Where is she where can she be goddamn it I knew I shouldn't have let her take the car what if something has happened I'll never forgive what if she's off with that Fred Spanger I knew that something like this she would never do that would she would she I don't think so but I don't really she's made eyes at him before I know I've seen she thinks she's so damned slick I'll find her and beat her ass and I'll kill Fred too is that the car no damn it nothing I'm going crazy up here please come home please come home I'm sorry I didn't mean to start the fight I didn't mean to you were right Cynthia please come home I need you I want you I love you oh Jesus I'm sorry "Where the hell have you been?"

"I still got lots of tomatoes out here, honey. You want to make some juice out of them?"

"I'm sick of these goddamned tomatoes. Leave them out there to rot for all I care."

"What?"

He turns around in amazement. Then there it is, flying straight and true. Splat! The tomato slaps against his shoulder, and Cynthia is laughing, laughing. "You little bitch." No anger, merely exhausted pleasure. A new tomato is on the return journey. Smack! against the side of the house. There is salvo after salvo. A miniature war with shiny crimson snowballs. And they make love in the dirt, muddy tomato juice covering their sweaty bodies, laughing, laughing.

"Anthony, please, talk to me."

I'm not going to answer. She doesn't deserve an answer. I would never do anything like that to her. And I just don't care. I don't care about her anymore. I really don't. Jesus. I really don't.

So he carried the body of his wife to the clearing in the woods, again. And he returned for the pick and shovel, again. And he chased off the fox, and he dug the hole. Again. But this time he had to widen the hole.

He laid the new body next to the old one, covered them up, returned to the house, ate his dinner, watched some TV, fell asleep on the bed, his muscles throbbing.

And in the morning he had it all to do again.

And so it went, day after day, the grave constantly widening, like a canyon being formed by a raging river. And why? He didn't know. Was he crazy? Was he cursed? He didn't know and he was afraid to consult with anyone, fearing that a trip to the gravesite would reveal a single decomposing body, and he would get an indefinite stay at a convalescent hospital.

So he did it, day after day, never complaining, always wondering if it were real.

But some things cannot be done forever. So . . .

"No no no no. Goddamn it, stop it. I can't do this anymore. I can't. I can't."

Anthony swung the pick high and brought it down into the flesh of one of his wives. Bone crunched and rotting skin split. Again and again he swung the pick. Brains spilled out, eyes popped loose, limbs separated. Anthony stood in front of something he had only seen in newspapers and books: a mass grave. Jumbled remains formed a mishmash of human anatomy.

And Anthony swung the pick, again and again and again.

"It isn't fair," he said to himself. "I don't deserve this. I never really wanted her dead. There were times when I thought I did, times when I thought everything would be easier if she was gone. I was just afraid to leave her, that was all. But it was a long time ago when I had those kinds of thoughts. When I was younger, *young*. When I wanted to hop into bed with every pretty thing I laid my eyes on. But I didn't think that for a long time. It isn't fair."

"What do you want from me? Goddamn it, how can I give you what you want if you never tell me?"

Cynthia's voice vacillated between a grating whine and a screeching nag. How did these things get started? How did this one get started? Anthony had no idea. But now his wife was pressuring him because he had stated that he might be a little unhappy.

"I just think I might be happier—that we both might be happier—if we separated. Let's at least try it for a while and see what it's like."

"Why? So you can go out and go to bed with half a hundred floozies while I sit around waiting for you to get bored? What am I supposed to get out of this?"

"You could go out too, you know. I'm not the only one who could take this opportunity to sow a few wild oats."

"Get stuffed, Anthony. One of these days you're going to grow up and realize what a relationship is all about. You have to work to get the good things. If you think you're going to be happier running from one woman to another, then go ahead and try it. But you better divorce me first, because I'm not going to sit around and wait. I'm not going to be your goddamned insurance. You're on your own."

Weeks later he had begun to acknowledge the accuracy of what she had said, although it would be years before he truly believed it. They hadn't separated; Anthony had decided to give it one more try. And it worked. All of a sudden they were in love again, jumping into bed every chance they got, staring into each other's eyes, doing silly things to make one another happy. It was as if they were starting all over again, as if this were the beginning of a new relationship. And Anthony was compelled to see that his relationship with Cynthia was an ever-repeating circle. It wouldn't stay bad forever, nor would it stay good. Back and forth: good bad, good bad. But every time was different; each time things began to correct themselves and they fell in love all over again. He didn't have to whore around to get involved with scores of women; he could do it with his wife.

Anthony walked into the other room. She was lying on the bed, the flesh dropping off. No more beauty, no more childishness, no more happiness. There was nothing in that husk to remind Anthony of what she once was, what she had meant to him. He had stayed with the woman for so many years. And now he was beginning to regret it.

He had begun to leave the bodies in the room until he could no longer stand the smell. As long as there was one present, no new ones appeared. So this way he only had to bury her every few days. If only he could stand the smell.

But maybe he didn't have to.

When he returned from the store he set to work

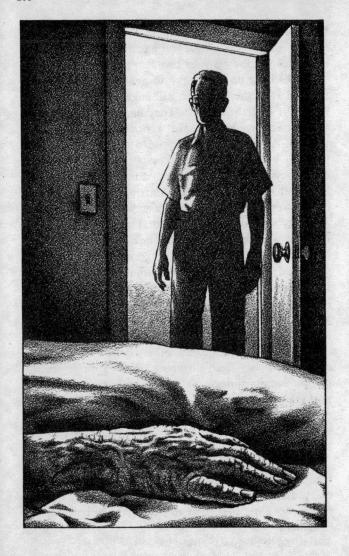

immediately. He wrapped the body in layer after layer of plastic. "What the hell you need all those drop-cloths for?" the clerk had asked him. But Anthony hadn't answered.

After he was finished wrapping the body, he could only just see traces of his wife (one of his wives) obscured by the intervening plastic. Then tape. He bound the body with masking tape, roll after roll ("Trying to corner the market?" the clerk had asked), until he had completely shrouded the body.

He went around the room, caulking the windows, making sure that every tiny crack was filled and sealed. Then he stepped out and closed the door. He paused for a moment, wondering if this would do any good, if he were truly mad. Would she show up tomorrow in his bed? But he also felt as though he were closing off his life from the woman he had loved for so long. Somehow it seemed like betrayal to seal the door. But he did it.

And he covered the windows outside the room, smoothing out the stucco and repainting the entire house. And he paneled over the doorway, so that guests (if he ever had any) wouldn't try to see what was behind the door. And soon every trace of the room was gone; nothing was left to show that there had been windows in that wall or a door in this one. Anthony hoped it was over.

The man awoke, lonely and sad. It would be another warm day, but that didn't really matter because there was no one with whom he could share that. It had been a mistake. He wished he could snatch back the years and start once again. He couldn't even remember what had driven him to live his life as a hermit. To have spent sixty of his eighty years all alone was nothing short of insanity; at least that was the way he viewed it now, he must have thought differently back when he had been a young man.

He ate breakfast, then wandered outside to tend to his garden. The tomatoes were coming in nicely this year, and for some reason this thought brought incredible sadness. He paused for a moment, gazing in the direction of the woods, but then he shook off his uneasy feeling and went back to work, striking the ground with the hoe over and over again.

At lunch time he made himself a sandwich and ate it in the shade of the old apple tree. He looked at his house, noticing once again how it was too big on the outside for what it held on the inside. *There could be a room right there,* he thought, staring at the large blank wall. He could remember, he thought, too, that for a while some time ago he had thought there was something to smell there, too. But just like every other time these thoughts had occurred to him, he shook them off, much as he had shaken off the strange feeling about the tomatoes.

His house was plenty big as it stood now; there wasn't any need to expand. Maybe he would need some extra space if he didn't live alone.

The Thing From the Old Seaman's Mouth
by
Victor L. Rosemund

About the Author

There can only be three prize winners per quarter or the contest loses an essential quality. But it seemed a shame when Victor Rosemund's story did not place among the first quarter's winners, so here it is nevertheless. We think you will find The Thing From the Old Seaman's Mouth *to be almost maniacal in its intensity; an emotional experience that will not soon leave your memory, as it did not leave ours.*

Victor L. Rosemund, 35, began writing seriously five years ago, taking courses at San Diego State University. Since beginning, he has written over a million words, including sixty stories and three novels, each taking a minimum of four drafts. Except for an Honorable Mention in a Twilight Zone *magazine writing contest, his appearance here is his only public success to date. Of writing, he says to other beginning writers: "Write, write, keep on writing and never give up. Don't get bitter. Love it or leave it." Those of us who still clearly remember our own apprenticeship, however long ago in time, can only agree.*

Saa'd Jefferson Kunte, back flat against the wall's stucco-rough side, damns heaven and hell for his own stupidity. The thing from the old seaman's mouth has him trapped between the twelve-foot-high brick wall and this suck'n house. The only way out, the way he came in.

Black, square, rock-hard, Saa'd's face looks impassive. But beneath the skin he is soaked with sweat. He tries to catch his breath while counting the number of sirens wailing closer in the distance. One. Two. Three. He imagines, eyes glittering coldly in the dwindling light, the blue bellies' shocked faces when they discover the bodies he left behind. A smile, cracking the lava-like surface of Saa'd's face, discards his own, imminent death.

Ten grunts wasted. Just plain blown away back there in the liquor store.

The smile widens into a fissure, a shit-eating grin: The mother-fucking cops are in for a surprise. "Body count that," he whispers savagely at the aloof night.

The square-barreled Colt is a hard, solid weight in Saa'd's hand. The heavy .45 is still hot with killing.

The two hundred and thirty-five dollars bulging in his pocket feels good; good enough so that he momentarily hardens, anticipating what he will buy with the money. The dead grunts back at the liquor store Saa'd

Illustrated by A. R. Conway

considers bonus bogies. In El Salvador they had been Sandinistas, guerrillas, leftists, dead meat. The only difference is that these were West Coast geeks and honkies instead of commies. Not that the fuckers didn't all die alike. Afraid of the nigger, of the Colt's brutish asshole. Screaming, the beautiful screaming, when he begins to shoot.

Dying rabbits.

Around in front of the house, a metal trash can goes flying, rattling down the sidewalk as if struck by a freight train. A bolt of electricity hums through Saa'd, tight as a wire. Night's cold fingers have already ripped the sun out of the sky, and the horizon swirls with that strange mix of purple and orange that makes it look like a bleeding wound.

Two years in Central America, then back to California and three months of partying, drugs, and women. Until he runs out of money. To get more, Saa'd does the only thing he knows to do. Dusted on PCP, he holds up the Balboa Liquor Store. Everything goes down smooth until the old seaman refuses to get on the floor with the others, to quiver like a grunt should quiver.

Polynesian, the seaman's skin is so dark brown that it looks ashy to Saa'd, who hates the thick, dark chocolate eyes, their pupils invisible behind folds of heavy skin; slanted eyes, geek's eyes. Wiry, snow-white hair beneath an ancient watchman's cap. Short, barrel body. Old and solid as oak. A round, cheeky face weathered dry by the sea. Doesn't even flinch when Saa'd triggers out a .45 round into the old man's gut. Not even surprised, as if he were just keeping an appointment. But dead.

Saa'd, busy grabbing money from the cash register, doesn't really register the thing creeping out through the dead man's open mouth, pooling in the filth on the floor, alive like a fetus delivered out of hell. Doesn't react to it until nearly stepping on it on his way out. Then the smell, worse than vomit or stale pussy, slams him. Reloading the .45, Saa'd shoots the putrid mess when it seeps across his boot. The heavy slug makes a wet, slapping sound against the thing's greenish flesh, severing it.

Should've blown it all into slime when I had the chance, Saa'd thinks, stucco digging into his back. But, hell! Half of it blown into scum should've been enough.

Saa'd doesn't blame himself. Not since butchering up his old man for raping his eleven-year-old sister. Saa'd's one rule: You're hard or you're dead. You take what you want. And, man, you don't never, ever give noth'n for noth'n.

Inching forward along the wall, Saa'd keeps his mind blank. Thinking isn't going to get him out of this one, will only clutter up his reactions. But before he can squeeze up one more step, the thing from the old seaman's mouth slithers into view from around the corner of the house. Its size is doubled since the liquor store. From a viscous pus, it has firmed into a lizard-like slug. Already, rows of clawed feet grow along both sides of its body. A plume of oil-colored scales breaks the skin under its belly. Antennae sprout. Pincers pop through.

The thing doesn't slow but comes right for Saa'd. It slithers over the ground in a sideways manner, like a stunted sidewinder. Saa'd empties the .45 at the thing. Each thunderous round jerks the black man's hand back and makes the house tremble against him. Three slugs miss. One ricochets off the thing's shiny black mantle. Underestimating the monster's speed is nearly fatal to Saa'd. At the last moment he hurtles over it. But with its pincer, it strikes his trailing foot, knocking him off balance. He lands awkwardly, wrenching his right ankle.

Hissing like a burned-out radiator, Saa'd hobbles around the front. The liquor store is five blocks behind him. Saa'd knows the area as well by night as by day. He is like a rat in a junkyard, in his element. The single-story houses are post WWII, but they look as though they might have been part of it. Stink'n stucco piles of crap, Saa'd calls them. Baby, he says, poverty is uptown around here.

And here, knows Saa'd, is where it is all going to end.

Lamed, he can't match Charlie hunting him. Only speed might've saved him, given him enough of a lead to hot-wire one of these heaps along the curb. With speed gone, Saa'd figures his chances stay right where they've always been; in the gutter, zero.

An angry wave of pain from Saa'd's ankle causes him to stagger. It's broken. To counter the pain, he drags up a fresh image of brains and blood and hairy bits of meat splattering against the liquor store's filthy floor. For a moment, the stimulus works. But the ankle won't support his weight. In agony, then, Saa'd stumbles over a trash can.

The thing from the old seaman's mouth skitters on its new legs after Saa'd. Its sleek, cigar-shaped body looks like glazed clay. Hundreds of tiny feet propel it after Saa'd. He hears the sound of its claws hissing across the cement sidewalk.

Saa'd lands hard against the cement curb. The pain in his chest can only be a cracked rib. The thing, coming up behind Saa'd, dashes up his leg.

Sucking air, Saa'd uses the broken foot to kick at the thing clawing its way up his other leg. He fights quietly, but with the savage intensity of the street fighter he is.

With its hundreds of tiny claws like fishhooks, the

hunter snags into Saa'd's skin and holds on to him through his pants. The head-pincer snaps, clicks like an empty machine gun. Finally, it catches Saa'd's foot. Rills of pain etch their way through Saa'd's face. The knife-sharp pincers carve through boot and flesh and bone— metal shears through tinfoil. Severed boot and toes fall to the ground.

Sirens scream with unceasing abandon in the background. The streets stay empty.

With a final desperate kick, Saa'd punches the thing off his leg with the heel of his boot, and he slams the trash can down.

Mad, rabid, violent, the thing from the old seaman's mouth rockets around inside the metal can. Saa'd, weighing down the can with his chest, holds on to a bucking bronco. The can's bottom lip rakes his broken rib. Hot knives plunge into his lung.

Blood from the severed foot sprays across the street and sidewalk in thick drops. An old car, fuming black smoke out the back, passes in the street. Jewel-like, Saa'd's blood gleams red in its headlights. An old face peers out at Saa'd. The old eyes shine with fear, and the car speeds up.

Saa'd, snarling his teeth in a death grin, points the .45 at the face, and he pulls the trigger. The empty gun responds with silence. Saa'd laughs wildly, as though at luck. He throws the Colt after the car.

Shaking, rattling, banging, the trash can walks Saa'd down the sidewalk, slams him around as if the thing inside it is crashing in every direction at once. Saa'd's grip weakens. A pincer rips through the metal skin at the point of Saa'd's left wrist. The pincer closes, severing Saa'd's hand cleanly. New blood spurts out in thick surges.

Saa'd gurgles more blood from his punctured lung.

His grip gone, he's thrown off the bucking can.

Whooshing air, he lands on his back in the middle of the street, beneath the burned-out eye of the street light. His head thuds, dully, against the greasy asphalt, bounces.

Hundreds of churning, driving legs, the thing from the old seaman's mouth swarms out of the trash can. It zips up Saa'd's leg and and jams itself into the stoned man's gaping mouth.

Saa'd's black eyes explode white with terror. His body jerks convulsively.

Unwittingly keeping time with the wailing sirens, Saa'd Jefferson Kunte writhes out of control in the greasy, gravelly road while vengeance sups its way home.

Without Wings
by
L. E. Carroll

About the Author

L. E. Carroll holds a doctoral degree in music, and works in Pennsylvania as a director of music and theater. She also teaches high school, graduate school, and privately. In addition, she has published scholarly nonfiction, with a book and a number of articles in print. In addition, she is engaged in musicological research on a project guided by the city of Philadelphia. With her brother, she is also writing an SF novel, and has, she says, scads of stories sitting around. Clearly, she has found some uncommon source of energy.

This story, which became a finalist in the second-quarter contest, is nevertheless one of the few stories she has ever mailed out, and her first contest entry anywhere; its publication here represents her first professional fiction appearance. So whatever arrangement she may have made, with whatever rulers of destiny, is just now beginning to come to full fruition. She says that the idea for Without Wings *came to her when a catastrophic spring snowstorm closed the opening performance of a musical she was directing. Other than that, she claims no relation to the heroine of her story, although she would like to meet Margaret's visitor. We think there may be more truth to her fiction than that. In any event, to the ranks of the traditional Deal-With-The-Devil story, we now proudly bring a brilliant variation. . . .*

I suppose it was the sheer absurdity of the situation, but I could not restrain myself and laughed unashamedly. The little creature appeared quite distraught at this and hopped off the piano, landing not on the floor but rather hovering in midair.

"Now see here," he sputtered, "you do not seem to be taking this seriously. I reiterate: I am fully prepared to offer you happiness—within reason, of course—in exchange for . . ."

". . . for my soul!" Again I felt the laughter bubble up and spill out, this time accompanied by wild tears. "How trite. How uninspired. How . . . how gauche! Faust to the contrary, this is simply too recherché."

"Faust? Faust? Oh yes, indeed." The creature glided back to the piano. "Except, of course, that Dr. Faustus sold his soul to our—er—our competition."

At this I dried the tears and looked at the apparition more intently. If not for his height (he was only about one foot tall) he would be an arrestingly handsome young man. He wore designer jeans and a pastel pullover. He waved his right hand and a small keyboard-type affair appeared. He began to tap at it.

"You are," he intoned, "a drama instructor and theater director in a rather somnolent college town. Rather an uninspired life. Your great sadness is a string of rather tawdry little affairs with . . ."

"Now, hold on a minute!" I exploded. "Who are you to . . . oh, I'm sorry. You are a devil, aren't you? You know all those things. Well, I can't see why you're bargaining with me."

"Devil? DEVIL? Dear St. Philomena, she really thinks I'm a devil!" At that the creature stood up, backing into and upsetting the piano lamp.

"For a devil," I sneered, "you are rather clumsy."

"Ego te absolvo," he intoned. "I forgive you. After all, how could you be expected to recognize me in this . . . this abomination of an outfit." He settled himself on the music rack and then continued. "Marketing and PR felt we needed a more modern image. However, this might satisfy your predetermined perceptions."

He waved his left arm and suddenly became the image of the Guardian Angel I had cherished in childhood.

"Long white robe, sandals, halo, and . . ." here he snapped his fingers, ". . . and wings. Does this satisfy you?"

Actually, to my adult eyes, he looked rather silly, but if I was to suffer such an unusual hallucination, I would enjoy it. "What," I asked, "no harp?"

He sighed. "Oh, very well." Another snap of the tiny fingers and a small gilded harp materialized. "Now do you recognize me?"

"A devil disguised as an angel," I howled. "What an absurdity!"

"Now, look here," he cried, placing the harp down and readjusting the slightly tilting halo, "why do you persist in calling me a . . . a . . . Saint Ermentrude assist me! . . . a devil?"

"What else could you be? You want my soul, don't

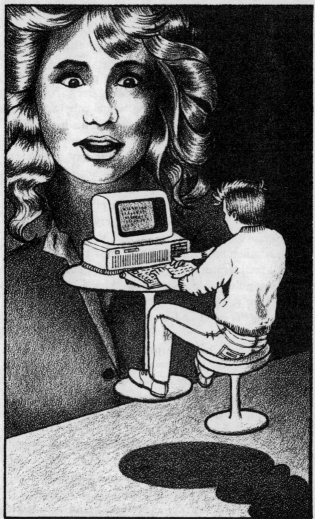

Illustrated by J. R. Rockwell

you? Who else could offer me fame and fortune for my soul? Assuming, of course, that such things as souls exist, and I'm not entirely convinced they do, you know."

"It *is* one of your problems." He paced beside the music rack. "Now look here, Margaret," he began, nearly tripping on the flowing white robe and once again dislodging the golden disc above his head. "You had better get this understood. Devils simply do *not* go around striking up bargains for souls any more." He looked right at me and I was amazed at the clear blueness of his eyes.

Idly, I fingered a *Dies Irae* on the piano.

"Now stop that," he pleaded. "*Resurrexits* are more to my calling."

I was still unconvinced. "You *must* be a devil. I've read all the literature. Devils bargain for souls."

He grumbled, folding the long-skirted robe over his hands. "Do you mind? This robe is much too loose."

I shook my head and once again he waved his arm, changing this time into a narrower one-piece outfit, tannish, without halo, harp or wings. Yes, I observed with a start, a much narrower outfit. I was surprised to notice—I could scarcely help it—that he had a surprisingly fine figure. I congratulated myself on calling up such an impressively designed hallucination.

"Ah, much better," he sighed. "Now, Margaret Merrivale, listen to me. Devils do not go about striking deals for souls because today they already have more than they can handle. Why, Processing and Admissions may strike if the work load doesn't ease up. There is scarcely a politician, administrator, tax accountant, film critic, creditor or courtesan who is not in *his* employ. Why, even you are headed toward . . ."

"Me? How dare you lump me in with tax accountants and film critics! I've never done anything to deserve . . . to deserve . . ." I could not finish.

"Hellfire?" he completed calmly. "Ah, Margaret, it doesn't take much. A lack of charity. No simplicity. Greed. No faith." The mini-console reappeared and he tapped at it furiously. "Now, there was that affair with a certain English professor. . . ."

"I didn't know he was married," I defended.

"Nevertheless, the marriage dissolved. A rather nasty settlement. Tssk. Do you deny the affair?"

"Of course not, but . . ."

"No buts. Ah, some lies to the IRS, neglecting to vote, a—what is your word—a kinky affair with an undergraduate, and, tssk! the things you did with the French horn player! Oh, my." He studied the screen intently. "Hmm. Some drinking, but not much, a little blasphemy—nothing out of the ordinary—and . . . oh my, here it is, the very worst: no Faith. The direction, I'm afraid, is clear."

I frowned.

"Shall I continue?"

"No."

I considered the situation. Of course, I had to be hallucinating. I was overworked and depressed. As a drama teacher, I trained my students to see things that weren't there, but this was decidedly different from the sense-memory exercises I did in class: I had not consciously conjured up this vision. Had I done it subconsciously? Was this an escape valve for my frustration? Was it perhaps a subliminal self-analysis at work?

While I considered, I grew more tired. The musical I was directing was scheduled to open the following night, and I was weary after a trying dress rehearsal. Surely I had created this dream out of fatigue and anxiety. I did wonder how it would end, so I persisted, "If you already *have* my soul, why are you here?"

"Saint Alexandra, give me strength!" he cried. "Has the woman no ears? *We* don't have your soul; *they* do. Or rather, they will. We want it. We have precious few these days. We are fully prepared to offer you certain compensation in return for a less frivolous life style."

"Compensations?"

"Certainly. How about a nice new word processor?"

I decided I had reached bottom at last. "Sorry. I have no desire to be angelic."

"Saint Aloysius, hear my plea!" He gurgled. "Then may—so to speak—the devil take you!"

With that, he vanished.

I shook my head, rubbed my eyes, and, certain that my delirium had ended, headed for much-needed sleep.

The next day dawned bright and sunny, a perfect April day holding the promise of spring to come. An omen for our opening, I decided happily, and whistled the title tune on my way to class.

The day and my mood deteriorated rapidly. The members of my first class, with the exception of one timid freshman, had simply cut. I attributed this to early spring fever. The second class was unusually unruly and argumentative. The graduate assistant I was seeing broke our lunch date, and I received a notice that my request for tenure had still not been acted upon.

Despite all that, I headed to the campus theater, still heady about opening night. There I discovered a faulty winch, saw that the braces on the proscenium flats had pulled loose, discovered that someone had slit the sand-bags, was told that the smoke powder had vanished and that the program inserts had been misplaced. Worse, all the makeup had been placed by an unthinking undergraduate directly above the heater, and it had all melted into a colorful glob.

This was more than the usual opening night discomfitures. I was tempted to consider my dream of the night before. I grumbled as I set about correcting the problems.

Everything was in order when the cast arrived for makeup. They were astonished to be accompanied by a fierce and unexpected blizzard. Winter's last triumph had upstaged our opening. Wind, snow, sleet—nothing had been spared. The radio meteorologist could not explain it. We were indeed forced to close before we opened. I sent the cast home and waited to turn away the few hardy audience members who braved the strange weather and to exchange their tickets for another night's performance.

When finally I arrived home that night I was wet, weary and more exasperated than ever. In place of my usual opening night exhilaration I was in a ferocious depression.

I brought some Chivas to the den, watched it glisten in a crystal goblet, then downed it quickly. I installed a fire and began to attack some Schubert on the piano. I was in a particularly violent rendition of the B-Flat Impromptu, unevenly fitting threes against fours when a little voice interrupted.

"A-hem. Are you willing to negotiate now?"

There, atop the open piano score, sitting crosslegged, was my visitor of the previous night. He was once again in a designer outfit.

"Where's the robe and wings?" I snarled.

He sighed. "Regulations. This is guaranteed to be more appealing."

I didn't argue. Fortified by more Scotch, I attacked. "And you call yourself an angel! How could you ruin my show like that! A snowstorm in April, for heaven's—pardon—sake. And the sets sabotaged. My poor cast. How *could* you?"

He looked sincerely crestfallen. "Actually, I didn't do it, you know. *We* can't do that sort of thing. We are, after all, the, uh, the good guys."

"If you didn't, who did? Not your 'competition,' surely!"

"Well, no. Life events, you see, Margaret, are cyclical. You were simply due for some disasters, that's all. A little overdue, actually."

I suppose I believed him then. Only an angel would say such an absurdity.

"Okay," I played along, "I would like to break out of here, go to Broadway, sing, act. . . . No, strike that. I want to direct. I want to be famous. And money. Lots of money. Oh, have I got plans for the money! Okay, cute stuff, what's the deal?"

"Ignatius of Loyola, spare me!" he wailed, tapping at the console that once again materialized beside him. After a moment he looked up sadly. "We can't send you to Broadway. Too many temptations. As to the money, I'm afraid this says you would spend it on . . . on . . . oh, my." He became agitated, his sad blue eyes affecting me in a startling manner.

I calmed him down. "Okay. Just what *can* you offer me?"

"Well," he sniffled, "we can give you . . . um, protection."

"Protection? From what?"

"From despair. From lack of faith. From yourself. From *them*."

I didn't like the sound of that. Rather sermon-laden. "Explain."

"Well, we'll help you reach inside yourself and do your best. . . ."

"Are you from the Moral Majority?" I interrupted.

"Certainly *not!*" he huffed, and continued ". . . to reach inside yourself and overcome your self-made obstacles. You have, you know, a great light within you. . . ."

"I *know* I've heard this somewhere. Oral Roberts? Fulton Sheen? Billie Graham? Purlie?"

He ignored me. ". . . and when temptation strikes, we can help to . . ."

"Oh, God," I interrupted, meaning no offense, "you're offering me a conscience!"

"No, no," he hurried. "A conscience merely advises you. When and if you follow it, you might still be unhappy. We'll make sure that you stay away from temptation, that you do only the good and true and beautiful, but that you'll always be happy."

"WHAT?"

"Hmm," he tapped buttons again. "Off-the-wall is okay. You need to have a goal in life, a sense of purpose. Now, as to leisure time, zany is okay. Illegal and blatantly immoral are out."

"*Blatantly* immoral?"

"Well, Margaret, morality is faddish. Sex is all right. *HE* did, after all, invent it, and some indulgence is acceptable. We are, however, in favor of fidelity. Just keep it nice and normal. Kinky is out. Definitely out."

"A nice, normal fling?" I laughed.

"Just sign here." He suddenly held a tiny parchment and quill. As I took them in hand they grew in size. That did not surprise me. The quill itself did.

"A quill? What about your more modern image?"

"Some tradition is maintained here," he murmured. "Our Supervisor is very sentimental about some things."

I read from the parchment. *"I, Margaret Merrivale, being of sound mind, do will my Soul to Everlasting Bliss by enrolling in the Celestial Happiness Associates Insurance Plan. . . .* WHAT? Celestial Happiness Insurance? Come ON!"

"Marketing," he sighed, "does win some."

I continued to read. *". . . whereby I will be guided to live a clean, honest, hard-working, guided life and . . ."* I put the paper down. "Are you people crazy? You've got to offer me something better than clean, honest, and hard-working."

"I am offering you," he looked embarrassed, "heaven when you die, Margaret."

"But I want something now!"

"Tssk. There is the insurance policy."

"This is absurd. I am not interested."

He fluttered off the piano and mumbled. "It's no use. I just am no good at this. Why, I haven't had any recent courses in contract law or collective bargaining. We are just so shorthanded. You are my first case, you know; I used to be on playground duty. We are *so* behind our quota." He shrugged, righted himself, and turned his attention to a blinking light on the once-again materialized mini-console.

"I have to go. They're giving me a shot at a deal down on Locust Street. A real prize of a conquest. Lots to repent. Meanwhile, think it over. Show the paper to a lawyer—or a rabbi or priest. I'll be back when I can."

With that abrupt change of mood, he waved both arms and vanished.

I looked at the parchment. It certainly felt real.

Except that the lettering was quite uncommonly beautiful, it was an ordinary parchment.

Because I held it in my hand, I was certain this was no hallucination. I believed. But could I show this to a lawyer? A rabbi? A priest? I would certainly be referred for "professional help," and I would not be the first theater director to trade in a stage for a padded room. I shuddered. Perhaps, I thought, if I told them that I needed advice, that this was a prop in a play, or that I was writing the play . . . that was it! A play. I had always wanted to write a play. What a terrific plot. I left the piano and headed to the typewriter.

The next night the snow had melted and the performance opened on time, to a standing-room-only house. The cast outdid themselves and as director, I was euphoric.

Each night I continued to type my manuscript, and forgot the source of my inspiration. We had a very successful run, and by the end of it I had once again decided it had been a tension-induced dream.

Several nights after the musical closed, I was still at the typewriter and the creature—I have since learned that his name is well-nigh unpronounceable, so I have named him Michael—appeared once again.

"Go away," I said harshly. "I'm working on my deal-with-an-angel story and I don't need or believe in you. I am going to sell this and make a fortune. And I will *do,*" I added significantly, "as I please."

Wordlessly, he produced the keyboard and punched at it. I looked up and awaited the inevitable speech. It came.

"Ah, Margaret, this project is just the direction your life needed. A project. Good, honest, hard work. Writing. Very commendable."

I left the typewriter and went to his console. The readout was colorful but indecipherable.

"You're pleased?"

"Oh yes. And your play will sell. You will make a modicum of profit. Writing, Margaret, is not that lucrative. That will keep you out of harm. You have a chance to do good for mankind . . . even if you play it for comedy. But Margaret, where will you get other ideas? And you really need a life partner. Let's discuss your life style now. . . ."

"I'll sell it?" I shrieked. "Really sell it? Even if I don't sign with you?"

"Yes." He left the console and hovered over the typewriter.

"Of course," I said, "at this point, I don't know how the play will end."

"No."

Suddenly, however, I knew just how my story—my dream, my fantasy, my hallucination, my whatever— would end. No more married English professors for me. No more kinky undergrads or bizarre French horn players. No more alone, no more . . . A life partner, he said. Fidelity, he said. I looked into the clear, sad blue eyes.

"I want you," I announced.

"Well, of course I can arrange to oversee your progress periodically. . . ."

"No," I repeated softly, "I want *you*."

He was startled, suddenly realizing what I meant. "You want a twelve-inch angel? I told you, nothing kink——"

"The parchment changed size," I said, half-closing my eyes and leaning toward him.

"Yes. Uh, no. We take material shape only for short periods."

I warmed to my subject. "In the fullness of time," I chanted grandly, "before my world was, you were." I waved at him. "Isn't that right?"

"Er, yes, uh, no . . ."

"What is one lifetime in an eternity?"

He tapped at the console. "It is a short time to me, but . . ."

"It would certainly solve all my problems. An angel to oversee, a life partner, fidelity . . ."

"No. Besides, I don't have a body."

"And what is this?" I gently poked him in the midsection.

"Oof! This, Margaret, is an illusion, a visual display based upon your own personal preferences, as determined by our compu——"

"Wonderful! On my own personal preferences." Gad, I had good taste!

He frowned in earnest. "This is most irregular."

"Do you want my soul?" I am certain I leered.

He did not answer but tapped at the computer keyboard again, then waited. Suddenly he looked toward the right wall and spoke to someone I could neither see nor hear. "Are you sure? I've never . . . but she . . . No, I don't know how to . . . but angels don't . . . I . . . really? How? Oh, my! Did you ask Him? He did? And She did? Oh, my. For how long? This simply can't get out, you know. . . . Oh, my."

He faced me again. "You'll sign if I stay?"

"Yes."

"Well, we are very behind in quota. There is not much market for clean, hard-working lives today, as you know. I did lose that prospect on Locust Street. Hmmm. Well, now, fidelity is the rule. And nothing kinky, understand?"

"Nothing kinky." I smiled, for I knew the word was still subject to definition. "And you did say I'd be happy."

"Oh, yes, indeed, very happy." He handed me the quill. He grew with it, changing in size until he was several inches taller than I. I approved. Most definitely, a well-designed specimen. I went to him, playing with the buttons on his shirt. "You really can stay?"

"Well, we can try for a while. Margaret, your pulse is racing. You must take care. Properly speaking, this is not my body, it is an illusion. SO, technically I am not . . . you are not . . . we . . . uh . . ."

I threw the quill down and put my lips to his, pressing my body close. I no longer cared if I was crazy, if he was a fantasy, or if indeed something incredible and other-worldly had occurred. I only knew that Michael was right about one thing. As he began to respond, I knew I was going to be very, very happy.

On Science Fiction
by
Jack Williamson

About the Author

Born in 1908 and living a hard-pressed early life on southwest desert farms, Jack Williamson is now a retired professor of literature in New Mexico, with a campus library named after him. Since the age of 20 he has also written memorable science fiction and fantasy for the top editors in the field, before, during and after the Golden Age. Just as energetically, he has pursued his notable parallel career as an educator, authoring a major analysis of H. G. Wells, and several works on teaching science fiction. The winner of top awards for his nonfiction studies as well as for his stories, Williamson can still become profoundly excited by the opportunity to pass his expertise on to younger hands, as the following essay demonstrates.

For the new writer, science fiction can be the last green oasis in a grimly forbidding desert. Getting a start is commonly hard, maybe harder than it used to be. When I was beginning, back in the 1920s, there were scores of pulp magazines; devoted to every sort of fiction, they bought millions of words a month. Their editors encouraged new talent, best of all by printing what we wrote.

As a class, the pulps had a bad name. Writers who wanted to do Literature offered their output to the "quality books," *Atlantic* and *Scribner's* and the like. The lions of the day got a dollar or more per word from such "slicks" as *Colliers* and the *Saturday Evening Post.*

The pulps paid around a lot less, the best of them a few cents a word, the worst only a miserly fraction thereof. By and large, they got what they paid for. That was entertainment, often but not always cheap or crude, for people who had no TVs yet and who hadn't forgotten how to read.

Entertainment. The editors demanded stories real and dramatic enough to hold interest, stories about people they could like or hate, people in action, impelled by motives of love or lust, greed or ambition or revenge, motives readers could understand. Writing for the pulps, we learned—and got paid for learning—the basics of literary craftsmanship.

Those basics aren't everything, but they are fundamental. No matter how high your artistic aim, it's pretty certain to fail until you are able to engage the interests and emotions of the reader. There were great pulp editors who taught some of us how to do that. For one, Captain Joseph Shaw of *Black Mask,* whose best-known students included Dashiell Hammett, Raymond Chandler and Erle Stanley Gardner.

Even under lesser editors, even those from whom that fraction of a cent a word sometimes came grudgingly, the pulps were a great school for us. First of all, they gave us the heady triumph of getting into print. Something maybe more useful, they gave us feedback, often in letters from their readers, the flak often better for us than the praise. They made us professionals.

All that has changed. Though today's markets are paying more money than ever for more kinds of writing, most of them are specialized and hard for the beginner to reach. The pulps are gone now, crowded out by TV and comic books and paperbacks. Scripts for films and TV may sometimes bring fabulous prices, but they can't be written except by people in close touch with producers and agents and directors.... In other words, they can't be written by persons who haven't yet become part of the Hollywood universe that most of us will never see.

Speculative fiction is perhaps the last oasis still existing in the unfriendly desert of fiction writing. A good many magazines still buy it, sometimes for exciting prices. The editors are still generally as friendly and helpful as their busy days allow. In the past few years, science fiction and fantasy novels have begun making best-seller lists; some are even made into high-budget films.

Even for those of us who never get all that gold, there are great rewards. Speculative fiction readers are an open-minded lot, ready to welcome nearly anything you want to write—if you can make it hold their interest and make it fit the conventions of the genre. Your protagonist can be a man or a woman, a child or an alien. Your theme can be nearly any statement you may choose, or your story can be pure fantastic fun. You can try for poetry and polish, or invent your own new future slanguage, though I suggest you try for a transparent simplicity.

The classic advice for the beginner is "Write what you know." In speculative fiction that may look odd, because so few of us have ever ridden spacecraft or time machines. Yet there are ways in which it does apply.

First of all, you must know SF. That doesn't mean that you need to know a great deal of science, but for most of us science fiction is an exploration of things we accept as possible. You should read enough SF to have some sense of what will look excitingly new and what has already been worn to a boring death. If the editor has seen the same threadbare idea a dozen times that week, it isn't likely it will be bought again—unless you can offer some special feature good enough to make the difference.

That vital added attraction can often come out of what you know, what you believe, what you feel. A theme that moves you can move the reader, too. If a fresh background comes from your own experience, or perhaps from your reading of history or anthropology or mythology, the reader is likely to find it as fascinating as you do. If the characters—even the robots and the aliens—reflect the traits and speech and behavior patterns of people you know, the reader will share your sense of their reality.

With the story contests and this anthology and the new magazine, *To the Stars,* L. Ron Hubbard is opening new trails into the new worlds of SF—worlds still alluring to me, even after exploring them for nearly sixty years. As one of the judges, I enjoyed reading the stories. I must admit that I found the winners hard to pick.

Something that was driven home to me some years ago, when I was involved with the Nebula Awards from the Science Fiction Writers of America, is that there are no purely objective measures of literary excellence. This is a fact I suppose we ought to be grateful for. If literary tastes were all identical, a dozen writers would be enough to satisfy everybody, with no opportunities left for the rest of us.

A judge can and should try to be objective. There are questions you can ask. Is it worth saying? Does it express truth to life and right? Is it well said, with effect and economy? The answers may help guide your own response, but they are still subjective. The ultimate test always remains: Do you like it?

I am neither surprised nor offended if some of the other judges made decisions different than mine, because our tastes and values differ so much, and because the top stories were themselves so different—excellent in such different ways. The winners all display craftsmanship and promise. They express emotion and reflect aspects of reality. They create illusions of shared human experience. We liked them. I think you will.

—Jack Williamson

Shanidar
by
David Zindell

About the Author

David Zindell has worked hard to become a writer, and is still attending workshop classes in the Denver area, under the tutelage of Ed Bryant. He has also attended the Haystack Writers Conference in Oregon, where he studied under Bryant, Gene Wolfe, and Michael Bishop. A more impressive trio of instructors drawn from contemporary science fiction could hardly be imagined.

Where writing comes from, however, is from within the writer. Skills can be taught, potential errors and dead ends can be warned against, and expert criticism can be rendered. But talent cannot be instilled, and neither can the patience and determination required to hone the skills.

Thirty-one years old, Zindell has an analytical mind, with a B.A. in mathematics. His minor in anthropology is clearly reflected in Shanidar, which won First Prize in the third quarter. Previously, he had placed one story, in Fantasy Book. In a very real sense, everything he has seen and thought in his life has pointed him in the direction of writing fiction professionally, and whatever success he enjoys will have been steadfastly earned. But first he had to feel the possibilities within himself, and see to it that they found the very best nurture possible. And that brings us to Shanidar.

Illustrated by A. R. Conway

I have heard the eschatologists deny the future of our kind. Man, they say, is a bridge between ape and superman, a rusty old bridge that we can neither preserve nor restore, any more than we can stop the stars beyond the Vild from exploding or turn the snows of deep winter into rain. For man, or for a man, there can be no new beginnings. The story I tell here is a story of restoration and resurrection, of how the philosophers of this doomed city were both right and wrong, a story, if you will, of endings and beginnings which sometimes are, as old men such as I well know, one and the same thing.

For me, the end of civilization came on the seventieth night of my fiftieth—or was it fifty-first?—deep winter in this City of Pain. Icefall, some called it, or Unreal City, city of lights and mists, the topological and, some say, spiritual center of a thousand decaying worlds. The eschatologists called it Neverness, which means, I think, "Last City" or "Lost City." I prefer the latter name though it isn't names that matter. What matters is ice and snow and cold so deep that your breath shatters into ice crystals on the hard air, and flesh—should any man be foolish enough to let the air of this forsaken city touch his naked flesh—flesh turns to stone as you watch. What matters is men who deny the importance of flesh, men who seek new beginnings.

He came into my cutting shop on a quiet night when the air was black and still, the only sound the far-off hissing and humming of the machines as they hovered over the city streets, melting and smoothing the ice for the following day. He was a pale young man with brown, lively eyes beneath the white hood of his parka, and he wore a beard so dense and black that you would have thought him born on Gehenna or Sheydveg and not, as he claimed, on Summerworld where the men are nearly hairless and their skin is as dark as coffee. With his heavy brows and large, muscular face he nearly had the look of the Alaloi which had been the fashion—you will presently understand why—some twenty years ago. As he stood there in the stone hallway knocking the slush from his skates, he explained that he had need of my services. "You are Rainer, the cutter?" he asked me in a low, conspiratorial voice. I told him that was what the people of the city called me. "I want you to use all your skills," he said. "I want to become an Alaloi."

I led him into my tearoom where he ejected the blades from his skates and flopped his dripping mittens on top of the marble table which I had imported from Urradeth at great cost. And though I didn't feel much like playing the host—my white tunic was spattered with blood and brains and I had matters to attend to—I offered him kvass or coffee and was surprised that he chose coffee.

"Kvass fogs the brain," he said, ignoring the frescoes on the stone walls around him and staring me in the eyes. "Drink makes men forget their purpose."

I sent for the domestic and I asked the young man, "And your purpose is to look like an Alaloi?"

He shook his head. "My purpose is to *become* an Alaloi. Completely."

I laughed and I said, "You know I can't do that; you

know the law. I can change your flesh as you please but——"

"What about Goshevan?"

"Goshevan!" I shouted. "Why do the young men always come asking about Goshevan?" The domestic came and I embarrassed myself by shouting out an order for coffee and kvass. As it rolled away, I said, "There are more stories told about Goshevan than dead stars in the Vild. What do you know about Goshevan?"

"I know that he wanted what I want. He was a man with a dream who——"

"He was a dreamer! Do you want to know about Goshevan? I'll tell you the story that I tell all the young men who come to me seeking nightmares. Are you sitting comfortably? Then listen well. . . ."

The domestic brought our drink bubbling in two of those huge, insulated pots that they blow on Fostora. It clumsily poured the dark liquids into our delicate marble cups as I told the young man the story of Goshevan:

"There lived on Summerworld a young noble who took a greater interest in antiques and old books—some say he had been to Ksandaria and bribed the librarians into selling him part of the Kyoto collection of Old Earth—than he did in managing his estates. He was an erudite man who claimed that the proper study of man was man—not how to produce five tons more coffee per cubage. One day he tired of his life and said, 'My s-sons are weak-faced maggots who exist on the diseased flesh of this rotten civilization. They p-plot with my wives against me and laugh as my wives sleep with other men.' And so Goshevan sold his estates, freed his slaves, and told his family they would have to make their living by the sweat of their hands and the inspiration of their brains. He paid for a passage on a Darghinni long ship and made his way toward the Vild.

"Now everyone knows the Darghinni are tricksters and so is it any wonder they didn't warn him of the laughing pools on Darkmoon? Well, warn him they didn't, and Goshevan spent two seasons on that dim, lukewarm planet coughing at the lungmelt in his chest while the surgeons painstakingly cut the spirulli from his muscles and waited and watched and cut some more.

"When he was well, he found a Fravashi trader who was willing to take him to Yarkona; on Yarkona he shaved his head and wrapped his body in rags so that the harijan pilgrims he befriended there would allow him a corner on one of their sluggish prayer ships in which to float. And so, gray of hair and stinking of years of his own sweat and filth, he came to Neverness like any other seeker.

"Though it was late midwinter spring, and warm for that season, he was stunned by the cold and dazzled by the brightness of our city. And so he paid too much money for snow goggles and the finest of shagshay furs lined with silk belly. 'The streets are colored ice,' he said disbelievingly, for the only ice he had ever seen had been brought to him in exotic drinks by his slaves. And he marvelled at the purples and greens of the glissades and the laughing children who chased each other up and down the orange and yellow slidderies on ice skates. The silvery spires and towers were frozen with the ever present verglas of that season, scattering the white spring light so that the whole city gleamed and sparkled in a most disconcerting manner. 'There is beauty here,' he said. 'The false beauty of artifice and a civilization gone to rot.' And so, dressed in deep winter furs and wobbling on his newly bought skates, he struck out into the streets to preach to the people.

"In the great square outside the Hofgarten where the people of the Unreal City, high and low, meet and take their refreshment, the scryers, eschatologists, and cantors as well as the harijan, splicers and whores, he said, 'I s-speak to that inside you which is less than m-man but also m-more.' And he raged because no one would listen to a short, overdressed farsider who stuttered and could barely stand on his skates. 'You p-pilots,' he said, 'you are the p-pride of the galaxy! You travel from Simoom to Urradeth and on to Jacaranda in less time than the Darghinni need to prepare the first of eighteen jumps from Summerworld to Darkmoon. You penetrate the Vild, lost in your mathematics and dreamtime and tell yourself you have seen something of the ineffable and eternal. But you have forgotten how to take pleasure in a simple flower! You foreswear marriage and children and thus you are more and less than men!'

"When the pilots turned away from him to drink their kvass and eiswein, he told the historians and fabulists that they knew nothing of the true nature of man. And they, those haughty professionals of our city, snubbed him and went on talking about Gaiea and Old Earth as if he were invisible. So Goshevan spoke to the programmers and holists, the Fravashi aliens and Friends of God, the harijan, the wormrunners, the splicers, and at last, because he was filled with a great sadness and longing, he zipped up his furs and went deep into the Farsiders' Quarter where he might pay for the company of a friendly ear.

"Because he was lonely and had been without a woman for many years, he took his pleasure among the whores of the lesser glidderies, which at that time were stained crimson and were narrow and twisted like snakes. Because his soul was empty he smoked toalache and awoke one fine morning to find himself in bed with four courtesans from Jacaranda. They asked him if all dark little men were as potent as he and advised him that the joys of conjoining with the alien Friends of Man were such that no man who had known only women could comprehend them. Goshevan, horrified at what he had done and forgetting where he was, began swearing and shouting and ordered that the courtesans be sold as field slaves. He threw a bag of diamonds at them, clipped in the blades to his skates, and raced up and down the back glissades for two days before he came to his right mind."

I paused here in my story to refill our cups. The young man was staring at me intently, watching my every move with those piercing brown eyes and, I felt, stripping my words bare for lies. The room was very quiet and cold; I could hear his slow, even breathing as he nodded his head and asked, "And then?"

"And then Goshevan made a decision. You see, he had hoped to win people over to his dream, which was to go out into the wasteland and live as what he called 'natural man.' The Alaloi, of course, had been his model. When he found he could not emulate them, he decided to join them."

"A noble vision," the young man said.

"It was insane!" I half-shouted. "Who were these Alaloi he so admired? Dreamers and madmen they were—and still are. They came to this world on the first wave of the swarming, when Old Earth was young and, some say, as radioactive as plutonium. Cavemen! They wanted to be cavemen! So they back-mutated their chromosomes, destroyed their ship, and went to live in the frozen forests. And now their great-grandchildren's great-great-grandchildren hunt mammoths for meat and die long before they've seen their hundredth winter."

"But they die happy," the young man said.

"Who knows how they die?" I said to him. "Goshevan wanted to know. He sought me out because it was said that once as a journeyman I had pioneered the operation he wanted, cutting on my very own self to prove my worth as a flesh changer. 'Make me into an Alaloi,' he begged me, in this very room where we presently drink our coffee and kvass. And I told him, 'Go to any of the cetics in this quarter and they will cure you of your delusions.' And he said, 'I will p-pay you ten million talanns!' But his farsider money was worthless in the Unreal City and I told him so. 'Diamonds,' he said. 'I've two thousand carats of Yarkona bluestars.' 'For that price,' I said, 'I can add eight inches to your spine or make you into a beautiful woman. I can lighten your skin and make your hair as white as a Jacaranda courtesan's.' Then he looked at me cunningly and said, 'I'll trade information for your services: I know the fixed-points of Agathange.' I laughed at him and asked, 'How is it you know what the pilots of our city have been seeking for three thousand years?'

"Well, it happened that he *did* know. With the riches from the sale of his estates, he had bought the secret of the location of that fabled world from a renegade pilot he had met on Darkmoon. I consulted our city archives; the librarians were *very* excited. They sent a young pilot to verify my information, and I told Goshevan we might have to wait two or three hundred days before we would know.

"Ten thousand city disks his information was worth! The pilot who rediscovered Agathange was very good. Phased into his light ship, the *Infinite Sloop*, proving the theorems of probabilistic topology—or whatever it is that our famous pilots do when they wish to fall through the space that isn't space—he rushed through the fallaways, fenestering from window to window with such precision and elegance that he returned from Agathange in forty days.

"'You can be a rich man,' Goshevan said to me on a clear, sparkling day of false winter. 'Do as I ask and all the disks are yours.'

"I hesitated not for a moment. I took him into the changing room and I began to cut. It was a challenge, I lied to myself, a test of knowledge and skill—to a dedicated cutter, it wasn't disks that mattered. I enlarged the basal bone of his jaw and stimulated the alveolar bone to maximal growth so that his face could support the larger teeth I implanted. The angle of the face itself I broadened so that there would be more room for a chewing apparatus strong enough to crack marrowbones. And of course, since the face jutted out farther from the skull, I had to build up the brow ridge with synthetic bone to protect the eyes. And though this shaping took the better part of winter, it was only the beginning.

"As he writhed beneath my lasers and scalpels, all the while keeping his face as quiet and blank as a snowfield, I went to work on his body. To support his huge new muscles—which were grown by the Fravashi deep-space method—I built him new bones. I expanded the plates and spicules of the honeycombed interior and strengthened the shafts and tendon attachments, adding as much as three millimeters to the cortices of the longer bones such as his femur. I stippled his skin. I went beneath the dermis, excising most of his sweat glands to keep him from soaking his furs and freezing to death at the first hint of false winter. Because his dark skin would synthesize too little vitamin D to keep his bones calcified during the long twilight of deep winter, I inhibited his melanocytes—it is little known that all men, light or dark, have nearly the same number of melanocytes— I lightened his skin until he was as fair as a man from Thorskalle. The last thing I did for him, or so I thought at the time, was to grow out his fine, almost invisible body hair so that it covered him like brown fur from toe to eyebrow.

"I was very pleased with my handiwork and a little frightened because Goshevan had grown so strong— stronger, I think, than any Alaloi—that he could have torn my clavicle from my chest, had he so desired. But *he* was not pleased and he said, 'The most important thing there is, this thing you didn't do.' And I told him, 'I've made you so that no one among the Alaloi could tell you from his brother.' But he looked at me with his dark fanatic's eyes and asked me, 'And my s-sons, should my s-seed by some chance be compatible with the Alaloi women, who will there be to call my weak-jawed half-breed sons brother?' I had no answer for him other than a dispirited repeating of the law: 'A man may do with his flesh as he pleases,' I said, 'but his DNA belongs to his species.' And then he grabbed my forearm so tightly that I thought my muscles would split away from the bone and said, 'Strong men make their own laws.'

"Then, because I felt a moment of pity for this strange man who only wanted what all men want— which is a son after his own image and a few moments of peace—I broke the law of the civilized worlds. It was a challenge, do you understand? I irradiated his testes and bathed them with sonics, killing off the sperm. I couldn't, of course, engage the services of a master splicer because all my colleagues shunned such criminal activity. But I *was* a master cutter—some will tell you the best in the city—and what is gene-splicing but surgery on a molecular scale? So I went into his tubules and painstakingly sectioned out and mutated segments of his stem cells' DNA so that the newly produced germ cells would make for him sons after his new image.

"When I finished this most delicate of delicate surgeries, which took the better part of two years, Goshevan regarded himself in the mirror of my changing room and announced, 'Behold *Homo neandertalis*. Now I am less than a man but also more.'

" 'You look as savage as any savage,' I said. And then, thinking to scare him, I told him what was commonly believed about the Alaloi. 'They live in caves and have no language,' I said. 'They are bestially cruel to their children; they eat strangers, and perhaps each other.'

"Goshevan laughed as I said this and then he told me, 'On Old Earth during the holocaust century, a neandertal burial site was discovered in a place called Shanidar near the Zagros mountains of Irak. The archeologists found the skeleton of a forty-year-old m-man who was missing his lower right arm. Shanidar I, they named him, and they determined he had lost his arm long before he died. In the burial site of another neandertal, Shanidar IV, was the pollen of several kinds of flowers, mixed in with all the bone fragments, pebbles and dust. The question I have for you, Cutter, is: how savage could these people have been if they supported a cripple and honored their dead with bright colored wildflowers?' So I answered, 'The Alaloi are not the same.' And he said, 'We will see, we will see.'

"Here I freely admit I had underestimated him. I had supposed him to be a lunatic or at best, a self-deluder who hadn't a chance of getting ten miles away from our city. The covenant between the founder of Neverness and the Alaloi allows us this single island—large though it might be—and to our city fathers, this covenant is holy. Boats are useless because of the icebergs of the Sound, and the windjammers of would-be poachers and smugglers are shot from the air. Because I couldn't picture Goshevan walking out onto the Starnbergersee when it freezes over in deep winter, I asked him somewhat smugly how he intended to find his Alaloi.

" 'Dogs,' he said. 'I will attach dogs to a sled and let them pull me across the frozen sea.' And I asked, 'What are dogs?' 'Dogs are carnivorous mammals from Old Earth,' he said. 'They are like human slaves, only friendly and eager to please.' And I said, 'Oh, you mean huzgies,' which is what the Alaloi call their sled dogs. I laughed at him then and watched the white skin beneath his hairy face turn red as if slapped by a sudden cold wind. 'And how will you smuggle such beasts into our city?' I asked him.

"So Goshevan parted the hair of his abdomen to show me a thin band of hard white skin I had taken for an appendectomy scar. 'Cut here,' he said, and after nerve-blocking him, cut I did until I came to a strange looking organ adjoining the large intestine where his appendix should have been. 'It's a false ovary,' he said. 'Clever are the breeders of Darkmoon. Come. Cut again and see what I've brought with me.' I removed the false organ, which was red and slippery and made of one of those pungently sweet-smelling bioplastics they synthesize on Darkmoon. I made a quick incision and out spilled thousands of unfertilized ova and a sac of sperm floating in krydda suspension to keep them fresh and vital. He pointed at the milky sperm sac and said, 'The seed of Darkmoon's finest Mutts. I had originally hoped to train hundreds of sled teams.'

"How Goshevan brought the dogs to term and trained them, I do not know because I didn't see him again for two winters. I thought perhaps that he'd been caught and banished or had his head split open and had his plasm sucked out by some filthy slel necker.

"But as you will see, Goshevan was a resourceful man and hard to kill. He came again to my shop on the deepest of deep winter nights when the air was so black and cold that even on the greatest of the glissades and slidderies, The Run and The Way, nothing moved. In the hallway of my shop he stood like a white bear, opening his shagshay furs and removing the balaclava from his face with powerful, sweeping motions. I could see beneath his furs one of those black and gold, heated kamelaikas that the racers wear on festival days when they wish to keep warm and still have their limbs free for stroking. 'This is my noble savage?' I said to him as I fingered his wonderfully warm undersuit. 'Even a f-fanatic such as I must make some concessions to survival,' he said. And I asked him, 'What will you do when the batteries die?' He gave me a look that was at once fearful and bursting with excitement, and he said, 'When the batteries die, I will either be dead or I will have found my home.'

"He said goodbye to me and went out onto the gliddery where his dogs were up on their hind legs, straining at their harnesses as they whined and barked and pushed their black noses into his parka. From my window, I could see him fumbling with the stiff leather straps and thumping the side of the lead dog with his huge mittens. He adjusted the load three times before he had it to his liking, taking pains that the sacks of dog meal were balanced and tightly lashed to the wooden frame. Then he was off, whistling in a curious manner as he glided around the corner of the cetic's shop and disappeared into the cold."

The tearoom felt cold as I said these words. I noticed that the young man was pursing his narrow lips tightly as he fiddled with his coffee. All at once, he let out his breath in a puff of steam that seemed to hang in the air. "But that isn't the end of your story, is it, Cutter? You haven't told the moral: how poor Goshevan died on the ice brokenhearted and disavowing his dream."

"Why is it you young people always want an ending? Does our universe come to an *end* or does it fold in upon itself? Are the Agathanians at the end of human evolution or do they represent a new species? And so on, and so on. Is there any end to the questions impatient young men ask?"

I took a quick gulp of the bitter kvass, burning my lips and throat so that I sat there dumbly sucking in the cold air like an old bellows. "No, you are right," I gasped out. "That is not the end of my story."

"Goshevan drove his dogs straight out onto the frozen Starnbergersee. Due west he went, running fast across the wind-packed snow for six hundred miles. He came to the first of the Thousand Islands and found mountains shrouded in evergreen forests where the thallows nested atop the steep granite cliffs filling the air for miles with their harsh cawings. But he found no Alaloi, and he urged his dogs carefully across the crevasses of the Fairleigh ice-shelf, back out onto the sea.

"Fifteen islands he crossed without finding a trace of a human being. He had been gone sixty-two days when the crushing, deadly silent cold of deep winter began yielding to the terrible storms of midwinter spring.

During a snow so heavy and wet that he had to stop every hundred yards to scrape the frozen slush from the steel runners of his sled, his lead dog, Yuri the Fierce, pulled them into a crevasse. Though he dug his boots into the sloppy snow and held on to the sled with all his strength, the pendulating weight of Yuri, Sasha and Ali as they swung back and forth over the lip of the ice was such that he felt himself being slowly dragged into the crevasse. It was only by the quick slashing of his hunting knife that he saved himself and the rest of his team. He cut the harness from which his strongest dogs dangled and watched helplessly as they tried to dig their black claws into the sides of the crevasse, all the while yelping pitifully as they fell to the ice below.

"Goshevan was stunned. Though the snow had stopped and he was within sight of the sixteenth and largest of the Thousand Islands, he realized he could go no farther without rest. He erected his tent and fed the dogs from the crumbly remnants of the last bag of food. There came a distant hissing that quickly grew into a roar as the storm returned, blasting across the Starnbergersee with such ferocity that he spent all that day and night tending the ice-screws of his tent so that he wouldn't be blown away. For nine days he lay there shivering inside his sleeping sack as the wind-whipped ice crystals did their work. By the tenth day, the batteries to his heated kamelaika were so low that he threw them in disgust against the shredded, useless walls of his tent. He dug a cave in the snow and pulled the last two of his starving dogs into the hole so that they might huddle close and keep each other warm. But Gasherbrum the Friendly, the smartest of his dogs, died on the eleventh day. And on the morning of the twelfth day, his beloved Kanika, whose paws were crusted with ice and blood, was as still as a deep winter night.

"When the storm broke on the fifteenth day, Goshevan was so crazy with thirst that he burned his frostbitten lips upon the metal cup in which he was melting snow. And though he was famished and weak as a snow worm, he could not bring himself to eat his dogs because he was both father and mother to them, and the thought of it made him so sick he would rather have died.

"From the leather and wood of his sled he fashioned a crude pair of snowshoes and set out across the drifts for a huge blue and white mountain he could see in the distance puncturing the sky. Kweitkel it was called, as he would later learn. Kweitkel, which meant 'white mountain' in the language of the Devaki, who were the tribe of Alaloi who found him dying in the thick forests of its eastern slope.

"His rescuers—five godlike men dressed in angelic white, or so it seemed to his fevered, delirious mind— brought him to a huge cave. Some days later he came awake to the wonderful smells of hot soup and roasting nuts. He heard soft voices speaking a strange, musical language that was a delight to his ear. Two children, a boy and a girl he thought, were sitting at the corners of the luxurious fur which covered him, peeking at him coyly through the spread-out fingers of their little hands and giggling.

"A man with great shoulders and a beard as black as a furfly came over to him. Between his blunt, scarred fingers he held a soup bowl made from yellowed bone and scrimshawed with intricate figures of diving whales. As Goshevan gulped the soup, the man asked, 'Marek? Patwin? Olorun? Nodin? Mauli?' Goshevan, half-snowblind and weak in the head as he was, forgot that I had made him so that no one among the Alaloi could tell him from his brothers. He thought he was being accused of being an alien so he shook his head furiously back and forth at the sound of each name. At last, when Lokni, which was the big man's name, had given up trying to discover the tribe to which he belonged, Goshevan pointed to his chest and said, 'I am man. I'm just a man.' 'Iaman,' Lokni repeated. 'Ni luria la Devaki.' And so it was that Lokni of the Devaki welcomed Goshevan of the Iaman tribe to his new home.

"Goshevan gained strength quickly, gorging upon a salty cheese curdled from shagshay milk and the baldo nuts the Devaki stored against the storms of midwinter spring. And though Katerina, who was Lokni's wife, offered him thick mammoth steaks running red with the life's blood beneath a charcoaled crust, he would eat no meat. He, who all his life had eaten only soft, de-cerebrated cultured meats, was horrified that such gentle people took their nourishment from the flesh of living animals. 'I don't think I can teach these savages the few right-actioned ways of civilized man,' he said to himself. 'Why should they listen to me, a total stranger?' And so for the first time since Summerworld he came to question the wisdom of what he had done.

"By the time Goshevan had put on fifty pounds of new muscle, the storms of midwinter spring had given way to the fine weather of false winter. There came cool sunny days; the occasional powdery snows were too light to cover the alpine fireweed and snow dahlia which blan-keted the lower slopes of Kweitkel. The thallows were molting and the furflys laying eggs. For Tuwa, the mam-moth, came calving time, and for the Devaki, it was time to slaughter mammoth.

"Goshevan was sick. Though he had quickly learned

the language of the Devaki, and learned also to tolerate his body lice and filthy hair, he did not know how he could kill an animal. But when Lokni unsmilingly slapped a spear into his hand, he knew he would have to hunt with the eighteen other men, many of whom had come to wonder about his strange ways and questioned his manhood.

"At first the hunt went well. In one of the lovely valleys of Kweitkel's southern foothills, they spotted a mammoth herd gorging on arctic timothy and overripe, half-fermented snow apple. The great hairy beasts were carousing and drunkenly trampling through the acres of alpine fireweed which were everywhere aflame with bright reds and oranges and so beautiful that Goshevan wanted to cry. They drove the trumpeting mammoths down the valley and into a bog where three calves fell quickly beneath flint-tipped spears. But then Lokni mired himself near the edge of the bog, and Wemilo was trampled by an enraged cow. It fell to Goshevan to help Lokni. Though he reached out with his spear into the bog until his shoulder joint popped, he failed to close the distance. He heard voices and shouting and thunder and felt the ground moving beneath him. As he looked up to see the red-eyed cow almost upon him, he realized that the men were praying for his ghost, for it was known that no single man could stand against Tuwa's charge.

"Goshevan was terrified. He cast his spear at the mammoth's eye with such a desperate force that the point drove into the brain, and the great beast fell like a mountain. The Devaki were stunned. Never had they seen such a thing, and Haidar and Alani, who had doubted his bravery, said that he was more than a man. But Goshevan knew his feat was the result of blind luck and my surgery, and thus he came to despise himself because he had killed a magnificent being and was therefore less than a man.

"In the cave that night, the Devaki made a feast to mourn the passing of Tuwa's anima and to wish Wemilo's ghost enlightenment on the other side of day. Lokni sliced his own ear off his head with a sharp obsidian flake and laid the bloody flap of skin on Wemilo's cold forehead so that he might always hear the prayers of the tribe. Katerina bound her husband's wound with feather moss while the other women scattered snow dahlias over Wemilo's crushed body.

"Then Lokni turned to Goshevan and said, 'A man, to be a man, must have a woman, and you are too old to take a virgin bride.' He went over to Lara, who was sobbing over Wemilo's grave. 'Look at this poor woman. Long ago her father, Arani, deserted her to live with the hairless people of the Unreal City. She has no brothers. And now Wemilo dances with the stars. Look at this poor beautiful woman whose hair is still black and shiny and whose teeth are straight and white. Who will be a man to this woman?'

"Goshevan looked at Lara and though her eyes were full of tears, they were also hot and dark, full of beauty and life. He felt very excited and said, 'A man would be a fool not to desire this woman.' And then he thought to comfort her by saying, 'We'll be married and have many fine children to love.'

"A hush fell over the cave. The Devaki looked at each other as if they couldn't believe their ears. And Ushi wondered aloud, 'How can he not know that Lara has three daughters and one son?' 'Of course I know,' Goshevan said. 'It only means she is very fertile and will have no trouble bearing me sons.' Then Ushi let out a cry and began tearing at her hair. Katerina hid her eyes beneath her hand and Lokni asked, 'How can it be, Goshevan, that you do not know the Law?' And Goshevan, who was angry and confused, replied, 'How can I know your law when I'm from a faraway tribe?' Lokni looked at him and there was death in his eyes. 'The Law is the Law,' he said, 'and it is the same for every Alaloi. It can only be that the storm stole away your memory and froze part of your soul.' And then, because Lokni didn't want to kill the man who had saved his life and was about to marry his sister, he explained the Law.

" 'She may have but one more child. A woman may have five children: One child to give to the Serpent's Breath of deep winter, one child for the tusks of Tuwa, the mammoth. One child for the fever that comes in the night.' Lokni paused a moment as the Law passed from lip to lip, and all the tribe except Goshevan were chanting: 'A boy to become a man; a girl to become Devaki, Mother of the People.'

"Lokni cupped his hand around the back of Goshevan's neck and squeezed as he said, 'If we become too many, we will kill all the mammoth and have to hunt silk belly and shagshay for food. And when they are gone, we will have to cut holes in the ice of the sea so to spear the seals when they come up to breathe. When the seals are gone, we will be forced to murder Kikilia, the whale, who is wiser then we and as strong as God. When all the animals are gone, we will dig tangleroot and eat the larvae of furflys and break our teeth as we gnaw the lichen from the rocks. At last we will be so many, we will murder the forests to plant snow apple so that men will come to lust for land, and some men will come to have more land than others. And when there is no land left, the stronger men will get their sustenance from the labor of weaker men, who will have to sell their women and children so that they might have mash to eat. The strongest men will make war on each other so that they might have still more land. Thus we will become hunters of men and be doomed to hell in living and hell on the other side. And then, as it did on Earth in the time before the swarming, fire will rain from the sky, and the Devaki will be no more.'

"And so Goshevan, who really wanted only one son, came to accept the Law of the Alaloi, for who knew better than he the evils of owning slaves and lying with whores?

"He married Lara at the end of false winter. In her long black hair, she replaced the snow dahlias of her mourning time with the fire flowers of the new bride and set to sewing him the new shagshay parka he would need when deep winter came. Each Devaki made them a wedding gift. Eirene and Jael, the two giggling children who had first greeted him so many months before, gave him a pair of mittens and a carved tortrix horn for him to fill with the potent beer that was brewed each winter from mashed tangleroot. His finest gift, a work of breathtaking art and symmetry, was the spear that Lokni gave him. It was long and heavy and tipped with a blade of flint so sharp that it cut through cured mammoth hide as easily as cheese."

I finished my drink, pausing a moment to catch my breath. The sounds the young man's marble cup made against the cold hard table seemed gritty and overloud. I smelled cinnamon and honey; a minute later the domestic served raisin bread spread with honey-cheese and brought us fresh pots of coffee. Outside the tearoom, I could hear the soft clack-clack of steel skates against the ice of the gliddery. I wondered who would be so foolish, or desperate, to be out on such a night. The young man took my hand in his, staring at me so intently that I had to look away. "And Goshevan?" he asked. "He was happy with the beautiful Lara? He was happy, wasn't he?"

"He was happy," I said, trying to slip my old hand from the young man's grip. "He was so happy he came to regard his body lice as his 'little pets' and didn't care that he would have to pass the rest of his days without a bath. His stuttering, which had embarrassed him all his life and caused him great shame, came to a sudden end as he found the liquid vowels and smooth consonants of the Devaki language rolling easily off his tongue. He loved Lara's children as his own and loved Lara as only a desperate and romantic man can love a woman. Though she had none of the exotic skills of the courtesans with whom he had been so familiar, she loved him with such a strength and passion that he came to divide his life into two parts: the time before Lara, which was murky and dim and full of confused memories, and the time after, which was full of light and joy and laughter. So it happened that when, the following midwinter spring, she pointed to her belly and smiled, he knew with a sureness that he had not spent his life in vain and was as happy as a man could be.

"The deep powder snows of winter were falling as Lara swelled like the ripened baldo nuts which the women picked and stored in great barrels staved with mammoth ribs and covered with mammoth hides. 'It will be a boy,' she said to him one night in early deep winter when the slopes of Kweitkel were silvery with the light of the moons. When I was carrying my girls I was sick every morning of the three seasons of growing. But with this one I wake up as hungry as Tuwa in midwinter spring.'

"When her time came, Katerina shooed Lokni and Goshevan, uncle and father, to the front of the cave where they waited while the women did their secret things. It was a night of such coldness that old Amalia said comes but twice every hundredyear. To the north, they could see green curtains of light hanging down from the black starry sky. 'The firefalls,' Lokni said. 'Sometimes they are faint and green as you see and other times as red as blood. The spirit of Wemilo and all our ancestors light the deep winter night to give us hope against the darkness.' And then he pointed at a bright triangle of stars twinkling brightly above the eastern horizon. 'Wakanda, Eanna, and Farfara,' he said. 'Men live there, I think. Shadow men without bodies. It is said they have no souls and take their nourishment from light.' And so they sat there for a long time shivering in their shagshay furs, talking of the things men talk about when they are full of strange longing and wonder at the mystery of life.

"There came a squalling from the cave. Goshevan clapped Lokni on the back and started laughing. But the cries of his newborn son were followed by a low wailing and then a whole chorus of women crying. He felt a horrible fear and leapt to his feet even as Lokni tried to hold him back.

"He ran to the warmest, deepest part of the cave where the men were not supposed to go. There, in the sick yellow light of the oil-stones, on a blood-soaked newl fur, he saw his son lying all wet and slippery and pink between Lara's bent legs. Katerina knelt over the struggling infant, holding a corner of the gray fur over his face. Goshevan knocked her away from his son so that she fell to the floor, winded and gasping for air. As

Haidar and Palani grabbed his arms, Lokni came to him and with such a sadness that his voice broke and tears ran from his eyes, he said, 'It is the Law, my friend. Any born such as he must immediately make the journey to the other side.' Then Goshevan, who had been full of blind panic and rage, looked at his son. He saw that growing from the hips were two tiny red stumps, twitching pathetically where they should have been kicking. His son had no legs. And to Lokni, who had gathered up the baby in his arms, he said, 'The Devaki do not kill each other.' And Lokni said, 'A baby is not a Devaki until he is named.' Then Goshevan raged so that Einar and Pauli had to come hold him as well. 'I name him Shanidar,' he said. 'Shanidar, my son, whom I love more than life.' But Lokni shook his head because life is so hard the Devaki do not name their children until four winters have passed. With his forefinger, he made a star above the screaming baby's head and went out to bury him in the snow.

"Lokni, whose white parka was stained crimson with frozen blood, returned alone with his hands shielding his eyes as if to protect them from false winter's noonday sun. Goshevan broke free and picked up the mammoth spear which had been his wedding gift. He threw it at Lokni in desperation, too blind with pain and fear to see the point enter his stomach and emerge from his back. And he ran outside to find his son.

"An hour later he returned. And in his arms, frozen as hard as a mammoth leg, he held his quiet, motionless son. 'Lara,' he said. And like a drunkard, he stumbled towards his wife. But Lara, who had seen what had passed between her legs and what her husband had done, opened the great artery of her throat with her hide scraper before he could get too close. And when he cried out that he loved her and would die if she died, she told him that the essence of the Law is that life must be lived with honor and joy or not lived at all. So Lara died as he watched, and the best part of him died with her. Knowing that his life had come to an end, he unknotted the ties of his parka, exposing the black matted hair of his chest so that Einar and Alani and the others might more easily spear him. But Goshevan had learned nothing. Lokni, lying on his back with the blood running from a great hole in his abdomen, said, 'Go back to the City, foolish man. We will not kill you; we are not hunters of men.'

"They gave Goshevan a team of snarling dogs and a barrel of baldo nuts and sent him out onto the ice. And he, who should have died a hundred times, did not die because he was full of the madness which protects desperate men, and a new idea had come into his head. So he made his way back across the ice of the Starnbergersee. This time, he ate his dogs when they died and didn't care that his beard was crusted with their black, frozen blood. He came once again to Neverness as a seeker; he came to my cutting shop, wretched, starving, covered with filth and dead, frostbitten skin rotting on his face. He came to me and said, 'I seek life for my son.'

"He stood in this very room, above this table. From a leather bag full of snow and rimed with frost, he removed a twisted, pinkish lump of frozen meat and laid it on the table. 'This is my son,' he said. 'Use all your skills, Cutter, and return my son to me.'

"Goshevan told me his story, all the while cradling in his arms the leather bag to which he had returned his poor son's corpse. He was mad, so mad that I had to shout and repeat myself over and over before he would cease his ranting. 'There isn't a single cryologist in the city,' I told him, 'who can bring your son back to life.'

"But he never understood me. He went out onto the slidderies and glissades, telling his story to every cutter, splicer and cetic who would listen to him. Thus it came to be known throughout the city that I had tampered with his DNA and tampered badly. I was brought before the akashics and their accursed optical computers which laid bare my brain and recorded my actions and memories for all to see. 'If you ever again break the laws of our city,' the master akashic told me, 'you will be banished.' To ensure that I would obey the law, he ordered me to submit to their computer on the first day of each new year 'so long as you live.' Curiously, although I had scandalized most of the city, my 'Neandertal Procedure' became immediately popular among the many farsiders who come to Neverness seeking to be other than what they are. For many years thereafter, the glidderies of our quarter were filled with squat hairy supermen who looked as if they could have been Goshevan's brother.

"And Goshevan, poor Goshevan—though he pleaded with and threatened every cryologist in the quarter—death is death, and no one could do more for him than give him a hot meal and a little toalache and send him on his way. The last I heard of him, he was trying to bribe his way to Agathange, where, he said, the men were no longer men and miracles were free to anyone who would surrender up his humanity. But everyone knows Agathanian resurrection is just a myth dreamed up by some fabulist drunk with the fire of toalache, no more real than the telepaths of The Golcanda. And so Goshevan disappeared into the back alleys of our Unreal City, no doubt freezing to death one dark winter's night. And there, my young friend, the story ends."

Painfully, I stood up to indicate that our conversation was over. But the young man kept to his chair, staring at me silently. His eyes grew so intense, so dark and disturbed, I thought that, perhaps, all men who desire the unobtainable must be touched with some degree of madness. I felt the acids of the kvass and coffee burning in my stomach as I said, "You must go now. You understand now, you understand why."

Suddenly, he slapped the table. The tearoom echoed with the loud rattle of teacups and the young man's trembling voice. "There the story does *not* end," he said. "This is the end, the true end of Goshevan's story that they tell in the silver mines of Summerworld."

I smiled at him then because the story of Goshevan is now a legend, and the endings to his story are as many as the Thousand Islands. Although I was certain to be bored by one of the fabulist myths in which Goshevan returns triumphantly to the Patwin or Basham or some other tribe of the Alaloi, one can never be *truly* certain. As I am a collector of such myths, I said, "Tell me your ending."

"Goshevan found Agathange," the young man said with conviction. "You yourself said he was hard to kill, Cutter. He found Agathange where the men—I guess I really shouldn't call them men because they were many-sexed and looked more like seals than men—where the Agathanians brought Shanidar back to life. They fitted him with mechanical legs stronger than real legs. They made him fifty sets of replacement legs, in graduated lengths to accommodate his growth. They offered Goshevan the peace of Agathange's oceans, the wisdom and bliss of cortically implanted bio-chips. But Goshevan, he said he wasn't fit for an ice-world that was less than civilized and that he certainly wasn't worthy of a water world that was beyond civilization. He thanked his hosts and said, 'Shanidar will grow up to be a prince. I will bring him home to Summerworld where men such as we belong.'

"To Summerworld he came many years later as an old man with white hair and a stooped back. He called upon the favor of his old friends, asking for the loan of rich delta land so that he could reestablish his estates. But no one recognized him. They, those wily, arrogant lords swathed in their white summer silks, they saw only an old madman—who I guess must have looked more like a beast to them than a man—and a strange-looking boy with proscribed Agathanian legs. 'Goshevan,' said Leonid the Just, who had once helped Goshevan put down Summerworld's forty-eighth servile revolt, 'was as hairless as an elephant. He stuttered, too, if my poor memory serves me right.' And then—are you listening, Cutter?—then Leonid ordered them sold into the silver mines. Sondevan, the obese slavemaster, removed Shanidar's legs and strapped a cart to his abdomen so that he could wheel himself along the steel tracks that led into the ground. And though Goshevan was old, he was as strong as a water buffalo. They shoved a pick at him and set him hacking at a vein of sylvanite. 'Goshevan,' said the slavemaster, 'was my father's name. He was small and weak and let the Delta Lords buy his land for a tenth a talann per cubage. This ugly animal is not he.'

"The mines were cooler than the rice paddies, but they were hellishly hot compared with the frozen forests of Kweitkel. Goshevan—do you remember how you removed his sweat glands, Cutter?—Goshevan lasted two hours before he keeled over from heatstroke and fell into delirium. But before he died, he told his son the story of his birth and explained the Law of the Devaki. His last words before the slavemaster's silver mallet caved in his head were, 'Go back!'

"So I've come back," the young man said. The cutting shop was silent around us. As I stood there on the cold tile floor, I could hear the ragged hissing of my breath and taste the bittersweet tang of coffee coating my tongue and teeth. Suddenly, the young man rose to his feet so quickly that he bumped the table with his hip, sending one of my priceless teacups shattering against the floor. He opened his furs and dropped his trousers. There, badly fitted to his hips as if by some ignorant apprentice cutter, I could see the prosthetic legs—the kind they make badly on Fostora or Kainan—where they disappeared beneath reddened flaps of skin.

"I've come back to you, Grandfather," he said. "And you must do for me what you failed to do for Goshevan, who was my father."

And there my story really and truly ends. I do not know if the young man who came to me was the real Shanidar. I do not know if the story he told of Goshevan's death is really true. I prefer to believe his story, though it isn't stories that matter. What matters is precision and skill, the growing of new limbs for the legless and the altering, despite the law of civilization, the tampering with a young man's DNA when the need to tamper and heal is great. What matters is men who aren't afraid to change the shape and substance of their flesh so that they might seek out new beginnings.

When, on the first day of midwinter spring, I am brought before the master akashic and banished from my mysterious and beloved city, I will not seek out Agathange, tempting though the warmth of their oceans might be. I am too old to take on the body of a seal; I do

not wish for the wisdom of cortically implanted bio-chips. To paraphrase the law: A man may do with his DNA as he pleases but his soul belongs to his people. It is to my people, the Devaki, that I must return. I have bitterly missed all these years the quiet white beauty of Kweitkel and besides, I must put flowers on my daughter Lara's grave. I, Arani, who once came to Neverness from the sixteenth and largest of the Thousand Islands like any other seeker, will take my grandson back across the frozen Starnbergersee. And for Goshevan, child of my lasers and microscopes, for my poor, brave, restless son-in-law I will pray as we pray for all who make the great journey: Goshevan, mi alasharia la shantih Devaki, may your spirit rest in peace on the other side of day.

One Last Dance
by
Dean Wesley Smith

About the Author

Dean Wesley Smith is 34, a former golf professional with an architecture degree who also studied law. Appropriately, when he designed a Moscow, Idaho, indoor shopping mall, he put a miniature golf course in its upper floor. The former operator of a paperback bookstore, he later joined another collector in setting up an art-gallery exhibit of pulp-magazine and newsstand paperback covers, presenting a major survey of popular American art over a period beginning in the 1920s. He has also been assistant manager of a billiard parlor. In the middle 1970s, something moved him to try writing poetry. In the space of a year, he published 26 poems in serious literary publications, appearing in Prize Poets, 1976, *an academic anthology. Frightened by the possibility of becoming a lifelong poet, he stopped cold and decided to turn to prose fiction.*

This led him to attending the Clarion Writers' Workshop in 1982, where he was a classmate of fellow Moscow-resident Nina K. Hoffman (see page 25). He has since been published once, with an ultra-short story in the Clarion Awards *anthology.*

Married to a nurse whose specialty is the care of old people, he has been working on One Last Dance *for several years. It placed high among the third-quarter finalists, and we think you will find it richly deserves publication here. We also think that in years to come, the Dean Wesley Smith touch on a story will signal many more reading moments in which we hover very close to the place where tears are a pleasure.*

Remember me? I was in your dream last night."

"Am I dreaming again?"

She smiled a faint smile as if he were a child and had stumbled on an adult secret. "Maybe." She shook her head back with a flip, freeing long brown hair from the collar of her open-necked blouse.

"Why?" he asked. "Why here?"

"This is where we agreed to meet." She spun playfully around, sweeping her arms at the trimmed grass, shrubs and half-filled parking lot. The light from the doors and windows of the time-worn nursing home caught in her hair as she twirled, reflecting a promise of cleanness and youth.

After one last slow spin, she stopped and faced him. "You really don't recognize me, do you, Bill?"

His memory whispered faintly, then came up blank. The answer was there, hovering in the shadows just behind the corners of his eyes. But he was old and lately had lost the ability to shine a light into those corners and come up with the right memory at the right time. He shook his head and looked down at the sidewalk and his walking cane.

"That doesn't matter," she said. "We'll give you new things to remember tonight. Now, come on. We're wasting time. Get rid of that robe and cane. We've got dancing to do."

Her laugh was high and fine, like a china bell. She curtsied to an imaginary partner. Then, pretending to dance with him, she skipped down the sidewalk toward town.

He looked back over his shoulder at the nursing home where he lived. Then back at her. Like a child standing at the gate of a circus waving for parents to hurry, she stopped and waved for him to come.

He was eighty-seven years old. He couldn't even remember getting out of bed, let alone walking down to the parking lot. How could she expect him to dance? And who was she? He shook his head. He'd been having a lot of dreams lately. What would this matter if it was just another?

He moved his cane ahead and let his right foot follow with a small step over a crack in the sidewalk. This was going to take him time, but damn it, it was his dream. He was going to follow, at least for a short distance.

His left foot caught up to his right and then the cane moved ahead again. Suddenly, he felt dizzy. God, he was dying! They were going to find his body in the morning sprawled in the bushes. What a way to go. He braced himself on his cane. Maybe he could make it back to his bed if the spinning would just pass. But it didn't. Yet it also didn't feel like what he expected from death.

His back straightened. His legs tightened. His arthritic left arm hung loose and without pain at his side. He rolled his shoulders and, for the first time in decades, enjoyed the looseness of tuned muscles. He blinked his eyes a few times. His vision cleared and the dizziness passed.

Now he knew he was dreaming. He was young again.

Down the sidewalk, Suzanne applauded and laughed.

Illustrated by David Dees

Now he remembered. Her name was Suzanne. They had met last night while walking the sidewalk. They had danced and talked until dawn.

He tossed his cane beside the sidewalk and pulled off the old bathrobe that smelled of hospitals. He had on tan slacks and matching shirt. Last night it had been blue pants and a white shirt. Suzanne had felt bad because she had gotten lipstick on his collar during one dance. She was afraid it wouldn't wash out. He couldn't even remember ever owning a shirt like that one, let alone taking it off last night.

He turned and looked up the hill at the old nursing home. The nurse had helped him into bed not more than twenty minutes ago. What was going on?

Suzanne's hand on his shoulder startled him. "Do you remember?"

He nodded. "Everything, except how I got here. How can I feel like this? I'm dead. That's it. Or dreaming."

"I don't know," she said. "What does it matter? I need to be here and I think you do too. I want to dance and laugh again. And I would like to do it with you."

The brick nursing home hugged the side of the hill above them like a shawl on a grandmother's shoulder. It offered him safety in his age. Safety in total care. Boredom in its very lack of living. He looked down at his polished shoes. A few moments before, they had been worn slippers. What did he have to lose? A little sleep? Maybe more?

She kissed him lightly. "Are you ready?"

He smiled and they held each other's gaze. He tried to set her every detail in his mind. He wanted to remember it all, tonight. Everything, all the way down to the fresh taste of rum and tonic he'd drink later.

"Don't worry," she said. "This will be fun."

"Damn right it will." He laughed, then took her arm. "But we'd better get going. I want to dance more than just the last dance."

Her bell-like laugh led them down through the spotlights of the street lamps, half-running, half-dancing between the dark homes of his grandchildren's world.

He tried never to take his eyes off her as they moved together through the music and the evening. He wanted to memorize her every smile and remember her every move.

They ate breakfast at the same cafe as the night before, then went for a stroll. It was after four and the sun was just starting to light the edges of the surrounding hills with a promise that neither of them wanted to keep.

"You know, don't you," he said as they slowly walked up toward the nursing home, "that I'm not going to be able to let this go?"

"I know," she said, looking up into his eyes. "Neither can I." A glimpse of age lodged in her eyes. She turned her head down and her face was lost in the flowing brown hair.

They walked the last block in silence, holding hands.

"How do we get back tomorrow night?" he asked her, stopping just short of his bathrobe and cane.

"We did tonight. Don't worry. We both want it. We'll be here."

"I hope you're right," he said. "Please be right."

He kissed her, then turned and picked up his bathrobe and cane.

The blurred pink face and white uniform of the nurse slowly focused into life distinct from the ceiling tiles over his bed.

"My, my, William, we were sleeping soundly this morning," the nurse said, pulling back his covers. "Why did you sleep with your bathrobe on?"

She hurried. She was always in a hurry this time of the morning. "Here, move this so we can slide you out of there." She picked up his cane and leaned it against the night stand. Then she grabbed his legs while supporting his back and levered him around into a sitting position on the edge of the bed.

"Thank you," he said. "I can handle it from here." She scurried from the room, rushing to disturb someone else.

It took him thirty minutes to use the toilet and shuffle around on his cane, dressing himself. For thirty minutes, the only thing he could think about was the dream. Maybe he was losing his mind, slipping back into the past as so many of his co-residents did. He had always thought it contemptible to refuse the present.

Yet it had seemed so real. Today, he could even remember Suzanne's name. Yesterday, he could barely remember the dream. Today, his entire body still tingled from the sensations of being young, of dancing, of rum and tonic.

Dream or no dream, he was going back this evening. He laughed out loud. That is, if he could get back.

Slippers in place, he moved step by step through the door and turned with his cane leading the way, down the hall, joining with the other slow traffic all heading for breakfast.

The dining hall was a large, high-ceilinged room with long tables lined in three straight rows. Many residents had already arrived and were sitting quietly at their places. As he started toward his usual chair, a nurse came up and asked him to help with the bibs.

Sometimes twice a week, he got to help put bibs on the less mobile residents. Normally, he loved to do it because it always made him feel useful. But this morning, all he could think about was the dream. However, if he turned the nurse down, she might not let him pass them out again.

"Of course," he said. He took the bibs over his free arm and started toward the first row. His job consisted of handing bibs to residents who could tie them themselves and putting bibs on the ones who couldn't.

He finished one side of the table and started down the other. The first two he simply handed bibs. The third was a women severely bent over in a wheelchair. He had always tied hers on for her, so he hung his cane over the handle of her chair and moved around to her side.

"Here's your bib," he said bending down and putting both strings around her neck. Then he stood and tied them, lifting her long gray hair loose from under the strings.

"Thank you, Bill," she said quietly, almost too softly for him to hear, and then looked up at him. She held his gaze for only a moment and then looked quickly back down at her lap and again her long hair fell forward and covered her face.

He stared at her for a moment, then started toward the next person down the table. It couldn't be. That crippled old lady couldn't be Suzanne. Suzanne was alive and beautiful and loved to dance.

He stopped with his back to her and looked down at his cane and his own wrinkled hand. He could still feel the smoothness of her hand in his as they walked up the sidewalk and then kissed.

He turned, went back. "Suzanne?"

The old woman turned her head and looked up at him with a faint smile. She had brown spots covering the shriveled skin on her cheeks. Suzanne's cheeks had been smooth, soft to the touch.

"I'm sorry," he said. "I thought you might be——" He stopped. He was going crazy. This couldn't be Suzanne. He hadn't met anybody last night. He was too old to dance.

"I'm sorry," he said and turned away from the wheelchair. "I must finish."

Behind him he thought he heard a faint "Bill?" But, when he stopped at the next person and handed them their bib, the hunched-over old lady had her head down and her hair covered her face.

That night, after the nurse had lifted his legs into bed, he lay awake hoping that Suzanne would come and get him. Hoping that his dreams would take him back to the feeling of control of his own body and the light-headedness that came with being in love.

But he couldn't sleep.

And Suzanne didn't come.

After an hour, he pushed his own legs out of bed. With only his bathrobe on, he made his way down the dark hall to the front door that overlooked the parking lot and the city beyond.

There was no one there. The sidewalk was empty. The street lights cast spots, making the sidewalk seem like an empty stage nightmarishly long.

The night nurse found him standing outside at midnight and scolded him as she escorted him back to his room and lifted his legs into bed.

When the nurse came in the next morning, he asked to be left in bed for the day. He couldn't face the fact that maybe that old lady had been Suzanne. Suzanne had just been one of his dreams. A wish-fulfillment that had no basis in reality. He might be dying, but he wasn't going to allow himself to lose his mind first. There were too many people here who lived in their own private worlds, ignoring who and where they were. He knew who and where he was. He was old and living in a nursing home. He couldn't dance.

At two, there was a faint tapping on his door and the old lady from breakfast wheeled herself slowly into the room.

"Excuse me, Bill," she said. "I didn't see you at breakfast or lunch. I just wanted to check if you were all right."

Bill felt his stomach tighten into a hard ball as he propped himself up on his elbows and turned toward her. She had pulled her long gray hair back and tied it so that it flowed out over the back of her wheelchair.

"I'm fine."

The old woman looked down at her hands curled in arthritic balls in her lap. It must have been very painful for her to wheel herself in here with those hands. The silence pushed between them like a closing door. She started to say something, but Bill interrupted her.

"What's your name?" he asked.

She pulled her head up until she could look him squarely in the eye. "Suzanne," she said.

He let himself fall back flat on the bed. It was just a horrible coincidence.

"Bill, are you all right?" she asked, moving her chair up to the side of his bed. "What's wrong?"

"Nothing." He turned to look at her. She was making an effort to keep her head up and level with his. He could see the pain drawing even more lines across her time-beaten face. But her eyes were open and clear. He knew those eyes. He had looked into them before.

"I had a dream," he said slowly. "For two nights I dreamt that I danced with a girl named Suzanne. I was young again."

"I also dreamt that I danced," Suzanne said. "I danced with you."

"How could we share the same dream? That makes no sense."

"Maybe it wasn't a dream."

He turned toward the window with its bar-like venetian blinds. "It was a dream. It was my dream."

Again the silence filled the space between her chair and his bed. One part of him wanted to tell her that he believed her. That part wanted to dance again tonight. But his mind overruled his heart and said it could not be real. He was old. That was a fact. He had danced when he was young. Now, it was his turn to die. And he would die without losing touch with reality.

"I'm sorry you feel that way," she said, softly. "It was my dream too. I just wanted to be happy. To dance with you. But we can't go back unless you believe. I will miss the laughing."

"Look at yourself," he said, rolling toward her. "You can't dance. Why pretend? Why not just accept that you're old and leave it alone?"

"Bill, it makes me sad to see you cling so stubbornly to this time and place. Look inside. Do you really feel old?"

"I am old."

"No. Look inside to the very soul that is Bill. Forget the shell. Do you feel old in there? Or do you feel like I do, as if there just hasn't been enough time? I'm not old. I'm just a young girl still trying to learn, trapped in a body that everyone thinks is too old to do anything but

sit. I don't want to sit. I want to dance every dance every night."

"Then explain how we——"

"I can't explain anything. Just believe that inside you're still young. Don't listen to what the nurses or your family tell you. Their bodies are still young. They haven't realized that sometimes the youngest part of your life is when your body is old."

"But if it wasn't a dream, how do we get back? I was out there last night and it didn't work."

"Believe that it will," she said. She let the space between them fill with silent thought for a moment, then broke it with a whisper. "I remember when I was a kid, I really believed that Judy found a real world over that rainbow." She laughed softly. "I still do."

"So do I," he said.

"Good. I'll meet you tonight." Without a look back, she used the palms of her twisted hands to turn her wheelchair away from the bed and move it through the door.

He lay there staring at the empty door where she had been, not noticing the traffic that moved up and down the tiled hall. If all that it needed was that he believe, then he would believe. He could do it. There was nothing to hold him here.

He took one hard look around his little room: tile floor, so the beds and the wheelchairs could move better, bars on the bed so that he didn't fall out at night, one small desk that he never used, and a mirror that he was afraid to look into. This was reality? How the hell did he get here?

The nurse woke him to ask if he wanted to go down for dinner, or have it brought in. He had been dreaming about the time, against his wife's will, that he had taken a hot-air balloon ride. He had been twenty-seven and he remembered thinking that maybe if the balloon got loose, he just might find . . . The balloon had been tethered to the ground and it didn't get loose.

"I'll pass, tonight," he said. "I'm going out later for dinner and dancing."

The nurse smiled at him and clicked the guard rail up on his bed.

He lay there and looked at the little holes in the white-tiled ceiling and thought that he really did believe. He thought of the taste of rum and tonics and the smell of Suzanne's perfume. He concentrated on his feet and let them feel the dance floor moving under his light steps. He listened to the music. Music that surrounded him and that he knew.

And it was the music of the last dance that took him.

The cold night wind played its fingers through his full head of brown hair. He clapped his hands together and laughed, then quickly took off his robe and tossed it and his cane into the bushes. He wouldn't ever need them again. Suzanne was waiting for him on the sidewalk, smiling.

He turned to her. "Remember me?" he asked.

"Of course," she said. "You dance very well."

Measuring the Light
by
Michael Green

About the Author

Michael J. Green is 31, married, with three children, and holds a master's degree. He works part-time as a librarian in Vermont, and part-time as a dishwasher. A few years ago, he began to try writing. Here is his first published story.

His story, a contest finalist, is the sort of speculative fiction that goes back as far as storytelling's most tenuous beginnings. Its theme is rooted in humankind's thus-far endless struggle to cling to the best of its nature in a world that often seems to evoke the worst. Where that nature comes from, with its madness and its mercy, its complex expressions of regimentation and its simple underlying faith that people are good and ought to be left alone, is a paradox that few creative minds have not grappled with.

Even in the history of modern science fiction, during and since the Golden Age on American newsstands at mid-century, this timeless theme has recurred countless times; under the hardware and the technological depictions, there is the constant concern with what it means to be human, and with what is in the stars, that we are situated among them with the capacity to wonder, and dream.

Here is Michael Green's dream. . . .

On the day the eggs rose in Koeningsborg, Hans Reuner slept late. It was the howling of his neighbor's dog that finally woke him, its persistence dispersing the last images of a vaguely pleasant dream. Reluctantly, he slid from beneath the covers and walked across the bedroom to the back window. Placing his palms against the sill, he leaned forward and peered out into the bright morning. Already the sun was an hour or so above the line of pines beyond the fields.

"Gaspar!" he shouted.

The dog immediately ceased barking and appeared in the doorway of the barn, looking anxiously from side to side across the yard.

"Go home," Hans yelled down. "Hey!"

But the dog simply glanced up, whimpered, and then vanished again through the door, to resume its agitated noise.

Perhaps something has happened to the hens, Hans thought, turning away and reaching for his pants. As he descended the stairs he recalled the morning some weeks past when he had entered the coop to find a small pile of blood-tipped feathers sitting atop one of the nests, and the remainder of the birds huddled quietly in the corner as if mourning their comrade's unfortunate fate. Fresh eggs or not, he always found such occurrences disturbing.

The moment he stepped out through the kitchen door, letting it swing shut behind him, he was aware that all was not as it should be, that there was a strange and unnatural element of excitement in the air. At the same time he became conscious of a curious sense of inner calm. Alerted no doubt by the slamming of the screen, the dog reappeared in the barn doorway, hesitated for an instant, and then came bounding toward him.

"What is it?" Hans asked, stroking the raised fur along its shoulders. "What's wrong?"

In answer Gaspar leapt about and charged across the yard, yelping once again. Following, Hans hoped that, after all, this would prove to be merely a matter of a lost hen or two, and nothing more. He crossed the threshold into the shadowed interior.

It wasn't so much the size of the sphere that astonished him, at first, as it was its color—the most beautiful azure blue, like a piece of pure sky. Its surface was etched with an intricate lacework of minute geometric designs. A low mound of earth and stone encircled its base; apparently the thing had emerged from underground. Filling the room from the feed trough to somewhere back beyond the coop, the incredible structure loomed over him. A muffled resonant thrumming, barely audible, pulsed softly within its core.

Without turning away from the orb, Hans walked slowly over to the nearest stall, took up a pitchfork, and returned to the doorway. The dog, after relieving himself nervously against a precariously angled beam, sat nearby and whined.

What, Hans wondered, could this possibly be? Various hypotheses immediately came to mind, though, such as an alien craft of some kind, sent to probe

Illustrated by David Dees

Earth's subterranean depths, or perhaps a time capsule constructed by an as yet undiscovered, highly advanced proto-race, buried all these years beneath his land and now everted.

After several moments of hesitant deliberation, he stepped forward and gently poked the sphere with the pitchfork. The rusted metal sank effortlessly into the semi-luminous material, meeting absolutely no resistance until it reached a depth of approximately six inches, at which point it would proceed no further. Then a faint electrical charge traveled the length of the tool and tickled his palms. Startled, Hans cried out and jumped back, stumbling over a small boulder. The fork remained hanging horizontally in the air for a number of seconds, and then, when it finally fell to the ground, all but the last inch or so of the prongs had vanished. Cautiously, Hans got back on his feet. It occurred to him that if he had any sense at all, he would leave this place at once and inform someone of his miraculous find. Bending over, he scooped up a handful of crisp pigeon droppings and tossed them at the sphere.

The instant they disappeared beneath the surface, so smoothly Hans wondered if he might not still be dreaming, a woman's voice called sharply from outside, "Gaspar." And then again, "Gaspar!"

Without so much as a glance orbward, the dog leapt up and ran from the barn.

"In here, Mrs. Kindlemier," Hans shouted. "Quickly." However at the sound of her slow shuffling footsteps, he thought that it might perhaps be best to spare her the shock of seeing the sphere unprepared. He turned and started out, but already the old woman stood in the doorway.

"Honestly," she said. "This dog of mine is more

than . . . I."

Hastily, Hans walked toward her. "Don't be alarmed, Mrs. Kindlemier. I'm not exactly sure what——"

"Good Lord," she exclaimed, looking past him, her eyes wide with surprise. "Not another one."

This of course was the last thing he expected her to say. For several moments he continued staring blankly at his neighbor and she at the sphere. Meanwhile, emboldened by the presence of his master, Gaspar made a series of snarling feints along the circumference of the dirt mound.

"What?" Hans finally managed to say.

"Gaspar," she said. "Hush." And then, once the dog had settled down, she replied, "Elisabeth, my eldest, just telephoned from town. It seems something very similar to this has emerged in Krolow Park. Her husband—you've met Georg—claims we've been invaded."

That's not unexpected, thought Hans. Judging by the few conversations he'd had with her son-in-law, a minor functionary of some sort in the town government, the young man claimed to know everything. More out of a personal distaste for Georg than for any other reason, Hans said nothing.

Mrs. Kindlemier stepped closer and cocked her head to one side. "Either my aid is acting up again, or that thing is beating like a heart."

"Watch this," said Hans, retrieving his fork. Gripping the end with the tips of his fingers, he carefully prodded the orb. Once again it sank to a depth of five or six inches and then stopped. He released it instantly. "There's some kind of a current in there, I can feel it through the handle." The pitchfork momentarily remained suspended, and then fell, once again noticeably shortened.

"Whatever it is," Mrs. Kindlemier said, touching his arm sympathetically, "it has certainly ruined your barn."

It was true. Until now, he hadn't really noticed. On both sides the beams and braces along the stalls were leaning dangerously outward. A section of the hayloft had collapsed as well, onto a pile of the previous owner's discarded furniture, smashing a glass-fronted bookcase that Hans had been meaning for months to carry inside and refinish. From high above the crown of the sphere came the sound of warbling pigeons, safe in their sun-lit spire.

"The chickens," said Hans.

With Mrs. Kindlemier and the dog trailing behind, he circled the barn and entered through the rear door. Apparently, the eruption of the globe had shaken open the hatch to the pen and the hens had escaped unharmed to their fenced yard outside.

"Look," said Mrs. Kindlemier.

A perfectly circular area, approximately half a meter in diameter, was clearly distinguishable at the orb's equator. Silver-gray in color, it lacked the delicate tracery of shimmering gold woven beneath the surface of the remainder of the sphere. A door? thought Hans. What next? For the first time he felt a small patch of fear blossom around his heart. Suppose the orb should iris open and something hostile emerge? It was a scenario he'd rehearsed perhaps a thousand times during his sixty years, most often during childhood, and yet now that it was actually about to happen, the long-awaited encounter with an extraterrestrial life form, he was more than a little ashamed to find himself poised on the verge of flight.

"I'd better phone Georg," Mrs. Kindlemier said,

startling him.

"No," Hans replied, still regarding the portal. "Don't. I'm sure he's busy enough as it is, and I——"

"But for all we know," she interrupted, her voice thickening with what Hans interpreted to be fear, "this thing may be about to explode."

He turned and looked at the old woman standing beside him. "I don't think you should worry, Mrs. Kindlemier," he said, as calmly as he could. For there was little doubt in his mind now that the orb was in fact a vehicle, of alien origin surely, although if pressed he wouldn't have been able to explain exactly what it was about the sphere that confirmed this. "I think it's a ship," he went on. "And that," he gestured upward, "must be a door."

At that instant the thrumming ceased and all was still within the barn. A feather floated down from above, crossed a shaft of slanted sunlight, and vanished into the orb.

"Someone must be told at once," Mrs. Kindlemier suddenly exclaimed, giving in at last, with the onset of the orb's ominous silence, to her own desire to flee. Abruptly she turned and left the barn, and Hans, for the moment totally absorbed in the flickering play of luminescence across the face of the ship, let her go. It was of such an amazing delicacy and ethereal beauty that it seemed preposterous to suppose that such a craft as this could have possibly burrowed up through the Earth's crust from any significant depth. It must have materialized, somehow, just beneath the surface and then subsequently risen, perhaps after having used the planet's solidity as a targeted braking device to terminate an interstellar voyage undertaken in a disembodied state. It occurred to him, though, that any theories he might devise at this point would most likely be substantially founded upon his fondness for reading science fiction rather than the objective reality before him, here in this barn, and so, in a conscious attempt to broaden the factual basis of any further conjectures, he gathered another handful of dried pigeon shit and tossed it at the orb. This time it bounced off.

Then the docking process must be complete, he decided. It's fully reassumed its corporeality.

Hans spent the next half-hour smoking his pipe, futilely awaiting additional developments. Then he fed the chickens, went back into the house, poured a glass of cold cider, and called his neighbor. "Mrs. Kindlemier," he said. "This is Hans. Did you talk to Georg?"

"No, I didn't," she replied nervously. "I've tried several times, but both lines at town hall are busy, and there's no answer at my daughter's, either."

"I'm driving in to see what's going on," he told her. "Would you like to come along?"

"Oh, yes," she answered, obviously relieved. "I'd feel much safer in town."

"I'll be right over."

After returning to the barn and taking nearly a dozen photographs of the still dormant spacecraft, Hans backed the car down his driveway and hurried next door. She was waiting for him on the front porch. "Thank you," she said, climbing in slowly and giving him a tired but heartfelt smile. She folded her hands awkwardly on the bag in her lap and sighed. "I'm too old for such excitement."

"Listen," he said, putting the car in gear. "If that thing is what I think it is, no one else in history has gone through what we just went through."

But then, remembering the other sphere in Krolow

Park, he switched on the radio and heard the newscaster from the Palmstrom station state that, at last count, close to three thousand spheres had appeared worldwide. "From Moscow to New York, from Hong Kong to Hamburg" reports of more sightings of the mysterious orbs were pouring in continuously. The latest tally for Western Europe alone was two hundred and twelve. Locally, there were two in Carinthia, two in East Klagenfurt, and one each in Morgenstern and Koeningsborg.

"At 5:16 this morning," the announcer went on, "in villages, towns and cities in every corner of the world, mankind witnessed what many have called the most miraculous occurrence of all time. Simultaneously, as if in response to an as yet undetermined signal, thousands of blue spheres, all measuring approximately thirty meters in circumference, appeared from underground. What they are, where they've come from, and why they're here, remain unknown. Ah, I understand we now have that eyewitness account I mentioned earlier, from an area farmer named . . . Tryon, in Morgenstern, who apparently watched one of these things emerge. Our mobile unit is——"

"Karl," a new voice said, "would you mind telling us again exactly what you saw?"

"Well," the farmer answered, "I was in the back barn there, milking, when I heard a loud crack and came running out, just in time too, to see this here elm topple over and fall against the house. Right where the tree was, the ground sort of swelled up some and broke apart, and then out popped this damn thing, nice and easy, all smooth and shiny, like a giant egg. By that time the wife was hollering inside, so I went in and got her to safety. When I came back around front here, I heard it ticking, like a bomb I thought, so I telephoned the authorities."

"Jesus," said Hans. "Maybe Georg is right after all, and we are being invaded." If it hadn't been for Mrs. Kindlemier, he would have gone back home immediately.

The first announcer returned. "Any thoughts, Paula?" he asked. The woman who usually hosted the weekday evening classical hour replied by observing that the number of sightings would most likely continue to escalate dramatically. "Let's not forget," she pointed out, "that for much of the world it's still the middle of the night, and as daylight comes to North and South America I suspect that we'll see an additional thousand or so confirmed reports, at least, that is, if the established pattern of distribution remains constant. Another interesting thought to keep in mind here, Ben, is the discovery we heard about previously, of two spheres off the coast of Scotland."

"By the French sub."

"That's right. Lord knows how many of these things surfaced beneath the sea."

There was an uncomfortably long pause, and then, "What about the theory Dr. Haider, of the Geological Institute, mentioned earlier, Paula, that the spheres come in pairs?"

"Yes, there's that too, Ben. If it's true, and it certainly seems to be, that nearly eighty percent of the orbs have appeared in pairs of two, separated in all cases by no more than three kilometers, then there should in fact be a companion sphere for each of the five hundred or so sightings of lone spheres reported thus far."

"So what you're saying then, is that perhaps all we've heard about so far this morning is simply the tip of the iceberg."

"Exactly. And there's one more point," the woman said, rather perfunctorily. "There have been no instances of any sightings yet, at least not any officially acknowledged ones, from New China, the Middle East war zone, South Africa, or the Brazilian war zone."

"Or your barn," Mrs. Kindlemier said softly, staring down at her hands.

Yes, my barn, thought Hans, easing the accelerator down as he retrieved a cigarette from a pack crumpled on the dashboard. What the hell was happening?

They drove the rest of the way to town in silence, listening to the sometimes strained voices on the radio. Finally, from a rise, over the pines on the slope of a hill, they saw the red rooftops of the village, and towering beyond, far above the high green fields dotted with white and black sheep, blue mountains crowned with snow.

Before dropping Mrs. Kindlemier at her daughter's house, Hans drove past the park. Clearly visible from the roadway, the sphere had emerged near the band shell. The surrounding lawn was filled with townsfolk. Clusters of loud teenagers lined the curb and children were everywhere, running and laughing through the milling crowd, slipping gracefully through the clean spring air on their bicycles. An ambulance was parked beside the central fountain, its amber lights flashing. When the car in front of them stopped to let off its passengers, Hans leaned out and gestured to a pair of approaching policemen. "Excuse me," he called. "Where can I——"

"Keep moving, old man," the younger of the two answered him. "Get that car out of the way."

"Oh, my goodness," Mrs. Kindlemier exclaimed,

turning to look through the rear window. Hans glanced back and saw two American army trucks rounding the corner, followed by a Bundeswehr jeep with a mounted machine gun. As the vehicles screeched to a halt and armed soldiers started jumping out, someone began broadcasting on a bullhorn from the direction of the orb. "Your attention, please! Your attention, please! Would everyone immediately leave this area! There's no, I repeat, no reason to panic!"

"You heard him," the cop said, rapping the bumper of Hans's car with his baton. "Party's over. Move it."

"Well," said Hans, easing forward through the traffic. "I knew they were bound to get here sooner or later." He lowered the still droning radio and lit another cigarette. "They'll probably quarantine the whole damned town." Though actually, he thought, it was surprising that the Americans hadn't arrived much earlier, their nearest base being only about twenty kilometers away. "I think maybe after I drop you off I'll walk back over and see what they're up to."

"Look at them," Mrs. Kindlemier said, as a young couple ambled across the intersection, the man carrying a plastic cooler and his companion a folded lawn chair. "You'd think it was a holiday."

"Maybe it is," Hans replied, turning and looking back at the shimmering cerulean curve rising above the spectators, who, en masse, now seemed to be pressing even closer to the globe, as if drawn by a subtle and pervasive gravity. "Maybe it is."

When he finally pulled up in front of her daughter's home, Hans requested of Mrs. Kindlemier that she say absolutely nothing to anyone about the sphere in his barn. "I don't want my farm being invaded by soldiers," he told her. "Especially American soldiers."

After expressing her doubts regarding the wisdom of such a decision and receiving his assurances that he would contact the authorities, and herself, at the slightest indication of any possible danger, Mrs. Kindlemier agreed to remain silent and, thanking him once again for his consideration, slowly climbed from the car and shuffled up the driveway.

Before returning to Krolow Park, Hans stopped at the market for a few needed items. As the clerk rang up the prices, Hans scanned the headlines of the Essen newspaper resting on the counter. PREMIER VOZNESENSKY CONDEMNS U.S. ATTACK; and BRASILIA AFLAME AGAIN; and TENS OF THOUSANDS PERISH DAILY IN MYSTERIOUS EGYPTIAN PLAGUE, with an accompanying photograph of a deserted boulevard in Cairo. "And this," he said, folding the paper under his arm.

"Might be these spaceships'll stop all this talk of war," the clerk said, nodding his head toward the stack of papers. "That's four ninety-eight. Before it's too late."

Hans handed the little bald man the money and smiled. "I doubt it."

He drove downtown and left the car in the primary school parking lot. Eating a green pepper purchased at the grocer's, he cut across the playing fields, climbed a steep rise, and entered the park from the rear. There were quite a number of people about, walking aimlessly along the pathways and sitting near the pond, conversing or tossing scraps of bread to the geese. Two policemen, talking to a huddle of young women, were standing on the old stone bridge that led to the band shell area, which Hans would have to cross in order to avoid detouring around the long way. He ducked his head and attempted to squeeze past the girls unnoticed.

"Sorry pal," one of the officers said. "That part of the park's closed."

"I know," Hans spoke up, "but I'm trying to find my granddaughter's puppy. You haven't seen a beagle around, have you? She says she lost it on the main lawn. Ran away in the crowd, I guess."

"Sorry," the patrolman answered, taking a step closer and placing his hand firmly against Hans's chest. "Can't let anyone through."

"Oh, come on," said Hans. "She's carrying on like crazy; I've got to find it. Besides," he pointed toward the band shell up on the hill, "there's still some people over there." A group of stragglers was in fact coming down the hemlock-bordered trail toward the bridge.

"Go ahead, then, Pops," the other policeman said. "Go look for your dog. But if I were you, I'd make it quick. Hey, you!" he shouted at the others. "Over here."

Instead of continuing on the path, as soon as he turned the first corner Hans slipped through a break in the shrubbery and cautiously made his way to within sight of the sphere. There were a dozen or so military men surrounding its base and a handful of what appeared to be civilians, scientists most likely, gathered around one fellow who was studying the orb through a large camera or scanning device. It was in every respect, at least from this distance, an exact replica of the ship that had emerged in his barn. The portal or door, silver-gray and perfectly centered along the globe's equator, stared out across the now empty lawn. Over by the band shell more soldiers were smoking and setting up additional equipment. A helicopter arrived, circled twice, and then went off as suddenly as it had appeared. For nearly half an hour, safely hidden amidst a patch of thick brush, Hans watched them measure, record, and after much debate, probe the sphere with a variety of instruments. Then one of the uniformed men wandered toward him, and as he unzipped and started urinating, Hans stood and walked away.

Angling through the woods and leaving the park via the Pointek Avenue entrance, which was also guarded, he returned to his car and drove straight home, switching off the radio (now tuned to a listener-sponsored station) upon hearing a nationally renowned artist proclaim that the spheres were in actuality the uppermost anchors of the world's interior framework, exposed at last because "we've finally worn this earth away."

Hans spent the remainder of the morning in the barn, observing the orb, waiting for something to happen. Finally, after taking a few more photos and tossing one last clump of crusty straw against the spacecraft, he went inside and made a ham sandwich. Opening a cold bottle of beer, he searched through the kitchen cabinets until he found his wife's transistor radio, which, he wasn't too surprised to discover, no longer worked at all, the metallic nipples of the batteries being coated with a fine growth of rust. Spreading the newspaper open across the dish cluttered table, he attentively read through the lead articles while he ate.

Officially, the war between Chile, Venezuela, and Brazil had begun over two years ago, the one between Iraq and Iran fifteen years ago, and the South African conflict—the smallest but in many ways already the most savage—only last winter. In all three cases the nations involved were ostensibly acting without any outside provocation or substantial support. Of course New China, America and the Soviet Union endlessly accused one another of causing and prolonging not only these wars but the dozen or so comparatively minor skirmishes and revolutions forever occurring elsewhere. While glancing through an account of the latest instance of superpower finger-pointing and doctrinaire posturing, Hans realized that the truth of the accusations was probably no longer of much importance. After a century of nearly continuous hostility worldwide, and certainly since the neutron bombing of Libya in eighty-eight, the general consensus seemed to be that any localized regression to a state of abject barbarity, whatever the cause, was preferable by far to an all-out nuclear exchange; in fact, little conventional wars, however numerous, were apparently the sole viable alternative, however temporary, to a final, unconventional one. Lately though, with the direct American intervention in the Philippines and the blatantly Soviet-sponsored coup and resulting massacre in Bangladesh, why, things seemed to be getting just a bit out of control.

Hans refolded the paper carefully, snapped it sharply against his knee, as he'd been taught to do as a boy, and lobbed it into the kindling box beside the hearth. So much for the news, he thought, finishing his beer. I might as well tend to my garden.

All his adult life, somewhere in the back of his mind, he had wanted to live at a place where he could raise an abundance of vegetables, and somehow, although he still didn't know exactly why it had taken him so long to do so—he had moved onto the farm two years ago, right after his wife's death and his subsequent early retirement from teaching at the university—it wasn't until this spring that he had finally planted his first seeds. There was something undeniably miraculous about watching sprouts break ground and flourish. And now, standing beside the fence with a splashing hose in his hand, almost in spite of himself he looked back at his years of city life, so active and apparently fruitful, as being, well, rather barren.

After wetting the garden thoroughly, Hans pulled weeds for close to an hour, placing whatever fat worms he came across into a dirt-filled coffee can for to-morrow's visit to the Badenbeal canal. He considered asking Mrs. Kindlemier to accompany him, for a change of pace, and then decided against it. No doubt she would be remaining in town in any case, minding the grandchildren she always spoke so highly of. His thoughts turning to his own offspring, his daughter killed in the first Prague uprising and his young son, a NATO soldier, lost in the Battle of the Sphinx, as it had come to be called, Hans put the hose on again, rinsed his hands, and returned to the barn to smoke his pipe away from the hot sun.

He saw instantly that the sphere was unmistakably brighter, more translucent. The luminous webbing beneath its surface had all but vanished, and the portal was much darker than previously. A soft vibrant humming again arose from the interior. Pipe gripped firmly between his teeth, Hans set up a tall stepladder and cautiously ascended to look into the window. Except for his own reflection staring back, there was nothing to be seen.

He spent the remainder of the afternoon reading in the hammock, mowing the back lawn, and then reading once again until he finished the novel, checking the orb at regular intervals throughout, only to find it unchanged each time. Feeling quite drowsy as a result of drinking a second beer, Hans closed the book, and then his eyes, and fell asleep.

The birds gathering noisily in the treetops for dusk finally woke him. He lay still for several moments watching the branches shift against the gold-edged clouds overhead, trying to recapture as many images as he possibly could from his dreams, a habit retained from childhood. Then the morning's occurrences sprang to mind and he swung himself out of the hammock and hurried across the yard to the car. Sitting sideways behind the wheel, his feet on the ground, he lit his pipe and listened to the radio, changing stations whenever the talk grew too shallow or repetitive.

According to the latest accounts, the estimated number of confirmed sightings now totaled six thousand and fifty, some five thousand four hundred of which were pairs, or twin spheres, separated by no more than three kilometers. Every reliable source described the globes as being identical in size, shape and color. No government acknowledged reports regarding any sightings had yet emerged from New China, the second largest and most populous country in the world, or from the Middle East or Brazilian war zones. In addition, numerous nations which had previously issued periodic bulletins, including the Soviet Union and most of Eastern Europe, were now mysteriously silent about any subsequent developments. There were countless instances of bogus orbs being reported, apparently in some cases even on an official level, especially in Central America. Riots had broken out in Calcutta and Ankara, Manila and Miami. The Berlin stock market, plummeting to a twenty-year low in five hours, had closed early in chaos. NATO forces were on red alert; the Pope was due to speak at any moment; war had begun between North and South Korea, Thailand and Vietnam; and all schools in Palmstrom, East Klagenfurt and Koeningsborg were dismissed until further notice. Having heard enough, Hans shut off the ignition and walked slowly to the barn, wondering how it all would end.

Once again the sphere appeared to be significantly lighter in color, clearer and more luminous. The lacework of silver tracery was no longer distinguishable beneath the surface, and it was quiet. Hans brought in the chickens, fed them, checked their water and then went over to the orb and touched it with his hand. It was warm.

He climbed the ladder and looked into the window. It too had changed. Although now jet-black, like a pure disk of ebony, it had assumed a state of porous granularity, a foggy murkiness beyond which could just be seen the shadowed outline of a narrow channel receding into the bowels of the orb. Shifting his weight, Hans leaned closer and peered down the passageway. A vague shape, barely visible behind the thin veil covering the portal, suddenly stood and walked toward him.

He jumped from the ladder and ran for the door, a loud groan escaping from his lips, a strangulated cry for help. When he kicked a plank of wood lying in his path and fell to his knees on the floor, he looked back expecting to see a new kind of death come sweeping down and enfold him in its cold burning wings. Instead, Bertolt, a stray tomcat who occasionally visited the farm, leaped out onto the top step of the ladder, sat, and began sleepily licking its paws. It wasn't until it finally descended, stretched and then skulked away that Hans recovered from the shock.

But how, he wondered, brushing the bits of straw off his legs as he stood, could he be certain that that in fact was Bertolt? He whistled to the cat softly, but already it was gone.

Hans climbed the ladder once more, more cautious than ever, and looked again into the orb. When he eventually reached out and felt the doorway, and then passed his hand through the amorphous field of darkness, a flickering sensation of pleasure washed up his forearm to his chest, causing his scalp to tingle, his scrotum to retract, and his eyes to tear. Pulling away rapidly, he just about tumbled headlong to the ground. It's alive, was his first thought.

He repeated the experiment several times, experiencing a similar rush of mild energy with each instance of contact. "I'll be damned," he said aloud. Then he heard the telephone ringing in the house, and since there were very few people who could be calling, he climbed back down the ladder and hurried from the barn.

"Hello, Hans? How are you?" Mrs. Kindlemier said. "Has anything happened to the sphere?"

"Are you home?" he asked.

"Yes," she answered, and after a moment of silence, continued. "You see, I decided that since I've lived here most of my life, well, I'd just as soon die here too."

"Why? What's going on in town?"

"Nothing, it's the rest of the world I'm worried about. Have you been listening to the radio?"

"I know."

"It's just terrible. What's wrong with people these days?"

"Did you tell anyone about the sphere?" he asked.

"No," she replied. "I didn't."

"Good," Hans said. "Thank you. I saw the one in town, by the way, and it's identical to ours." He paused. "Were there still a lot of soldiers around, when you left?"

"No, not really. They've completely blocked off the

park, though, and Georg says the Americans are going to try to move the thing to their base tonight. Carry it away by helicopter, or something. He says they're actually quite light, and that they've already transported the orb in Morgenstern."

"Did he say what time?"

"They've started by now, I should think."

"Maybe I'll drive in and watch," he said. "If I can get close enough."

"You'd better be careful, Hans. Even Georg had some trouble with a guard, or someone, coming home. Elisabeth is very worried; I almost talked them all into spending the night here with me."

"Are you sure you'll be okay alone?" he asked. "Should I call you when I get back?"

"If you don't mind," she said. "And if it's not too late."

Touched by the sound of her kind voice in his ear, he promised he'd telephone by nine at the latest and tell her what he'd learned in town. "Don't worry," he said, hanging up.

He made a quick sandwich, searched for his keys until he remembered that they were still in the car, and left by the back door. While speaking with Mrs. Kindlemier he had noticed through the kitchen window that with the gathering darkness of nightfall the orb now filled the barn with an eerie iridescent light that was surely visible from the road. He crossed the yard and entered the doorway. Chewing a mouthful of bread and ham, he watched the quietly humming sphere thoughtfully, wondering for perhaps the hundredth time what purpose it possibly served by being here. Switching on the lights to mask its glow, he swung the doors closed and walked down the driveway. The Moon was up now, floating above the house like a watchful eye. He could smell the garden in the night air, rich and fertile with still fresh manure, and imagined, listening to the whisper of crickets across the lawn, thousands of spheres breaking silently through the cold lunar stone, sapphire seeds alive in a barren, gardenless void.

A half-kilometer from town he was stopped by a Bundeswehr patrol. "Excuse me, sir," a young soldier said, shining his flashlight directly into Hans's face. "We'd like to ask you a few questions."

"All right," Hans answered. "Should I pull over?"

"That won't be necessary." Another figure appeared from the shadows carrying a clipboard. "You live around here?" he asked.

After taking Hans's name and address, the second soldier explained that they were looking for a sphere which they believed to have surfaced in the area. "You know what I'm talking about?" he muttered.

"Yeah," said Hans. "I was in town this morning. But that's the only one I've seen, or heard about, around here."

"Got any neighbors that might've noticed something?"

"Only one, an old lady by the name of Kindlemier. Nothing there though. I just talked to her on the phone."

"Mind if we check your place out? That is, if we get up that way tonight?"

"No, go ahead," Hans replied.

The first soldier clicked off his light and stepped back. "Thanks for the tip," was all he said.

As he started to pull away he heard a radio crackle and come to life. Three or four men were lounging on the roadside, smoking and passing a canteen. One of them nodded his head and smiled at him, and Hans felt foolish for being afraid.

When he arrived in town he left the car at the bank and approached the park on foot. In the distance he could hear faint voices calling, but nothing more. Strolling down the sidewalk along a row of well-kept brownstones, beneath windows illuminated with an aura of domestic tranquility, Hans found it hard to believe that this was anything other than a perfectly normal, peaceful spring evening.

There was a police barricade erected at the next intersection, though, one block from the park. A small group of people were gathered under a streetlight on one side of the avenue and a handful of patrolmen on the other. After a moment's hesitation, Hans began walking toward the closest police car. He was just about to call over to an officer standing nearby when he heard the first tremors of a distant thunder coming down the valley. Realizing that there wasn't time enough left for him to talk his way through the blockade, he turned away and tried to think of a better solution. With each passing second the rhythmic pulsations grew more distinct. Glancing upward, searching the sky for the approaching helicopter, Hans saw the spire of the old Catholic church outlined against the moonlit clouds, rising high above the other buildings of the town. Having climbed the tower once before, with a flock of foreign tourists who regularly ascended its heights to marvel at the restored medieval interior and the quaint village spread below, Hans knew that from there he would have a fairly good view of the band shell area of the park. Quickly crossing the street and cutting through an arched alleyway that emerged behind the church's adjoining rectory, he hoped the door would be open.

And it was. In fact, there were quite a few people scattered in the pews, praying with bowed heads and rounded backs. Hans turned down a dark corridor, stepped over a low railing posted with the tower's hours of operation, and began climbing the stairs, resting only once at the mid-point landing. He reached the top just as one of the helicopter's searchlights sprayed wildly across the small stone-walled room, illuminating the brass bell that filled its center in a golden strobic flash.

"Hello," Hans called over the steady roar to the young woman standing before one of the windows.

"You're just in time," she replied loudly, not in the least startled by his sudden apparition. "Best seats in the house, too."

He circled the bell and looked down. The helicopter was maneuvering into position above the sphere, lowering three large grappling hooks as the wind from its blades swept through the trees like an invisible storm. The luminous orb, wrapped in a harness of wire and fencing, was nearly transparent now, a giant glass marble, a minute crystallized star. On its crown a lone soldier gathered in the dangling lines from the helicopter with a long pole and then set to work attaching them to a knot of steel rings at his feet, as his companions watched motionless from below like so many tiny toy figurines arranged in a playful tableau.

"Fucking morons," the girl said. Hans turned from the window and for the first time looked at her closely. She was very pretty, and he suddenly realized, crying. Miniature searchlights sparkled in her eyes and down her cheeks where the tears were slowly falling. "Don't they realize that this is our last chance?" she said, speaking forcefully, as much from bitterness as from a desire to be heard over the steady wash of noise that enveloped them.

Soon a second man climbed the ladder leaning against the orb, inspected one of the points of linkage, and then both men returned to the ground. Everyone cleared away as a soldier standing on the top step of the band shell lifted two red neon batons and signalled. With practiced ease, the helicopter rose until the steel threads falling from its belly pulled taut and lifted the bright egg gently from the earth, away over the trees, floating like Glinda's diaphanous bubble in Oz, Hans thought, until it finally vanished into the quieting night.

Where the orb had rested there was now merely a slight depression, within which large patches of grass could be seen, hardly disturbed, as though the sphere had risen from underground with only a minimum degree of force, passing through the stone and dirt by some mysterious osmotic process. Suddenly feeling very tired and alone, Hans ran his hands through his hair and sighed. "What did you mean before?" he asked the girl. "About this being our last chance."

She wiped her eyes again and shrugged. "I have this crazy theory," she said, still looking out the window. "It's been bugging me all day." The engines of the trucks were starting below as the portable arc lights flicked out, one by one, and the soldiers prepared to depart. "I think the eggs have always been here," she went on. "I think they were buried by someone as soon as life began on Earth. Or maybe later, not much later, but it doesn't really matter exactly when. All this time they've been down there though, not watching us, but waiting, waiting to see how we would turn out. And I think the last few years, hell, the last few centuries, have convinced them of the inevitable outcome. And now they're all leaving, escaping to another planet maybe, to try again, or just going back home, while we proceed to blow ourselves to smithereens."

"That's the best theory I've heard all day," Hans told her after a long pause. "Let's hope to God you're wrong."

He said good night and left her standing at the window, looking up at the stars, her long hair stirring softly in the breeze.

On the way home, in order to avoid hearing about the latest exchange of threats between the superpowers, which seemed to be on every other station, Hans listened to an interview with a Frankfurt physicist who outlined in detail the first steps to be undertaken in studying the spheres, which would involve a thorough analysis of their molecular structure and, he went on to predict, the probable discovery of matter of unusual isotopic composition that could not be explained by known or plausible processes within the Solar System.

"I don't follow you," said the announcer.

And neither do I, thought Hans, pulling into his driveway and switching off the car. At this point, at the conclusion of what would surely prove to be the single most important day in the history of mankind, did it really matter so much what the spheres were made of? Gripping the wheel and resting his head on his hands, feeling more tired than he'd felt in a long, long time, he thought not.

He entered the barn a few minutes later and stared absentmindedly at the orb. Except for the circular black window, it was now completely transparent, as if fashioned of the purest crystal. Minute scintillating lights flickered randomly beneath its surface, silver and white, and for an instant Hans had the illusion he was gazing down into an immeasurably deep well lined with stars.

Not knowing what else to do, he climbed the ladder and looked into the portal. Still obscured by the shadowy veil covering its opening, the narrow channel appeared unchanged. Hans passed his hand into the dark field, and, failing to feel the lazy wave of pleasure spread throughout his body, leaned closer, and saw that from the elbow down his forearm had emerged from the other side of the membrane. As if compelled to do so by an unconscious force, he climbed one step higher, shifted his balance, and then pushed his head and shoulders through the boundary of his universe.

He fell for what seemed like hours.

Then it stopped and he was floating weightlessly in an utterly silent, utterly black void, entombed by nothing, in a warm womb of absolute night. Bringing his arms close, he folded his legs up and tightly hugged his knees. He was no longer afraid. After the first insane moments of his screaming plunge through the endless passageway, kicking and flailing wildly, yelling and crying and then quietly sobbing, he had eventually resigned himself to his incomprehensible fate. Or perhaps it was simply that he had finally slipped into a condition of acute shock. In any case, he was now no longer afraid. Curled in a fetal ball, he rotated gently in the air, his breath coming and going, coming and going, his heart pulsing softly in his ears.

Whether or not he slept for a short while, he could not have said. In the state of unsensing nonexistence in which he found himself suspended, the difference between waking and sleeping, or for that matter living and dying, was scarcely to be perceived. Time passed, of that he was certain. At one point he spread his limbs and attempted to swim through the nothingness, but to no avail. Folding his arms across his chest, he lay still and waited, staring up, or down, into fathomless space. Soon all reference points receded and lifelong barriers between interior and exterior were removed. The darkness that encompassed him became an extension of internal space, reaching as far as the pivotal point of his personal balance allowed, until that too vanished.

Deprived of all stimuli, his mind slowly began fabricating a world of its own. What he at first took to be a particularly persistent gleam of phosphene in his eyes intensified until, like a curtain rising, he was abruptly conscious that he was seeing in the darkness. In fact, there was now a great deal of diffuse light shimmering around him, and he suddenly felt as though he had crossed an important threshold and was moving rapidly toward radical transformations. Incredibly intricate and flawless geometric images appeared from nowhere, self-amplifying and transitory, extraordinarily clear and at first rigorously independent of one another. Good heavens, Hans thought to himself, as they began multiplying and merging to form a unified three-dimensional grid of impossible complexity, I'm hallucinating like crazy! But despite the continuing perceptual pyrotechnics he was relieved to discover that he was not losing his rational awareness. Indeed, he was conscious of an increased clarity of mental process, to a degree never before experienced in his life.

When the magic abstract tapestry dissolved into unearthly landscape, embellished with surrealistic precision and, Hans was glad to see, a familiar amorphous sensuality, he began moving again, gliding above mad cliffs and chasms with effortless speed. A timeless, teeming jungle appeared, cut diagonally by a rainbow river. Then a glass city rose from a road-webbed desert. Blue, wide mountains. A storm-driven sea.

What eventually fell into place, as somehow Hans suspected it would, was the past. Friendly faces came and spoke to him. Hands reached out or just waved. Backs were turned. Once it was a green summer morning and he was digging in the damp sand and no one else was around. Tucked in bed late at night, he saw the lights from the passing cars fly across his ceiling, countable like the days. When he threw a rock at his brother Sigmund and broke one of his teeth, Hans was so upset he was given a treat. The first girl who lay on her back and opened herself to his lust. The thirty years of teaching about books and broken men and women, passing like an empty train through a busy town.

The first night he got drunk and then waded far out into a dangerous stream.

Sleeping in fresh snow and waking up alone.

Playing ball for seasons at a time, measuring the years by how good you are.

Sitting behind his naked wife, holding her and wiping her brow as she pushed their first baby out into the world.

"Easy," the midwife said. "Easy now."

She slipped one hand into Maria's body and pressed down with the other against her swollen belly. Hans offered his wife a drink of water, then took a sip himself and set it down again on the night table beside the ticking clock. It was three in the morning. Outside, the world was asleep.

"Here it comes," Maria said, arching and panting, forcing his back painfully against the headboard for the hundredth time.

Finally, the water broke and splashed onto the mattress. Quanita, the midwife, smiled. "Feel better?"

Then the contractions began in earnest as the head and shoulders passed through the interior portal and entered the passageway. After propping her securely against a wedge of pillows and blankets, Hans climbed between his wife's legs and prepared to catch the child.

Massaging her thighs with what he hoped was sufficient pressure, it occurred to him that what he was about to behold here was God's most precious gift to a man. In due time the wet wrinkled scalp appeared, then the little tired face and clutching hands, so fragile and afraid.

"It's a girl," Maria said, crying and reaching down. "My little girl."

Later, kneeling beside the quiet bed, watching the infant drink her first mouthfuls of milk, Hans knew what it meant to be alive.

Quanita called his name gently from the doorway. Kissing the child's wrist, he stood and left the room.

"Congratulations," she said, as he walked over to the kitchen table for a cigarette.

He turned and looked at her, striking a match and grinning boyishly, and saw a creature kilometers long, all alabaster and jade, stretching into infinity.

"Do not be afraid," it said inside his head. "I mean you no harm."

Hans felt the flame bite into his fingers, and then the match, the kitchen, and the world dissolved. Only the alien remained, beautiful and true.

"Your journey will be a safe one," it said. "We have gathered as many of your kind as we could."

As the creature vanished and the black vacuum reappeared, Hans felt himself rising, soaring into a vertical whirlwind until he was aware of nothing but his ascent. Then the darkness changed its nature and he realized he was seeing the surface, speckled with moonlit clouds, of

the receding Earth.

Rising vertiginously above her he saw an isolated city glimmering off to the east, a faint phenomenon on the shell of a small sphere floating in infinite space. A strange melancholy force was holding him, which was the planet's weight. He imagined the other eggs ascending in diamonded brightness, sailing upward toward the stars, each carrying a lone passenger, or perhaps several, within its core.

Then, oddly enough, he suddenly remembered that he'd neglected to telephone Mrs. Kindlemier upon returning home. But she must be sleeping by now, he told himself. And he thought of all the others below, sleeping peacefully in their beds, or graves. For a moment, it seemed as though the entire planet must be resting from its labors.

A Way Out
by
Mary Frances Zambreno

About the Author

Lifelong Chicago-area resident Mary Frances Zambreno has never formally studied creative writing. She has, however, taught writing as a public high school English teacher. After that, she returned to the University of Chicago to work toward a doctorate in Medieval Literature, which she estimates is a year away, bringing with it what will be a long job-search. A part-time librarian and part-time college teacher now, she can read Spanish, French, Italian, Latin and Anglo-Saxon, as well as being able to write strikingly in English. She entered the second-quarter contest in hope of gaining third place. She won Second, thus—to paraphrase her reaction—making her creditors half again as happy as she'd thought.

It seems to us that Ms. Zambreno splendidly represents that unheralded world of patient, educated persons who sometimes wryly persist in an attempt to kindle a little light in a generally inattentive universe, and who often accurately expect very little in return. You will be impressed, we think, by how much she illuminates for us in A Way Out, and we rather expect that it will, from start to finish, hold your attention.

Stairs got taller and taller every flight. The old black woman paused at the half-landing, leaning against the cinderblock wall and panting heavily. Her cane braced against the opposite wall held her steady. Come on, old woman, you can do it; round the turn, then twelve more steps to the next floor. Floor sixteen, that'd be. She'd long since given up counting by days or weeks, and the hours all ran together into dark and light since her watch had stopped for the last time. Twelve more steps—that'd be two floors for the day. Not a bad score.

Once she'd run up and down two flights of stairs twenty, thirty times a day, back when Jimmy'd opened that little produce stand over on Fifty-seventh. Someone had to keep the books; Jimmy was a good provider, but the man was hopeless with numbers. Only you can't leave babies alone, so she'd run up, down, around— Lord, Lord, how long ago had that been? She pushed white hair behind her ear with one claw-like hand. Longer ago than she cared to remember. Those had been good days, before the business failed—failed all over. Even moving into this place hadn't been so bad. They'd lived on the fifth floor, with everything in the whole tall building clean and new. Hadn't stayed that way long, but still a project was just a place to live, those days, before folks started runnin' down at the heart; before the city added the top floors and sealed off the bottom for parking; before they closed all the stairways and built new ones where the elevators had been. That was what to look for now, an old elevator shaft. She knew she could find one, did she get to the roof—weren't no elevators anymore after that day; people just had to walk, and old folks stayed in their apartments, mostly. She'd mostly stayed on the twenty-seventh floor, then, but did she get to the roof she could find the right way down all right. Easy enough to tell new building from old on the roof; there'd been playgrounds up there once.

Come on, old woman.

She hooked her cane around the door at the top of the stairs. Sixteen, the faded yellow letters said; sixteenth floor. Well, now, that wasn't so bad, not bad at all for a woman who was, what? Ninety-five? Ninety-six? Hard to remember sometimes. The women of her blood had always been long-lived. There'd been Granny Cilla Mae, her mother's father's mother, who'd lived to see great-grandchildren grown and married. Old Cilla claimed to remember the days of slavery and even before, and to a thin pigtailed child pressed up beside a kitchen chair and marvelling it had seemed perfectly possible. Hundreds of years it would take to get those wrinkles and white hair; black folk didn't *get* such.

She had her own wrinkles now, and her hair—what she could see of it—was as white as the snows of her childhood. But she didn't have any grandchildren: her girl-baby had died birthing and then Jim Junior died in the war. The fight seemed to go out of his father when that happened; reckon most folks reached a limit somewheres.

The door opened on a dark hall. She didn't like dark halls—when the lights weren't working, people got bad.

Illustrated by Frank Ferrel

But it was daylight still—she could see the hall window from where she stood—and she could do with a drink of water. Could be the automatics were still working. On the fourteenth floor the lights had been on but the food was off, and she was hungry. Back on twelve, there'd been a family, warned her about going ahead, offered her food. Nice to know there were still good folk like that in the building . . . course, old people don't eat much.

She hunkered down next to the food processor. Agh, nothing—well, water of course—no, wait. Her old hands hunted around in the back of a machine never intended to be searched so. Food there; bread, and some sort of salted meat. Synthetic, of course, but it would do. Greedily, she tore at the bread with old teeth. Good thing her teeth were good. Don't know what she would do did she get gum rot.

The lights worked every other floor or so. The food processor, maybe every third. Occasionally she wondered if there was still someone pushing the buttons or if the whole system'd gone on automatic. Lord help them all if a gear failed or a wire broke. Hadn't been any repair crews in the old days, let alone now. Lord knew if there were even repair crews still alive, outside; certain they never came in. Sometimes she went to one of the unopenable-because-too-dangerous windows and looked out on the endless gray fog surrounding the building and wondered if there was anyone at all still out there. Had been a city out there once; reckon there still was. Reckon they hadn't dropped the bomb or everything would have gone all together—leastways, that's what folks always said. Might not be, though. Maybe the pollution killed everyone outside and left only those few pockets of inside-folks living. Lord knew it was ugly enough. Better past the twenty-seventh floor; up that high you could look down on the smog and pretend it was just clouds.

More likely folks outside had just plain forgot folks inside. Wasn't easy to get out of this place; in the old days most people hadn't even wanted to think about coming in. You didn't live in the projects if you could find even the meanest, rat-infested slum elsewhere. Only the cockroaches weren't too particular to live in a cement maze. Placidly chewing, she let eyes follow a trail of bugs running along a fake sideboard. That's it, roaches, you and me know where we goin'. Someone had taken up the tile on this floor. Probably lining someone's apartment somewhere. Made it easier on the roaches. Spray paint on the walls, the usual sort of words: "Sons of Satan" this time. Gang name, most like, new or old. Young folk.

Noise on the stairs; footsteps. Quiet, but old ears hear good. Folks comin' to use the processor, like—maybe the only one for several floors. She'd have to take food with, did she try for the seventeenth and a lighted floor before night.

The old woman didn't twitch as the hall door opened behind her, but her eyes shifted like black jewels.

"Hey!" Young folk all right. "What you doin' here, old woman?"

"Eatin'," she answered, not turning. Three, maybe four by the sound of them. About twelve or thirteen years, from the voice's height.

"You don't live in this territory."

She turned to look up. "Just passin' through."

Four, it was, all with oily skin caked from not washing. One had rust-red hair, tight curled and frizzy. The littlest wore a yellow shirt.

The boy who had spoken was the tallest; he wore shorts and no shirt, and a jagged pink scar cut down the smooth tawny hide across his breastbone. Young folk, fightin'. He sniggered. "Passin' through? From where to where?"

"From down," she pointed, "to up."

"Yeah? Well, you got no call usin' our food 'less you ask permission. This here's Sons' territory. We say what goes here."

"You wasn't here," she pointed out reasonably. The fourth boy's arm hung crooked—broken once and not healed straight.

"It's okay, Steen," Yellow Shirt said nervously. "She ain't no spy from up-bove. Ain't no women 'tall up there no more."

"Did I say she a spy?" Steen asked angrily. "Did I say? You just listen before you talk, boy."

Yellow Shirt dropped his eyes. "I was just——"

"You was just speakin' up, that's what you was doin', and *I* say what's for speakin' up round here!" He whirled back. "What you be, old woman? What you be *doin'* here?"

"Eatin' and passin' through," she said placidly, patiently. "Just goin' on up to the roof."

"You go on up to twenty and the Disciples'll get you," Crooked Arm said with relish. "Ain't got no food processors up there—they been eatin' people."

"That so."

"'Tis," he affirmed eagerly. "It's only us what keeps folks on these floors safe, ain't it, Steen?"

"Reckon so," his leader said. "I reckon *so*. We keep folks safe and folks listen to us. 'Cause we are *in* charge, man. Old woman, you better go down to fifteen. You be safe there."

"I don't think so," she said. "I'm goin' up."

"But they eat you!" Yellow Shirt protested. "Ain't you 'fraid?"

"Reckon not," she said, unobtrusively slipping a hunk of bread into the capacious double-hem of her apron. "Reckon not. Never been et before. Might be interestin'."

"Why you goin' up?" Red Hair said, speaking for the first time. "Down's easier."

"Been down. Been all the way down those stairs. Ain't nothing down there but a cement wall."

"So?"

"So now I'm goin' up. I'm lookin' for a way out; figure I can find one, do I start at the top." That had been her first mistake, starting down at the twenty-seventh floor. But going down was so much easier on her arthritic knees. "I won't bother you none. Just let me be to breathe and I'll be on my way."

"A way out?" the boy said slowly. "Way out where?"

She looked at him. "Outside," she answered. "Outside the building, under the open sky. . . ."

The boy named Steen sniggered again. "You crazy, old woman! Ain't nothing out there! They closed up the doors long, long time, fore we all was born."

"Fore you was born," she reminded him. "I'm old. I remember——"

"Yeah? Well, just you try that crazy old talk on the Disciples! They eat you, they will. And maybe," his sneer became leeringly suggestive, "maybe first they do other things. Reckon they most as tired of no women as no food, up there."

"Reckon I'll see," she said.

"Reckon you will, crazy old woman." One hard young hand took her by the shoulder. "Get outta the way—we *hung*ry."

She let him twist her, using his strength to keep from getting hurt, then limped over to the window. Sun near down, but she had bread in her pocket and her bottle was full of water. Calmly she rested against the window sill, waiting for the boys to leave so she could take her own slow way upward. Might be a good idea to carry extra food . . . could come in handy if folks upstairs was really so hungry they'd eat a stringy old carcass like hers.

The redheaded boy brought his food to within a few paces of her. She lowered at him suspiciously but didn't speak.

"You want water?" he asked finally.

"No."

"Good water—no rust."

"I had my fill."

He looked away from her down the hall to the half-circle of the others, spoke into his own shoulder.

"Why you goin' up?"

She shrugged. "I said——"

"I heard. You really been all the way to the bottom?"

"All the way."

"What floor you start with?"

"Twenty-seventh. Been down this way once already, on the other stairs. Now I'm comin' up on this one. Ain't no way out down there this side of the building. Used to be a crossover on the third floor, but they blocked it up with the parking wall."

"You really think you can get out from the roof?"

"Got to be a way out somewheres; air's gettin' in somehow, up and down all along the line, and the air-conditioning's been broke since before you was born."

He looked at her uncomprehendingly. "You go into the stairwells, do you want fresh air."

"Hey, Sappha!" Steen called peremptorily. "You goin' to sit there all night? You and Cam got first guard."

"There's lights upstairs," the boy whispered fearfully. "On eighteen, way back. Disciples don't start till twenty; you be safe on eighteen for tonight."

"Hey, Sappha!"

"I goin'——"

But the three others stood in a half-circle around him and her now; Steen almost purred.

"You talkin' up the old bag, Sappha? You feel maybe like samplin' Disciples' meat fore they get to tastin' it?"

"No, Steen, honest! I was just, was just askin'——"

"Askin' what?" His eyes turned to the old woman. "Don't think I'm buyin' your story, old woman. Could be you come from above the Disciples. Could be they 'acruited you for a spy."

"I never saw a Disciple, nor even want to," she said, eyes narrowing. "Last folks I saw was some few floors back, and I'm goin' up, not down. I won't bother you none. I'm just goin' for a way out."

"What you want do that for?" Yellow Shirt blurted out. "What's wrong with in here?"

She considered. "Nothing, I reckon. I guess I just got a hankering to find if there is anyone else out there, or if we been forgot all these years. Don't you ever wonder?" Black eyes dared them, the redheaded boy, dared them all.

"No," Steen said. "Ain't no way out, old woman. Never was——"

"Was once," she said. "We all got in somehow."

"——and never will be!" Finishing loudly. "We stay in our own territory, no sense to goin' off explorin' and maybe gettin' killed."

"You can get killed here, too," she reminded him. "Don't the Disciples kill you once and again?"

Indrawn breath told her she'd scored a hit, but she couldn't locate the source. Neither could Steen.

"What you goin' *do,* if you get out, hah?" he asked desperately. "Tell me, what you goin' *do?*"

"Same as I do here, I reckon, only outside."

"You crazy, old woman!"

"You already said that."

"I say it again! You crazy, and you goin' die, and there ain't no way——"

"Steen, don't!" Sappha stepped in front of him. "She only a crazy old woman. Let her go!"

"You challengin' me, boy? You——" He twisted the redhead's arm behind him. "I'm leader of the Sons! *I* say what goes!"

"Let him be!" the old woman said sharply. She raised her cane. "Sons my left foot—ain't none of you knows what the devil is anymore, save the little one you carries in you. I said let him be!"

Her cane swung.

"Hey, you old——!"

Steen lunged for the shadow against the end of the wall. She wasn't quick anymore, but you don't stay alive ninety-five or -six years without learning some tricks. Her cane looped down to catch at his ankle, adding the force of a fall to that of his own rush. He fell into the window, and the old, thick glass gave way with a truly horrific crunch and crash and then hands scrabbled in blood at the edge of jagged glass and then slipped and were gone——

She stared at the hole opening on to new night and breathed deeply. Smog. Better air than in the halls, at that. Boy hadn't even had time to scream. . . .

"Well, I guess that's *one* way to get out." Not the first time someone had looked at her and thought, *easy.* Not the last, likely.

The three boys left stared open-mouthed at where their leader had been.

"What's the matter with you, hmm, boy?" She poked the redhead with her cane. "You never see a window before?"

"I didn't know they *broke,*" he said, dazed. "No one hits windows."

"That's *'cause* they break. Hit anything hard enough and it'll break." She chewed her lower lip. The other two looked shocked and scared; this one looked all that and something more. "I reckon most human folks got heads hard enough to go through walls, do they want to bad enough."

She put her cane down solid, began to hobble away.

"Where—where you goin'?"

"Upstairs, to find me another way down. Don't like your friend's way."

"But what if you get all the way up, then all the way down, and it's still closed?"

"Why, I reckon I'll go up again. Got nothing better to do." She spoke to all of them, but it was to Redhead she was looking.

"You'll never make it," he said. "You'll die first. Someone'll kill you."

"Or maybe I'll just die," the old woman agreed. "And maybe that's the easiest way out of all. You ever think of that, boy?"

"No."

"Just you think of it, then. When you decide dyin' ain't such a thought, you let me know."

"What if there ain't a way out?"

She held very still. "Got to be."

"What if there ain't? What if there's no people outside, no food processors—no—no anything?"

"Hard questions, boy." She sighed. "Young folk always want answers to hard questions. No one can answer those for you; you got to go look for yourself, do you want to know. And standin' here talkin' won't get me no closer to a lighted floor for the night."

Painfully, she hooked her cane on the door handle, pushed in. The stairs got harder and harder to drag herself up, every flight, every step. Sixteen to eighteen and call it a day. Ought to be gettin' above the cloud cover soon. That'd be good; maybe even see some sky again.

"Well?" she said sharply. "You comin'?"

She had almost reached the landing before she heard his footsteps pounding behind her. Panting, she clung to the metal handrail and smiled. Young folk.

The Writer's Life And Uniqueness by Roger Zelazny

About the Author

One of the most interesting and individual stylists in the field, Roger Zelazny has been a full-time writer for a decade and a half. But for more than five years after his first published appearances, in 1962, he worked for the Social Security Administration by day and fitted in his writing when he could. By 1965, however, he was already recognized as a major SF writer, winning Hugo and Nebula awards for novels and shorter work; such creations as A Rose for Ecclesiastes *and* This Immortal *were then followed by the* Amber *chronicles as he settled into his career. His work is characterized by a "science-fantasy" touch—a blend of science fiction plots and fantasy images, so that he has become noted as one of our great makers of legends. That orientation is the foremost of his many contributions to the judging of our contest entries, and to the essay that follows.*

A day or so after my first professional sale as a writer the activity in my pleasure center died down sufficiently to permit me to begin writing again. I sold sixteen more stories that year and I learned a lot of narrative tricks. The following year I stretched my efforts to novelette-length, to novella-length. I felt then that I had learned enough to try writing a novel. I did it and I sold it and the moment was golden.

I did not quit my job to write full-time for another five years, however. I had seen others do this after an initial book sale—chuck everything and Be A Writer—with disastrous results. I realized that there was more to being a writer than the act of writing, that there were other lessons to be learned, that one could not rely on current sales for one's support, that one required an economic cushion and a plan for maintaining it. So I made my plans, I followed them and they worked.

There is no use in going into autobiographical detail about this. The times have changed, the markets are different. Only the principles stand. A writer still has to hustle in the beginning, and there seem to be as many different ways of going about it as there are writers. What I am saying is that the ones who succeeded and exhibited staying power had a plan. They followed it, they established themselves, they became secure. They sell everything they write now. They learned the extra-literary considerations as well as the writing reflexes necessary for the successful pursuit of the writer's trade. I counsel all of the new writers whose work is contained in this volume to begin learning about publishing, distribution, agenting, contracts, to talk with other writers and other people in the publishing business whenever possible, to learn how things work. The actual writing is in some ways the easiest part of this business once you've mastered certain essentials, and the business side is the hardest part of writing when you are getting started.

So much for the crass, commercial end of things. It deserves mention in a book of this sort, though, and if it causes even one beginning writer to think ahead to what it may be like to sell a book first and then have to write it and deliver it by a certain date, to wonder what it will be like to write on days when one doesn't feel like writing, to speculate as to the manner in which everything involved in one's occupation may be reflected on one's tax return and to consider the best ways of responding to interviewers, academic inquiries, crackpot callers and fan mail—and if the fruits of these cogitations help to make the difference between the writer's ultimate success or failure, then I am vindicated in prefacing my more general remarks with reference to the non-writing side of writing.

So I said it. Now I'll talk about writing.

In acting as a judge in the contests from which the stories in this volume emerged on top I saw some good writing and some good ideas. Unfortunately, these were not always conjoined. When they came together in one tale it was great; it made my job easier. But in my place, which story would you choose? A story that is well-written but light? A story with a good idea, a novel plot or a solid character but weak in the writing itself? This was my biggest problem. Usually the first-place story, as I saw it, stood well to notice, was possessed of several virtues. The second or third-place stories were generally the ones where this problem loomed to devil me when it did appear. I generally resolved it by favoring originality over slickness, under the theory that narrative skills can be improved upon but interesting and unique viewpoints are harder to come by. The other judges may have proceeded differently—but that was my feeling, and I might as well state it here. I'll even tell you why.

I have taught at writers' conferences and I know a lot of editors, and I have become familiar with that species of narrative best called a "borderline story"—a piece suitably composed but not terribly compelling. I will have to give away a dark secret, also, in order to make this point. On several occasions I have been shown a borderline story and asked, "What's wrong with this? Everyone's rejected it, and I don't think it's all that bad. I've seen worse in print." In each instance I've had to agree. It was okay. If I—or one of my established colleagues—had written it, it would have sold. But it was not strong enough for an initial sale. It would have been easy for me to point out some flaw or other (there is always *something* that can be improved upon) and suggest a rewrite to take care of it. But that wasn't what I was being asked. I decided to be blunt and honest on one occasion I can recall, and I said, "There isn't really anything wrong with it. Put it away and write some more. If you begin selling, dust it off and send it to the editor who's buying your stuff, even if that editor rejected it before." Two years later I received a copy of a magazine containing that story, unchanged. The author had had several stories appear in that magazine by then.

This one was autographed, beneath the words, "You were right." I have seen this sort of thing happen more than once. It is not perversity on the part of editors, but simply one of those Cold, Hard Facts of Life: While you'll need both in the long run, content usually has an edge over form.

With respect to science fiction and fantasy stories, I have often observed that they have all of the same requirements as a piece of general fiction with the added problem of stuffing in all of the extra background material dealing with an exotic setting or the functioning of the unusual concept which make the story a part of this *genre*—and to do it without losing the reader's interest. It pleases me to see that the authors of the stories in this volume have passed that hurdle and may be read for content without distraction by the stage machinery. They have learned certain basic reflexes and are ready to gain strength by focussing continuing attention on character and ideas. If this results in any borderline stories I counsel them to hang on to these for later study, to educate the ultimate editor—*i.e.,* the "internal editor" every writer must develop, a benign species of schizophrenia permitting one to create and to look over one's own shoulder and kibitz at the same time.

I have always felt that anything is a valid subject for a science fiction story, that any idea can be run through the various "If this goes on . . ." and "What if?" machines to produce stimulating and sometimes profound results. I have also felt that when a person dies an entire universe passes, since no two of us seem to inhabit the same universe in terms of perceptions and values. It is this unique quality which, if one can put a handle on it and transport it into fiction, provides the reason for and value of all of the world's literature. A story is a ticket to a new universe, and traveling in the worlds of science fiction and fantasy can be the glamour tour of the mental traveler.

It is a delight to a tourist such as myself to see the opening of new realms each time that someone learns the magic words and shows us the way. It is a sign, I feel, of the strength and attraction of this area of writing that so many new people have been moved to make the effort, and that some good things have been done as a result. For long range success I can only counsel perseverance. After luck, I think it is one of the best things a writer can have. Good luck to everyone in this book. I hope to see you again.

About the Artists

Appropriately, the artists whose work appears in these pages are themselves relative newcomers to the world of stories and story illustration . . . a world that thrived in the heyday of the colorful pulps, and is largely missed nowadays. Universally, they found themselves thrilled and excited by this opportunity. Here they are:

A. R. Conway, 27, has been an illustrator nine years, with his heaviest experience in nonfiction books and brochures. This is his first venture into SF story illustration, including the artwork for *Arcadus Arcane* and *A Step Into Darkness*.

David Dees, 27, has six years' experience, mostly in the creation of advertising art including motion-picture advertising. This is his first fiction illustration, too, including *One Last Dance* and *Anthony's Wives*, which he found "chilling."

Frank Ferrel, 29, devotes most of his time to motion-picture graphics, to computer-generated art, and major design elements of SF films. Despite his daily exposure to Hollywood glamor, he, too, found challenge and inspiration in such stories as *Tiger Hunt* and *A Way Out*.

J. R. Rockwell is a distant cousin of Norman Rockwell, the late dean of illustrative artists. Her work for *The Land of the Leaves* and *Without Wings,* however, is her first experience with fiction illustration, though it has left her an enthusiast for this sort of artistic experience. A graphic design graduate of the Basle College of Fine Arts in Switzerland, she is 36 and works as a book designer.

Dave Simons, who has worked as a comic artist for Marvel with such notable characters as Conan and Spider Man, is now stepping into the future by illustrating science fiction in *The Ebbing.*

ANNOUNCING

The Writers of the Future Contest™

A Contest for New & Amateur Writers

Sponsored by L. Ron Hubbard

FOR ORIGINAL WORKS OF SCIENCE FICTION OF SHORT STORY OR NOVELETTE LENGTH

☐ ALL WORKS ARE ADJUDICATED BY PUBLISHED AUTHORS ONLY.

☐ 1ST, 2ND, 3RD PRIZES: $1,000, $750, $500.

Don't Delay! Send Your Entry To:
Writers of the Future Contest
2210 Wilshire Blvd., Suite 343
Santa Monica, CA 90403

CONTEST RULES

1. All entries must be original works of science fiction or fantasy. Plagarism will result in automatic disqualification. Submitted works may not have been previously published.

2. Entries must be either short story length (under 10,000 words) or novelette length (under 17,000 words).

3. Contest is open only to those who have not had professionally published a novel or novella or more than three short stories or one novelette.

4. Entries must be typewritten and double-spaced.

Each entry shall have a cover page with the title of the work, the author's name, address and telephone number, and state the length of the work. The manuscript itself should be titled, but the author's name should be deleted from it in order to facilitate anonymous judging.

5. Entries must be accompanied by a stamped, self-addressed envelope suitable for return of manuscript. Every manuscript will be returned.

6. There shall be three cash prizes for each contest: 1st prize of $1,000.00, 2nd prize of $750.00, and 3rd prize of $500.00.

7. There will be ten quarterly contests commencing from January 1, 1984 and ending June 30, 1986.

a. Jan. 1—Mar. 31, 1984   f. Apr. 1—Jun. 30, 1985
b. Apr. 1—Jun. 30, 1984   *g. Jul. 1—Sep. 30, 1985
c. Jul. 1—Sep. 30, 1984   *h. Oct. 1—Dec. 31, 1985
d. Oct. 1—Dec. 31, 1984   *i. Jan. 1—Mar. 31, 1986
e. Jan. 1—Mar. 31, 1985   *j. Apr. 1—Jun. 30, 1986

To be eligible for a quarterly contest, an entry must be postmarked no later than midnight of the last day of the quarter.

8. Only one entry per quarter.

9. Winners of a quarterly contest are ineligible for further participation in the contest.

10. The winners of the quarterly contests will be eligible for trophies or certificates.

11. Should the sponsor of this contest decide to publish an anthology of science fiction and fantasy works, winners will be contacted regarding their interest in having their manuscripts included.

12. Entries will be judged by a panel of professional authors. Each contest may have a different panel. Entries will not be judged by L. Ron Hubbard or his agents. The decisions of the judges are final.

13. Winners of each contest will be individually notified of results by mail, together with names of those sitting on the panel of judges.

This contest is void where prohibited by law.

*Due to popular demand the contest has been expanded with the addition of these four new quarters.

Writers of the Future 1984 Contest Winners

First Three Quarters

First Quarter (January 1, 1984 to March 31, 1984):

1st place winner:	Story:
Dennis J. Pimple	**"Arcadus Arcane"**
2nd place winner:	Story:
Leonard Carpenter	**"The Ebbing"**
3rd place winner:	Story:
Nina Kiriki Hoffman	**"A Step Into Darkness"**

Second Quarter (April 1, 1984 to June 30, 1984):

1st place winner:	Story:
Jor Jennings	**"Tiger Hunt"**
2nd place winner:	Story:
Mary Frances Zambreno	**"A Way Out"**
3rd place winner:	Story:
Randell Crump	**"Anthony's Wives"**

Third Quarter (July 1, 1984 to September 30, 1984):

1st place winner:	Story:
David Zindell	**"Shanidar"**
2nd place winner:	Story:
Ira Herman	**"The Two Tzaddicks"**
3rd place winner:	Story:
Michael D. Miller	**"Tyson's Turn"**

COMING THIS YEAR...

**THE CROWNING ACHIEVEMENT
OF THE GRAND MASTER
OF SCIENCE FICTION**

L. RON HUBBARD'S

MISSION EARTH

**HIS SUPERLATIVE TEN-VOLUME
MASTERWORK,
UNPARALLELED IN**

**scope . . . concept . . .
imagery . . . action**

A brilliantly conceived fusion of high science fiction adventure, rich comedy-satire and hilarious social commentary in the great, classic tradition of Voltaire, Swift, Verne, Wells and Orwell.

An unprecedented event in publishing history, so momentous that a new word—dekalogy (meaning a group of ten volumes)—had to be coined to adequately describe <u>Mission Earth</u>'s sheer magnitude and mastery— 1.2 million words in ten epic volumes that surpass even his last triumphant, internationally acclaimed best-selling masterpiece—<u>Battlefield Earth</u>.

Filled with a dazzling array of other-world weaponry and systems and set in the here and now, <u>Mission Earth</u> is a spectacular cavalcade of battles, of stunning plot reversals, with heroes and heroines, villains and villainesses, caught up in a superbly imaginative, intricately plotted invasion of Earth—as seen entirely and uniquely through the eyes of the aliens that already walk among us.

Unlike anything in the annals of science fiction, <u>Mission Earth</u> is told with the distinctive pace and artistry that is the inimitable hallmark of L. Ron Hubbard, the unequaled master of storytelling.

To be released by Bridge Publications in the fall of 1985.

WATCH FOR IT!

"Nothing makes me happier than to hear from readers and writers."

Any message addressed to L. Ron Hubbard in care of the publisher at the following address will be given prompt and full attention.

BRIDGE PUBLICATIONS INC.
1414 North Catalina Street
Los Angeles, CA 90027